Best Hikes With
CHILDREN™

in Vermont, New Hampshire, & Maine

Cynthia C. Lewis
& Thomas J. Lewis

The Mountaineers

For little hikers everywhere

© 1991 by Cynthia C. Lewis and Thomas J. Lewis

4   3
5   4   3

Published by The Mountaineers
1011 SW Klickitat Way, Seattle, Washington 98134

Published simultaneously in Canada by Douglas & McIntyre, Ltd., 1615 Venables Street, Vancouver, B.C. V5L 2H1

Published simultaneously in Great Britain by Cordee, 3a DeMontfort Street, Leicester, England, LE1 7HD

Manufactured in the United States of America

Edited by Lorretta Palagi
Maps by Debbie Newell
Cover photograph: Gilson Pond, near the base of Grand Monadnock
All photographs by Cynthia C. and Thomas J. Lewis
Cover design by Betty Watson
Book design and layout by Bridget Culligan

Title page: Look what I caught!

Library of Congress Cataloging-in-Publication Data

Lewis, Cynthia Copeland, 1960–
    Best hikes with children in Vermont, New Hampshire, and Maine / Cynthia C. Lewis & Thomas J. Lewis.
      p. cm.
    Includes index.
    ISBN 0-89886-281-7
    1. Hiking—New England—Guide-books. 2. Family recreation—New England—Guide-books. 3. New England—Description and travel—1981–—Guide-books. I. Lewis, Thomas J. (Thomas Josef), 1958–
II. Title.
GV199.42.N38L485   1991
917.4'0443—dc20   91-26465
                                                          CIP

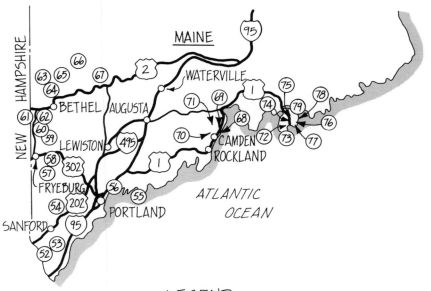

LEGEND

ⓟ	PARKING	♿ⓟ	HANDICAPPED PARKING
Ⓢ	START	～～	STREAM
••••••••	HIKING ROUTE	⋙	WATERFALL
- - - - - -	OTHER TRAIL	○	TOWER
―――――	PAVED ROAD	□	RESTROOM
― ― ―	DIRT/GRAVEL ROAD	⊓	PICNIC SITE
—②—	U.S. HIGHWAY	△	CAMPGROUND/CAMPSITE
—95—	INTERSTATE HIGHWAY	▣	VIEWPOINT
+++++++	RAILROAD TRACKS	⋮⋮⋮	BEACH
•—•—•—	STONE WALL	⸌ ⸌ ⸌	MARSH
+—+—+—	POWER LINE	⋰⋱	OPEN AREA

7

KEY TO SYMBOLS

 Dayhikes. These are hikes that can be completed in a single day. There is no camping shelter along the route.

 Overnight trips. These hikes encompass a designated campsite (often with a shelter) or follow a route that leads hikers close to a campground. They are not necessarily too difficult to be completed in one day.

 Easy trails. These are relatively short, smooth, gentle trails suitable for small children or first-time hikers.

 Moderate trails. Most of these are 2 to 4 miles total distance and feature more than 500 feet of elevation gain. The trail may be rough and uneven. Hikers should wear lug-soled boots and be sure to carry the Ten Essentials (see "Safety" in the introduction).

 Difficult or challenging trails. These are often rough, with considerable elevation gain or distance to travel. They are suitable for older or experienced children. Lug-soled boots and the Ten Essentials are standard equipment.

 Hikable. The best times of year to hike each trail are indicated by the following symbols: flower—spring; sun—summer; leaf—fall; snowflake—winter.

 Driving directions. These paragraphs tell you how to get to the trailheads.

 Turnarounds. These are places, mostly along moderate trails, where families can cut their hike short yet still have a satisfying outing. Turnarounds usually offer picnic opportunities, views, or special natural attractions.

 Cautions. These mark potential hazards—cliffs, stream crossings, and the like—where close supervision of children is strongly recommended.

Acknowledgments

We would like to thank Daniel and Cecelia Lewis for cheerfully offering their babysitting services while we completed the field work for this book. Sharlene and Clayton Copeland supported and encouraged us—as always—throughout our project. Thanks also to Marshall Randolph for allowing us to use his central New Hampshire home as a base of operation, and to Art Simington, our local hiking expert, for assistance and advice. Also thanks to the Hilltop Campground in Sullivan, New Hampshire, for their cooperation. Finally, we offer our sincerest gratitude to Donna, Margaret, Marge, Rick, Storm, Tish, and the other folks at The Mountaineers who worked so hard on our New England hiking guide series. It truly has been a pleasure.

Introduction

You have visited a video arcade for the last time, watched your last Ninja Turtles movie, and taken your final ride on a loop-da-loop roller-coaster. Meanwhile, the kids are boycotting art museums, flea markets, and anything that takes place on a stage and requires them to wear a necktie and/or dress shoes.

Is this the end of family togetherness? No, it's time to take up hiking!

Healthier than cable TV and cheaper than downhill skiing, hiking is within everyone's capabilities and will appeal to toddlers and teenagers, preschoolers and parents. We all love the outdoors, and hiking adds an element of adventure: What will we find around the next bend? A cave? A camping shelter? A waterfall maybe?

Even though hiking with kids requires a good deal more effort than hiking without them, it's worth the extra hassle. Kids notice clouds shaped like hippos and trees that look like witches; they delight in ant-hills and spider webs. Your daughter will point out everything in the forest that is her favorite color. (She'll also point out everything in the

Children enjoy the simple pleasures of the outdoors.

11

forest that is your favorite color, her cousin's favorite color, and her best friend Rachel's favorite color.) Your son won't remark or observe—he'll squeal, he'll shout, he'll exclaim! Kids react to these adventures the way we'd all like to—if only we didn't feel obligated to act so darned grown up. By taking little folks along, we're able to experience nature with renewed enthusiasm.

But Will It Be *Fun?*

Keep in mind the one basic rule for family hiking—it's got to be fun. Kids will expect it, and you will have to respond by gearing the trip toward their interests, needs, and capabilities. Try to envision the experience through your children's eyes and plan accordingly. If the first few trips are memorable, they'll be eager to embark on more family adventures.

Here are a few pointers for making hiking with young children enjoyable for everyone:

Bring a Little Buddy

A friend is a distraction from that blister on his big toe and a deterrent to whining—nobody wants to look wimpy in front of a school chum.

Set a Realistic Pace

A child's pace varies tremendously within the course of a walk from ambling along, examining every stone, leaf, and blade of grass, to racing ahead as if the lead runner in the Boston Marathon. By letting her set her own pace (within reason), you will convey the message that a hike's success is not measured in terms of miles covered but rather in the pleasure taken in each step.

Choose an Appropriate Hike

Easier is better than harder, when in doubt, but an athletic twelve-year-old will be bored with the mile-long amble through the woods that is better suited for a preschooler.

Give Compliments

Nothing means more to a child than his father or mother patting him on the back and telling him he's the best climber around. Such praise makes sore feet suddenly feel a whole lot better.

Make Frequent Stops

A trailside boulder, fallen tree, breezy peninsula. . . . Children may need more frequent rests than adults, but they tend to recover more quickly. Teach them to pace themselves; remind them as they dash out of the car that it will be a long climb to the summit.

Offer Snacks

Granola bars, bananas, cheese cubes, a mixture of nuts, chocolate chips, and dried fruits, boxes of raisins—bring along any favorite that will boost energy. Bring plenty of water, too.

Play Games on the Trail

Have fun! Suggest things for children to listen and look for—frogs croaking, deer tracks, acorns, birds flying south for the winter. Don't worry about making proper identifications; if you see something interesting just say "Look!" Take turns guessing its name. Offer incentives and distractions—"We're halfway there," "The waterfall is just over the hill"—and talk about the day's goals. Have fun—laughter lightens the load.

Encourage Responsibility

Children, like the rest of us, tend to meet the level of expectation. An older child given the responsibility of following the hike on the map, keeping an eye out for a loon through the binoculars, or charting direction with the compass will proudly fulfill his duties and be less likely to engage in horseplay.

Maintain a Good Attitude

Misery is contagious, so even if you are anxious because you think it might rain or your pack has somehow doubled its weight in the last half mile, don't complain in front of your kids. A bad attitude will kill a good time much faster than a pair of soggy sneakers.

Environmental Concerns

Sometimes the very qualities that make children so much fun to have along on a hike can present the most problems. Adults recognize that what our ancestors referred to as "dismal wilderness" is our most valuable and threatened resource, but to children the outdoors is a vast playground. While the seven-year-old is gleefully stripping a boulder of its moss blanket in search of worms and beetles, his younger sister is stomping among the wildflowers reciting a spontaneous ode to posies. But by springing to the defense of each cluster of ferns parents may be concerned that they will turn what should be a relaxed family outing into a battle. How can parents creatively direct their children's enthusiasm toward nature-friendly pursuits?

Older children can anticipate the consequences of their actions on the environment. They will learn respect for the wilderness and its inhabitants from their parents' examples. By recycling, buying biodegradable products, and supporting environmental concerns, parents integrate

A meadow sprinkled with wildflowers makes a lovely spot for a rest.

a conservation ethic into the family's daily life so that "clean hiking" and "clean camping" come naturally to their children. Youngsters so raised understand that as hikers and campers they are becoming, for a time, part of the wilderness; they are not seeking to dominate or ruin it. Willingly, they'll "take nothing but pictures, leave nothing but footprints, and kill nothing but time." Children old enough to distinguish "safe" from potentially harmful trash can be encouraged to pick up the litter of previous hikers as well.

Younger children are more likely than older ones to act recklessly and without concern for the environment and its inhabitants. Offering desirable options rather than simply forbidding certain behavior works best with most children. Instead of picking a wildflower, your daughter can smell it, examine the petals under a magnifying glass, or take a photograph. Binoculars, as well, focus attention on soaring birds or far horizons. Such equipment retains its appeal when it is reserved just for special outings. One of the greatest gifts we can give our children is to instill in them a respect for the other living things that share our planet and an understanding of their own importance in determining the future of our natural environment.

Here are some specific ways that hikers can leave the forest without a trace:

- Prepare to take trash out with you by bringing along appropriate bags or containers.
- Stick to the trails and, when presented with the choice of stepping on delicate vegetation or rocks, pick the rocks.

14

- Trails are most vulnerable during "mud season" in March and April; be especially careful then.
- Don't wash in streams.
- If restroom facilities are not provided, dig a small hole for human waste far from any water source and cover it with soil.
- Conform to the specific regulations of the state park, wildlife refuge, or other recreational area you are visiting.

Safety

While you cannot altogether eliminate the risks inherent in hiking, you can minimize them by taking proper precautions and by educating yourself and your children. You should carry the supplies necessary to combat the most frequent problems—a well-equipped first-aid kit, flashlight, map, and extra food and clothing (refer to the Ten Essentials in the "What to Take" section). Recognize your own limitations and those of your children: Don't attempt to climb to Glen Boulder (Hike 47) on your first family outing. If you're hiking with very young children, you will probably wind up carrying them, or at least their packs, for some of the way, so choose a hike that is well within your own capabilities.

Getting Lost

Prepare for the possibility of getting lost. Leave your itinerary with a friend or relative (or at the very least leave a visible note on the dashboard of the car). Carry enough extra food and clothing so that if an overnight is necessary, you are prepared.

Teach your kids to read maps and pay close attention to trail markers and landmarks. On most marked trails, they should be able to see two blazes (one ahead of them and one behind them) at all times. (Most trails are marked with paint blazes on trees or rocks. Cairns—small rock piles—indicate the route when the trail goes above the treeline.) Kids need to know that double blazes indicate a significant change of direction and triple blazes usually signal the end of the trail. Instruct them to look back frequently to see what the route will look like on the hike out.

You may want to insist on the buddy system or equip everyone with a whistle and establish a whistle code. Encourage little children to stay put as soon as they realize they are lost. Older children might be able to follow a river downstream or retrace their steps looking for particular landmarks. Above all, emphasize alertness and remaining calm. If you are unable to attempt a return to your car because you are lost or injured or both, make a fire using greens that will smoke and signal anyone looking.

Although we have described as accurately as possible the trail conditions and routes, they may be different when you embark on a given hike. Blazes are painted over, seasonal changes such as erosion or fallen trees cause a trail to be rerouted, bridges and boardwalks collapse. You'll want to change your plans if the trail seems too poorly marked to follow or if the condition of the trail is dangerous.

Bushwhacking

To veteran hikers, even wilderness trails begin to feel civilized. Often, these adventurous souls take to bushwhacking, using topographical maps to locate trailless peaks or leaving the blazed trail to make their own way through the forest. Despite the thrill of going where no one has seemingly gone before, we don't recommend bushwhacking for families. It's easy to get disoriented and tough to keep everyone together. You're more likely to spot wildlife if you stay on the trails because many animals follow the trails themselves. Crashing through the underbrush is likely to scare off any animals or birds in the area. You may also inadvertently trample delicate vegetation or disturb a nesting site if you leave the path.

Fire Towers

We have tried to note which fire towers seem dangerous, but you should inspect each one you intend to climb. Many fall quickly into a state of disrepair, some are sold to private owners, others are in the process of being torn down. No matter what its condition, never use a fire tower for overnight camping.

Warm-ups

The colder the weather, the more your muscles will need stretching before the hike. Kids don't need to warm up as much as their parents do, but it won't hurt them. Stretch your calf muscles and hamstrings by leaning forward against the car or a tree and slowly lowering your heels until they touch the ground. Hold, rest, and repeat. For your quadriceps (front of the thigh), support yourself with one hand while you grab an ankle behind you with the other and pull it toward your buttocks. Hold the position, then repeat on the other side. (You will want to repeat these exercises after your hike as well to prevent cramping.)

Hypothermia

If children are particularly engrossed in what they are doing, they may ignore discomfort or an injury. Watch for signs of fatigue—encourage a rest and food stop. Hypothermia (the most common cause of death for hikers on Mount Washington) may affect a child sooner than an adult exposed to the same conditions. Most cases of hypothermia occur in relatively mild temperatures of between 30 and 50 degrees, often in windy or wet conditions. If a child seems listless and cranky (early signs of hypothermia), and certainly once he complains of being cold, begins uncontrollable shivering, or exhibits impaired speech, add another layer of warm clothes or change him into dry clothes, wrap him in a sleeping bag, and offer a warm drink or soup.

Weather

Be conscious of weather conditions and do not hesitate to rechart your course due to a potential storm. Even the least challenging trail can pose a hazard in foul weather. And some of the toughest routes—especially those in New Hampshire's White Mountains—are nearly impossible to navigate in a blizzard or severe thunderstorm. The only thing worse than getting caught in bad weather while hiking is getting caught in bad weather while hiking with your children.

The higher the elevation, the colder, windier, and wetter it is likely to be. The summit of Mount Washington in the White Mountains, battered constantly by winds of between 26 and 44 miles per hour, sits in a cloud bank more than half of the time. We hiked to Washington's summit on a day when the temperatures in Boston topped a scorching 100 degrees. On the mountaintop, the temperature hovered around 50. The nearby mountains, though not as high as Washington, see similar contrasts between the conditions at their bases and those on their summits.

What to Take

The Mountaineers recommend ten items that should be taken on every hike, whether a day trip or an overnight. When children are involved and you are particularly intent on making the trip as trouble-free as possible, these Ten Essentials may avert disaster.

1. Extra clothing. It may shower, the temperature may drop, or wading may be too tempting to pass up. Be sure to include rain gear, extra shoes and socks (especially a pair of shoes that can be used for wading when bare feet might mean sliced toes), a warm sweater, and a hat and mittens.

2. Extra food. Too much is better than not enough. Carry sufficient water in canteens or fanny packs in case there is no suitable source on the trail.

3. Sunglasses. Look for a pair that screens out UV rays. A wide-brimmed hat or visor also works to shade your eyes.

4. Knife. Chances are you'll never need it, but if you do and it's with the string and masking tape in the top drawer to the left of the refrigerator, you'll be sorry.

5. Firestarter-candle or chemical fuel. If you must build a fire, these are indispensable.

6. First-aid kit. Don't forget to include moleskin for blisters, baking soda to apply to stings, and any special medication your child might need if he is allergic to bee stings or other insect bites.

7. Matches in a waterproof container. You can buy these matches in a store that carries hiking and camping gear.

8. Flashlight. Before you begin your hike, check the batteries (and bring along extras).

9. Map. Don't assume you'll just "feel" your way to your destination.

10. Compass. You don't need anything fancy—for under ten dollars, you can find a sturdy, accurate protractor-type compass at an outdoor equipment or sporting goods store. Teach your children how to use it too.

In addition to the Ten Essentials, a few other items can come in mighty handy, especially when young children are along.

Until you've hiked or camped during black fly season (May through mid-June), it's hard to describe how immensely annoying a swarm of these little buggers can be. Insect repellant doesn't deter them all, but it helps (be sure the repellant you have is appropriate for children). In addition to this protection, dress children in lightweight, long-sleeved shirts and pants. A cap may come in handy as well.

Mosquitoes flourish in low, wet areas like swamps and seem to congregate around little children who haven't perfected their swatting techniques. Repellant and head covers made of mosquito netting (with elastic to gather it at the neck or waist) may be hike-savers. If you're surrounded and defenseless, try tucking a fern into the back of your shirt collar and give the kids fern "flags" to wave around.

Toilet paper may come in handy; a yard or two per person is usually enough for a day hike. And don't forget to protect children from the sun. Kids can get sunburned even in wintertime, and their skin will burn faster at higher altitudes.

Binoculars, a camera, a magnifying glass, and a bag for collecting treasures are fun to have along and might keep children from trying to push each other into the brook.

Leave your poodle, portable radio, and the kids' toys at home.

Footgear

In selecting footwear, make comfort the number one priority. You do not want to find out two miles from the car that Mikey's boots (which were a *tad* small in the store but *were* half price) have turned his toes purple. Buying shoes that are too small, in fact, is probably the most common mistake new hikers make. Many stores specializing in outdoor equipment have steep ramps that you can stand on to simulate a downhill hike. If your toes press against the tip of the boot when you are standing on the ramp, try a larger size. Be sure to bring the liners and socks that you plan to wear on hikes for a more accurate fit. (In most cases, the sales people in sporting goods stores are very helpful and will be able to guide you to an appropriate pair of boots.) You probably want lightweight, ankle-high, leather or fabric-and-leather boots. Be sure they have sturdy soles and provide good ankle support and adequate resistance to moisture. In a few cases, sneakers or running shoes will be adequate, but on most trails, hiking boots are preferable. If you will be doing a lot of hiking, invest in a good pair that will hold up to rugged terrain. (Be sure to wear new boots at home for several days before hitting the trails.)

In the wintertime, insulated boots are a must, and in the spring or after a rainstorm, opt for waterproof boots. Snowshoes or cross-country skis can also be used for winter hikes on fairly level terrain, although we do not recommend winter hiking for children since it's not nearly as enjoyable for most kids as hiking in spring, summer, or fall.

Clothing

As with footgear, comfort is top priority. Think layers—they can be added or taken off as temperature dictates. Often, if you will be visiting a ravine or heading to a summit, factors such as wind and temperature will change noticeably. With layers, the moment you begin to feel warm you can remove an article of clothing to avoid becoming wet. In bug season, long sleeves are best, paired with long pants. Jeans, a perennial favorite among kids, aren't necessarily the most comfortable walking pants. When wet they are very heavy and cold, seem to take forever to dry, and unless well-worn can be stiff as cardboard. A better bet might be sweatpants or cotton slacks or tights. Be sure not to wear clothing that is too loose because it may snag on branches and brush.

If you'll be hiking in cool weather, consider the new synthetic thermal long underwear. Cotton tends to retain moisture, whereas polypropylene keeps it away from your skin. You don't want to perspire on your climb and then become chilled once you stop for a rest or head back to the car. Socks should be medium weight and wool (even in warm weather); try the rag-knit type found in most shoe or sporting goods stores. Wear a thin, silken liner under the socks. (Thick over thin will usually prevent blisters.) A hat will help keep the sun out of your eyes and the black flies out of your hair. And your head will be somewhat protected if a rain shower takes you by surprise.

A rain poncho with a hood that can be folded up into a small pack is essential for every member of the family. Bring a windbreaker if you're heading to a breezy summit. A few bandanna handkerchiefs are not quite as critical, but may prove handy for a multitude of annoyances such as runny noses, dirty hands and faces, cuts, and sunburned necks.

Packs

Older children will probably want to carry their own packs, while the little ones will want to move unencumbered. Child-size packs can be purchased at stores carrying hiking and camping supplies—be aware, though, that they may quickly become too small. Unless you have a num-

ZZZZZZZZZ...

ber of other little hikers who will be using it, you may want to just fill an adult pack with a light load. Kids like to carry their own liquids and snacks.

Adults should carry as light a load as possible since there will inevitably be times when a child needs or wants to be carried. Backpacks should have a lightweight but sturdy frame, fit comfortably, and have a waist belt to distribute the load.

Child-Related Equipment

Infants can be carried easily in front packs. We took our oldest daughter on a mountain hike when she was just three weeks old. The walking rhythm and closeness to a parent are comforting to the littlest tykes. Older babies and toddlers do well in backpacks. They enjoy gazing around from a high vantage point and are easily carried by an adult. Look for a backpack that also has a large pouch for carrying other hiking essentials. (To keep the "backpacked" toddlers amused, try filling a bottle with juice and several ice cubes—it's a drink and rattle in one!)

We have also used a carrier resembling a hip sling that will accommodate children up to four years old. Ours folds into a wallet-sized pouch and can be put on when your three-year-old has had enough walking for the day. Look for ideas in outdoor stores, toy stores, and stores specializing in baby furniture and supplies. Ask hiking friends what they have found useful and, whenever possible, try before you buy.

Additional Equipment for Overnights

You will need additional equipment if you plan to spend the night on the trail. Sleeping bags, foam pads, a small stove, cooking utensils, and a tent or hammocks are obviously needed. Generally, folks who work at stores stocking outdoor supplies are more than willing to help you outfit your family for an overnighter. In some cases, trailside shelters, tent platforms, or lean-tos will be available. Learn everything about the accommodations (including whether you need to reserve or rent space) before your trip.

Food

If you are staying overnight, you may want to buy freeze-dried food made especially for backpackers, although the kids might prefer more familiar nourishment. While a food's nutritional value, weight, and ease of preparation should take precedence over taste, kids—even hungry ones— may turn up their noses at something that just doesn't taste right. You can try one-pot meals such as chili or beef stew or try bringing foods that require no cooking at all. Cooking equipment is cumbersome and it usually takes more time than you expect to prepare for and cook the meal.

Dayhikers need easy-to-carry, high-energy snack foods. Forget about three filling meals and eat light snacks as often as you are hungry.

The time of year will affect your choices: You won't want to have to peel an orange with fingers frozen by the cold—you're better off with meat-balls. Non-squishable fruit is good—try dried fruit, raisins, papaya sticks, and banana chips. Fig bars, cheese cubes, granola, and nuts are also hiking favorites. Let the kids help you mix chocolate chips, peanuts, raisins, and other "gorp" ingredients since it's cheaper than buying the ready-made trail mix. My kids like granola bars, store-bought or home-made. Often, we buy a loaf of our favorite bakery bread and a hunk of mild cheese that will appeal to the kids, and then hard boil some eggs to take with us. Let your family's taste buds and your good judgment deter-mine what you bring.

Hikers need to drink frequently and the best way to ensure a safe water supply is to bring it along. The plastic water bottles used by bicy-clists are easily packed. It's never a good idea to drink water from an un-known source, even in the wilderness. If you must, boil it for 10 minutes or treat it with an iodine-based disinfectant to avoid giardiasis, an infec-tion that results from drinking polluted water.

The Hiking Seasons

Although we indicate in each hike's information block the months when the trail is considered hikable (see the "How to Use This Book" sec-tion), you can select an optimum time by being aware of certain seasonal hazards and pleasures.

Spring is the best time of the year to visit cascades, waterfalls, or any natural area where a heavy flow of water will add more drama and interest. But watch out for river crossings in the spring—August's tiny stream is often May's roaring, swollen river. Waterproof boots may be necessary since the ground is bound to be soggy. Step with care; trails are particularly susceptible to damage in the spring.

Mud season is as well known to New Englanders as hurricane sea-son is to those in the tropics. Many of the mountain access roads are dirt, and these may be tough to navigate (or may be closed) in early and mid-spring.

Because March and April snowstorms are often the fiercest of the year in northern New England, we have often recommended May as the earliest hiking month. Even during the first few weeks in May, you're best off exploring drier trails at lower elevations. The pleasant weather in the lowlands often does not reflect the harsher summit conditions.

One final springtime reminder: Be sure to bring insect repellant and wear long-sleeved shirts and long pants—black flies and mosquitoes work overtime in May and June.

Summer is a terrific time to hike to cool ravines, breezy mountain-tops, or lakeside parks where there are swimming or cookout facilities. It's also the best time to camp in northern New England, since the evenings will not be too chilly for kids. Of course, most folks recognize this and popular spots will be crowded. Whenever possible, hike midweek and avoid holiday weekends. Weekend hikers can get an early start to beat the crowds or head for more remote locations.

Winterlike conditions can descend on the higher elevations (such as in the peaks in the White Mountains) even in midsummer, so be prepared with extra clothing.

New England autumns draw visitors from all over the country. This is the bona fide hiking season, offering hikers pleasant temperatures and colorful views. You'll want to find spots from which to admire the blushing hills as well as to watch the annual hawk migration, a spectacular sight and popular fall pastime.

Late autumn ushers in hunting season, so we have suggested in most cases that you hike just until October. Our children are frightened by the sound of gunshots, and hiking with crying kids is not loads of fun. If you elect to share the woods with the hunters, be sure to dress every member of your family in brightly colored clothing, including the characteristic orange hats worn by hunters. Late fall can also bring an unexpected snowstorm. As is the case in springtime, valley weather conditions do not reflect the conditions on top of the mountains.

We have included several year-round hikes, most of them on flat terrain at lower elevations. While some families embark on winter snowshoeing or skiing expeditions along the mountain hiking trails, we don't recommend it for any but the hardiest and most experienced families. Many access roads are closed in the wintertime (lengthening the hike considerably in some cases) and it can be difficult finding trail markers. Often, snow and ice make the route dangerous. Expect the trip to take at least twice as long as the time we've allotted, and you'll have to be conscious of the limited daylight hours. If you do embark on a winter hike, stick to the easy, familiar trails, and follow a leader experienced in such outings.

Weather is likely to undergo abrupt and hazardous changes in the winter, especially in the mountainous regions. The exposure and windchill factor demand that kids be dressed as warmly and covered as completely as possible.

Camping

In the information block for each hike, an "overnight trip" symbol indicates that a designated campsite is located along a trail encompassed by that hike (or a campground is nearby).

Vandalism and overuse of the trails have led to strict regulations regarding backpack camping in all New England states. In the cases where we've identified an agency or individual for you to contact for more information, refer to the "Important Addresses" section.

Vermont

Camping on private property (and trails often cross private property) requires the landowner's permission, while camping on state or locally owned public land in Vermont is limited to those sites designated by proper authorities. Often, there are trailside shelters or lean-tos, toilet facilities, fireplaces, and a water source at these sites. The state's primitive-camping guidelines affect state land below the 2500-foot elevation level. For further information on primitive camping on state land, contact the Department of Forests, Parks, and Recreation.

Within the Green Mountain National Forest, campers must practice "clean" camping policies and follow strict fire safety procedures. The restrictions that apply in the national forest recreation areas are posted near these designated areas. Contact the Forest Supervisor of the Green Mountain National Forest or the Vermont Department of Forests, Parks, and Recreation for camping guidelines as well as information about public and private campgrounds. The reverse side of the *Vermont Official State Map and Touring Guide* (available free from local information centers or from the Vermont Travel Division) also lists many of the state's campgrounds.

New Hampshire

In New Hampshire, backpack camping is permitted within the White Mountain National Forest (WMNF) and in other specific locations, such as at campsites along the Appalachian Trail. Camping on private land requires the owner's permission. Campfires built in undesignated areas outside the WMNF require a permit. Camping and campfires are permitted in state parks only in the campgrounds.

Although "no trace" camping is permitted within the WMNF, the United States Forest Service (USFS) has instituted specific camping regulations for some of the more popular areas. These are designated as Restricted Use Areas (RUAs) and have rules that apply within their boundaries during certain times of the year. The RUA rules (which are posted at most sites) require that campers be a certain distance (usually 200 feet to 0.25 mile) from roads, trails, streams, lakes, shelters, tent platforms, and other locations. Camping and wood or charcoal fires are not allowed above the timberline (where trees are less than 8 feet tall). Portable stoves are preferred to campfires in nearly all locations. For current rules and RUA sites (the sites change based on usage), contact any Ranger District office or the USFS in Laconia.

A number of campgrounds managed by the WMNF offer limited facilities for a fee. Reservations are not accepted and the campgrounds are often full during the summer. (Details are available from WMNF offices.) Several state park campgrounds fall within the boundaries of the WMNF; for more information on these, contact the Office of Vacation Travel.

Maine

In the parts of Maine we've covered, hikers planning to stay overnight on the trail should camp in designated areas or obtain the owner's permission if on private land. Portable stoves are preferred in Maine (as in most areas of New England) because often there is not enough dead or downed wood available to use as fuel near the campsites. Fire permits are required if you're outside a designated fire area.

General "clean camping" rules apply: Set up camp well away from streams and trails; avoid clearing a site to pitch a tent; wash dishes and bathe far from ponds, springs, and other sources of water; bury human waste 6 to 8 inches underground and at least 200 feet from water sources; and carry out what you carry in.

Backpack camping is not permitted on Acadia National Park's Mount Desert Island, but the Blackwoods and Seawall campgrounds are located within the park boundaries. In addition, there are a number of private campgrounds on the island. Isle au Haut, accessible by ferry from Stonington, offers the only backpack camping sites within Acadia.

White Mountain Adopt-A-Trail Program

Did you ever wonder who maintains the 1200 miles of hiking trails that crisscross the White Mountains? In many cases, it's people just like you! If you and your family would like to support the efforts of the Appalachian Mountain Club (AMC) and the USFS, you might consider participating in the Adopt-A-Trail program. Trail adopters are responsible for basic maintenance tasks on a specific trail or section of trail that they choose. To find out what is involved and what trails currently need "parents," contact any of the coordinators:

Bob and Leah Devine
15 Hawthorne Street
Milbury, MA 01527
(508) 752-3537

Fred T. Kacprzynski
Volunteer Coordinator, USFS
P.O. Box 638, 719 Main Street
Laconia, NH 03247
(603) 528-8721

Reuben Rajala
Trails Program Director, AMC
P.O. Box 298
Gorham, NH 03581
(603) 466-2721

How to Use This Book

This, the second in a two-volume series, covers northern New England: Vermont, New Hampshire, and Maine. The guide is divided into three sections by state, with state maps that show the locations of the hikes.

Read the trip description thoroughly before selecting a hike. Each entry includes enough information for you to make an appropriate choice.

Name: This is the name of the mountain, lake, or park as it will appear on most road maps.

Number: Use this to locate the hike on the state map.

Type: There are two possible choices for each entry. *Dayhike* means that this hike can easily be completed in a day or part of a day for most families. There is no camping shelter or cabin along the route. *Dayhike or overnight* refers to trails on which there are lean-tos, shelters, or some place for you to stay overnight. The overnight location is shown on the trail map. This indication does not necessarily mean that the hike is too long or difficult to be completed in an afternoon.

Difficulty: Hikes are rated for children on a scale of one to three hiking boots (easy, moderate, and challenging). Ratings are approximate, taking into consideration the length of the trip, elevation gains, and trail conditions. It's best to gain experience as a family on the easier trails first. Don't reject a hike based on a difficult rating, however, before noting the turnaround point or reading about an optional shortcut.

Distance: This is the loop or round-trip hiking distance. If a side trip to a waterfall or view is included in the text and on the map, it is included in the total distance. An alternate route described within parentheses—whether it increases or decreases the total distance—is not factored into the total.

Hiking Time: Again, this is an estimate, based on hiking length, elevation gains, and trail conditions, that will vary somewhat from family to family. Short rest stops are factored in—longer lunch stops are not.

High Point: The number given reflects the height above sea level of the highest point on the trail.

Elevation Gain: Elevation gain indicates the total number of vertical feet gained during the course of the hike. When analyzing a hike, this notation will be more significant than the high point in determining difficulty.

Hikable: The months listed are when the trails are hikable. In northern New England, hiking earlier or later may mean that you'll encounter icy terrain or potentially dangerous storms. See the "Hiking Seasons" section to get a better idea of appropriate hiking months.

Maps: The name of the topographic map published by United States Geological Survey (USGS) is included for you to reference (see "Important Addresses" section). Many outdoor and office supply stores stock USGS maps, which are a good supplement to those in our guide since the contour lines indicate elevations and terrain features. Be aware, however, that the trails may have changed since the map was printed (some are quite old), so don't follow it exclusively.

Each entry is divided into three general sections: a summary or history of the hike and region, driving and parking instructions, and a complete description of the hike. The route is described for your hike in; any potential difficulties you may encounter on the return trip are addressed at the end of each entry. The symbols within the text, in the margins, and on the maps indicate turnaround points, views, campsites, picnic spots, and caution points. (See "Key to Symbols.")

Fees

In some cases, a fee is charged for entry or parking. These fees are generally minimal (between one and five dollars) and some, such as those for Audubon properties, do not apply to members. Be aware that fees increase and some places that only charged in season or didn't charge at all when we did our research may have changed their policies. It's best to come prepared with some cash.

Happy Hiking!

A Note About Safety

Safety is an important concern in all outdoor activities. No guidebook can alert you to every hazard or anticipate the limitations of every reader. Therefore, the descriptions of roads, trails, routes, and natural features in this book are not representations that a particular place or excursion will be safe for your party. When you follow any of the routes described in this book, you assume responsibility for your own safety. Under normal conditions, such excursions require the usual attention to traffic, road and trail conditions, weather, terrain, the capabilities of your party, and other factors. Keeping informed on current conditions and exercising common sense are the keys to a safe, enjoyable outing.

The Mountaineers

VERMONT

---

1. Haystack Mountain

Type:	Dayhike
Difficulty:	Moderate for children
Distance:	4 miles, round trip
Hiking time:	3.5 hours
High point/elevation gain:	3462 feet, 1050 feet
Hikable:	May–October
Map:	USGS Mount Snow

Attention nervous parents! We've found the perfect mountaintop for you! Haystack's partially treed, conical summit rewards you with the great views you've earned after a 2-mile climb while giving the kids what they want for their efforts: a safe place to explore and roam, romp and cavort. The climb is steady, but within the abilities of most kids, who will enjoy the walk through pretty forests and alongside babbling creeks. If you've been looking for a worry-free mountain to climb with your own Dennis-the-Menace or with a group of curious little tykes, read on!

 From the junction of VT-9 and VT-100 in Wilmington, travel west on VT-9. In 1.1 miles, turn right onto Haystack Road (at a sign for Chimney Hill). In another 0.2 mile, turn left onto Chimney Hill Road, following the sign to the clubhouse. In 0.2 mile, turn right onto gravel Binney

Brook Road. Drive 0.8 mile and turn right onto Upper Dam Road. Turn left at an intersection in 0.1 mile, still on Upper Dam Road. In another 0.1 mile (2.5 miles from VT-9), look for the Haystack Mountain Trail on the right side of the road. Park along the shoulder.

Haystack Mountain Trail is a multiuse route, blazed with blue diamond cross-country ski markers. The washed-out jeep road rises gently, soon reaching a Green Mountain National Forest sign. At 0.1 mile, the trail passes a metal gate heading northward. Amidst hemlock and spruce trees, the trail dips into a depression. Who can find something that is perfectly straight?

One-quarter mile from the start, water spills through a ravine to the left of the trail. Tossing twigs and leaves into the hurrying Binney Brook, the kids can experience white-water rafting from a giant's perspective. Cross Binney Brook just under the 0.5-mile mark, following the Haystack Mountain Trail as it splits left (southwest) at a sign and an orange arrow. (The jeep road continues straight.) Immediately, cross another branch of the brook over logs.

The wide trail drops gradually on soggy terrain following blue diamond and orange rectangle markers. Ferns cluster along the edge of the path. The kids can take turns thinking of an animal while the others take guesses. Give clues like "I have a tail" or "I have poor eyesight" or "I can swim" to help the guessers.

At 0.65 mile, the trail sweeps right (northwest) and dries out, climbing gradually, then moderately. Can you find patches of moss? Under what conditions does moss grow? As the trail levels, 0.8 mile from the start, look through the sparse trees for a glimpse of Haystack's pinnacle.

The trail crests on an open shoulder at 1.2 miles with good views northward to the top of Haystack. As you track on level ground through spruce groves, have the youngest child find the smallest spruce tree in the forest. Can the oldest one point to the largest spruce? In another 0.1 mile, soft, wet ground makes for mucky going as the wide path climbs between rock ledges. Play follow the leader as you hop from rock to rock, trying to keep your feet dry.

The Haystack Mountain Trail winds through pretty spruce woods, turning right (east) at a sign 1.4 miles from the start; a woods road continues straight. Still guided by blue cross-country ski markers, follow the gently rising trail as it snakes beside moss-covered rocks and under evergreen canopies.

At a trail intersection 1.6 miles into the hike, continue straight (east) following the blue triangles as a trail diverges right. Almost immediately, turn left (north) at a second intersection, while another path heads straight. This trail veers eastward, met suddenly by a tree-covered granite outcropping. From here, a number of footpaths wind up and around Haystack's cloistered summit.

For maximum views with minimal effort, turn left and scramble up a rock that affords excellent western views. Work your way southeast-

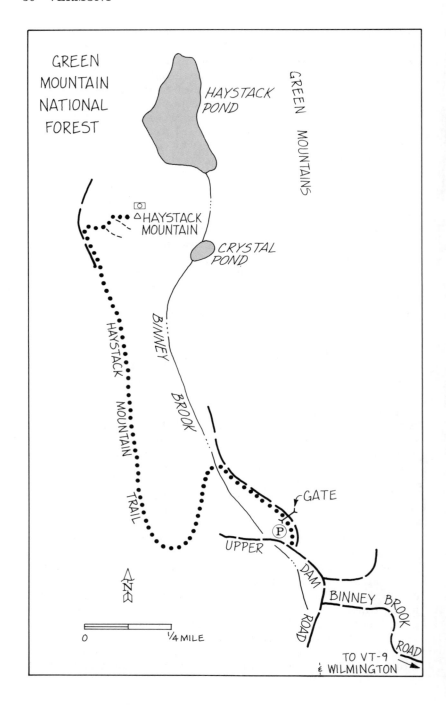

GREEN
MOUNTAIN
NATIONAL
FOREST

HAYSTACK
POND

GREEN MOUNTAINS

△ HAYSTACK
MOUNTAIN

CRYSTAL
POND

BINNEY BROOK

HAYSTACK MOUNTAIN TRAIL

GATE

P

UPPER DAM ROAD

BINNEY BROOK ROAD

N

0   ¼ MILE

TO VT-9
& WILMINGTON

ward to the open ledges at the height of the summit for superb views to the east, northeast, and southeast. Look for Haystack Pond, Mount Snow, Mount Ascutney (Hike 7) to the north, and Mount Monadnock (Hike 26) on the distant eastern horizon. On a sunny day, tell the kids to touch various objects and compare the surface temperatures. Does a rock feel as warm as a pine cone? Is the top of your head as warm as your backpack? What do you think affects the amount of warmth an object retains?

Let the kids freely explore, playing hide and seek among the "Christmas trees," scaling rock outcrops, and peering into crevices and caves. Return the way you came.

A garter snake darts across the trail on Haystack Mountain.

Climbing near the potholes midway up Hamilton Falls

2. Hamilton Falls

Type:	Dayhike or overnight
Difficulty:	Moderate for children
Distance:	6.2 miles, round trip
Hiking time:	5 hours
High point/elevation gain:	1610 feet, 1050 feet
Hikable:	May–October
Map:	USGS Londonderry

Hamilton Falls lies within Jamaica State Park, an area with as much fascinating history as natural beauty. Since the West River helped to link the Connecticut River and Lake Champlain, it was a significant transportation route for Native Americans. Archaeologists have determined that prehistoric Indian activity centered along the riverbanks for over 8000 years. When European settlers arrived, they farmed the riverside land and logged the surrounding forests, using the swift-running water to power their sawmills. In the late 1800s, the West River Railroad snaked beside the river, connecting South Londonderry and Brattleboro. Dubbed "36 miles of trouble," the railway was plagued by floods, storms, and other hardships. Today, hikers follow this old railroad bed for much of the way to Hamilton Falls.

If you visit in the spring, you may witness a white-water canoe or kayak race on the West River—you'll also see the falls at its most explosive time of the year. Summertime hikers will be able to end the walk with a swim at Salmon Hole, a beach area just west of the parking lot.

From VT-30 in Jamaica, turn north following a sign for Jamaica State Park. In 0.5 mile, enter the park and pay a small day-use fee. Drive 0.1 mile to a parking area on the left above the West River.

At the northern side of the parking area, a sign announces the Railroad Bed Trail, Overlook Trail, Ball Mountain Dam, and Hamilton Falls. The Railroad Bed Trail winds on level terrain along a wide dirt road (the roadbed of the former West River Railroad), sandwiched between the West River and a campground. Soon, the path curls eastward, running about 20 feet above the splashing river.

Urge the kids to watch for the huge, rounded glacial erratics rising out of the river that mark the 0.6-mile point. Take turns guessing the name of these boulders. ("Dumplings.") Shortly beyond the Dumplings, the Overlook Trail diverges right (east) on blue blazes. (Do not take the Overlook Trail now, but you may want to alter the return route to include this path because it offers lovely views of the West River Valley.)

As you continue, trailside benches provide welcome rest stops at river overlooks. If the kids can sit still long enough, they may see a grouse, beaver, or deer.

The trail strays northward, then curls northwestward around the "Ox Bow" where a stream joins the river from the right. Depart the Railroad Bed Trail 2.4 miles from the start and turn right (north) onto Hamilton Falls Trail, an old switch road marked in turquoise that leads to the falls. This trail climbs briskly and veers left toward (though up to 125 feet above) Cobb Brook. In 0.6 mile, follow a steep footpath that splits left at a sign for "Lower Falls," dropping quickly to the base of the falls.

The dramatic falls are nestled between high ridges with water spilling more than 100 feet in two tiers to crash onto a smooth, granite base. At the bottom are two pools, the shallow upper pool being the more suitable for exploration by young hikers. (Warn kids that these rocks can be slippery.) Older kids may be brave enough to jump into the deep, lower pool. Do you think that Indian children played in these pools hundreds of years ago?

If you would like to visit the top of the falls, return to the Hamilton Falls Trail and turn left, following the switch road to its conclusion in 0.1 mile, where you will turn left onto a dirt road. Just past the Hamilton Falls Lumber Mill, turn left onto a trail that leads to the top of the waterfall. Keep the children close as you watch the water cascading 125 feet to the potholes below.

Return to your car as you came. (If you detour along the Overlook Trail, add 0.3 mile to the total distance.)

Exploring Cobb Brook

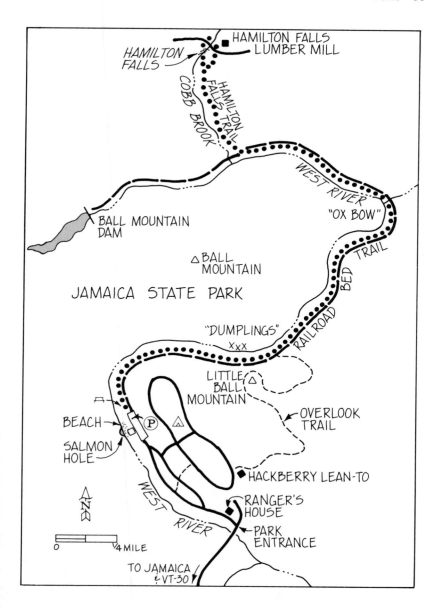

3. Prospect Rock

Type: Dayhike
Difficulty: Moderate for children
Distance: 2.8 miles, round trip
Hiking time: 2.5 hours
High point/elevation gain: 2100 feet, 1100 feet
Hikable: May–October
Map: USGS Manchester

Lots of folks enjoy being swept along a downtown avenue in a crowd of chattering tourists. Hikers, however, have discovered the pleasures of experiencing an area in a more solitary way. If you'd prefer to see the lovely town of Manchester from a hiker's perspective, climb to Prospect Rock as locals have done for many years. You'll follow the abandoned Rootville Road on a consistent, moderate grade for 1.3 miles, joining the

A hiker trekking the Long Trail pauses atop Prospect Rock.

Long Trail for the final 200 feet to the spectacular overlook high above Downer Glen.

Experienced hiking families shouldn't dismiss this as too short, nor should novices reject it based on the significant elevation gain. The views will impress even veteran hikers and, with frequent rests, kids who are new to hiking will be able to manage the climb.

From the junction of US 7, VT-30, and VT-11 in Manchester, follow the combined VT-30 South and VT-11 East. In 0.5 mile, turn right (west) onto East Manchester Road. In 100 yards, turn left (south) onto gravel Rootville Road. Drive 0.5 mile and park on the right-hand shoulder just before the water storage tank (at the end of the public road).

Alternatively, from the eastern junction of VT-11 and VT-30, drive 4.5 miles to East Manchester Road and turn left, then follow the above directions.

From the water storage tank, head east on gravel Rootville Road. Climbing briskly, follow the road as it curves south, passing a Green Mountain National Forest bulletin board at 0.15 mile. At 0.2 mile, a cascading stream joins from the right as the road becomes more rugged. The stream tunnels under the road at 0.3 mile and another branch crosses 0.1 mile later under a wooden platform. How do different objects sound when tossed into the water?

Kids, rub your cheek against a hemlock tree, then an oak. Do they feel the same? Do all hemlocks feel the same? How about all oaks? Trudge over rockier terrain on the washed-out road as you near the 0.5-mile mark. As the grade eases at 0.6 mile, look to the left, through trees, to a moss-covered boulder field.

Any stragglers? Appoint a slowpoke as hike leader and see how quickly he or she picks up the pace. An indistinct side road splits left at 0.7 mile as you continue to climb steadily along unblazed Rootville Road. Revive your weary young hikers by announcing that you are more than halfway to Prospect Rock!

One mile from the start, work your way up the rocky road along a tired stone wall. As a woods road diverges left (east), you continue straight (south). Enjoy a reprieve when the grade eases within a grove of spindly white birch trees. Pass through more stands of birch over the next 0.2 mile.

A cropped view of the Manchester valley appears shortly before the white-blazed Long Trail enters from the left on rock steps at 1.3 miles. Follow this foot trail as it cuts across the gravel road and ducks back into the woods on the right (west). In 200 feet, you'll arrive at Prospect Rock. You'll view the Manchester valley through a deep canyon with the Taconic Range as a backdrop. Look for Big Equinox (Hike 4) and Dorset Peak. While the older kids lay out the sandwiches, the younger ones can perfect their echoes.

Retrace your steps along Rootville Road to the car.

4. Big Equinox

Type: Dayhike
Difficulty: Easy for children
Distance: 1.2 miles, loop
Hiking time: 1 hour
High point/elevation gain: 3816 feet, 250 feet
Hikable: May–October
Map: USGS Manchester

Think of Big Equinox as a three-part package: the thrilling (if somewhat hairy) car ride up Sky Line Drive to the highest spot in the Taconic Range; the sensational 360-degree views from the mountaintop; and the foot trail that circles the summit through dense woods. The trail suffers from overuse in some places and neglect in others, but that does not detract from this top-of-the-world experience.

Developed by the late Dr. Joseph C. Davidson, the area has a distinctive character that sets it apart from other mountain trails (for instance, a memorial to Davidson's dog, Mr. Barbo, embellishes the Lookout Rock Trail). This is a terrific choice for a family seeking superb views without a demanding climb. Time your hike so you will return to the parking lot to watch the sun set into the layers of bluish gray mountains.

From US 7, take Exit 3 ("Historic US 7A") to VT-313 West following signs to Manchester Center and Arlington. In 1.9 miles, turn right onto US 7A North and VT-313 West. In 1.4 miles, continue straight on US 7A as VT-313 turns left. Seven and six-tenths miles from the first US 7A/VT-313 junction, turn left onto Sky Line Drive. At the entrance gate, pay a moderate per-car fee and drive 5 miles up the mountain, passing several picnic and parking areas, a monastery, and Little Equinox with its characteristic wind turbines. Park in the lot near the Sky Line Inn.

Enjoy the commanding views from the parking area of Vermont's Green Mountains, New York's Adirondacks, the Berkshires of Massachusetts, New Hampshire's White Mountain range and, yes, Canada's Mount Royal! From the northern deck of the Sky Line Inn, walk to the back of the building and drop down a set of stairs to a gravel path. Heading eastward on the Lookout Rock Trail, pass the base of the transmission tower, listening for the deep, resonating hum of the vibrating, wind-blown tower.

After the Burr and Burton Trail joins from the right in less than 0.1 mile, drop through a tunnel of spruce and hemlock trees along the rocky, eroded path. Though the sheltered trail offers limited views, your other

Grand view from the Sky Line Inn atop Big Equinox

senses will take over. Hear the ceaseless wind howling across the mountaintop, run your fingers over the lush mosses that border the trail, smell
Christmas in the evergreens.

The Beartown Trail splits left (north) as you continue straight,
reaching Lookout Rock at 0.4 mile. This protected ledge overlooks the
Manchester Valley from an altitude of 3700 feet and provides superb
views of Mount Ascutney (Hike 7), Mount Monadnock (Hike 26), and the
White Mountains. Retrace your steps for 50 feet to a tight Y-intersection
that was not evident on the hike in. Here, bear left onto the Yellow Trail
(blazed sporadically) and parallel the Lookout Rock Trail for 0.1 mile before curving left to scalp the upper edge of Equinox's eastern ridge.

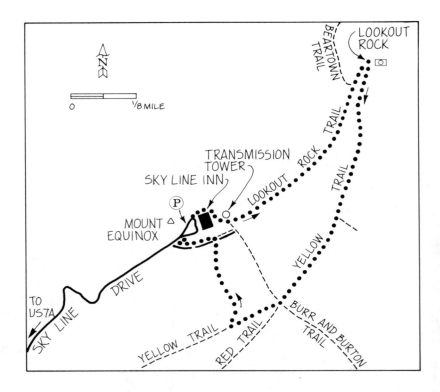

Dense spruce groves crowd the level trail. Although your distant views are limited once again, look nearby for neon green mosses and tiny spruce trees straining for sunlight. Shortly, an indistinct side trail splits left as you continue straight (southwest). One-half mile from Lookout Rock, bear right to follow the Yellow Trail as the Red Trail goes straight and the Burr and Burton Trail heads sharply left and right. As you continue to wind below the summit, the path drops gently, still crowded by thickets of spruce.

Shortly beyond the intersection, turn right (north) onto an unmarked trail following a weary sign pointing to the summit. The trail, climbing moderately through more open woods, is not well traveled and you will be forced to push aside encroaching branches and brush. In 0.1 mile, the trail opens onto a woods road. Turn left (west) onto the road and in 0.1 mile, you'll reach Sky Line Drive. A right turn brings you back to the Sky Line Inn parking lot. (The drive down the mountain is even more spectacular than the drive up!)

Note: Sky Line Drive, a toll road, is open from May 1 to November 1 from 8:00 a.m. to 10:00 p.m.

5. Natural Bridge

Type:	Dayhike
Difficulty:	Moderate for children
Distance:	2.8 miles, round trip
Hiking time:	2.5 hours
High point/elevation gain:	1940 feet, 1400 feet
Hikable:	May–October
Map:	USGS Dorset

Nothing motivates hikers like an intriguing destination. Natural Bridge, a piece of ledge that spans a narrow 20-foot-deep chasm, can be investigated close-up during dry spells. Because the trip to the bridge involves a number of turns and junctions, kids will be forced to pay atten-

Natural Bridge, by Mother Nature

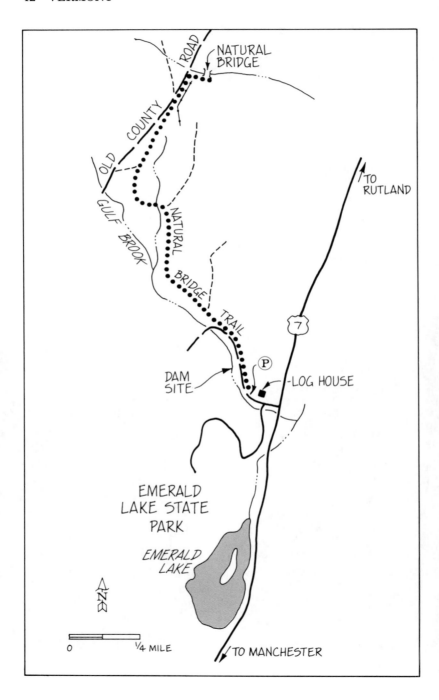

tion to the trail rather than to the weight of a pack or the stiffness of new boots.

From the junction of US 7, VT-11, and VT-30 in Manchester, travel 8.3 miles on US 7 North. Turn left onto the access road to Emerald Lake State Park. Drive straight for 0.2 mile (passing the left turn into the park) to a small parking turnout on the left beyond a log house, next to a stream.

Walk along the gravel road on the Natural Bridge Trail in a westerly direction beside a swift stream. Almost immediately, you'll pass a dam site. Tell the kids to pay close attention to landmarks such as this and to trail junctions because they will lead on the hike out. (Such an exercise teaches critical outdoor skills and focuses kids' attention on the natural surroundings.)

Blue blazes usher you along the wide road to a junction, 0.15 mile from the start. Bear right onto another gravel road, departing the brook on a stiff climb. Wind between birches on the right and hemlocks on the left. (Have the kids close their eyes and feel the bark on a birch tree, then on a hemlock. Does all bark feel the same?)

Guided sporadically by blue blazes, follow the woods road on a steady ascent to a fork at 0.4 mile. Follow the more-traveled road to the left, still climbing briskly. As you continue, the trail becomes increasingly overgrown. At 0.75 mile, the grade has nearly leveled as you approach an intersection. Turn left, cross a stream, and dip into a minor sag. At 0.9 mile, cross an often inactive stream. How many white limestone rocks can the kids count?

Just under 1 mile from the start, the road pushes out of the brush and begins a moderate-to-steep ascent. Look for the tracks of white-tailed deer. At the 1-mile mark, double blue blazes indicate that the trail curls right (north) and the climb lessens briefly. As the steeper pitch returns, a gravel path joins from the left (west); you continue to head northward.

At 1.2 miles, the trail meets gravel Old County Road. Turn right (northeast), rising gently. Almost immediately, you'll pass a less-traveled road that veers left on a moderate ascent. Continue to climb easily on Old County Road, passing through a stand of tall birches. The trail levels at 1.4 miles as a stone wall borders the right side of the road.

At the end of the stone wall (about 200 feet), follow the narrow trail that plunges right (southeast) down a wooded slope for less than 200 feet to Natural Bridge. (If you miss this turnoff, you will meet a stream that cuts across Old County Road in less than 0.1 mile.) You can drop into the gorge below the bridge during the dry season to explore—look at the potholes created by the swirling water! Do you have any budding circus acrobats who dare to inch across the narrow bridge?

Remember: On the return trip, have the kids lead the way back to the car. Allow yourself enough time for wrong turns—let the leaders discover their own mistakes. It's the only way to learn!

6. White Rocks Cliff and Ice Beds

Type: Dayhike
Difficulty: Easy for children
Distance: 2 miles, round trip
Hiking time: 1.5 hours
High point/elevation gain: 1280 feet, 450 feet
Hikable: May–October
Map: USGS Wallingford

When I was in junior high school, no one wanted to take Earth Science. We called the teacher "Mr. Rock" and dreaded the hours spent studying charts of the earth's layers and scratching one rock against another to see which was harder. I wish I had known about White Rocks Cliff and the Ice Beds then. I might have had a greater appreciation for lessons on the Ice Age and the movement of glaciers and the variety of rocks and how all of that affects today's landscape.

As you hike along the White Rocks Trail, you'll pass two overlooks with spectacular views of the cone-shaped slides of White Rocks. Dramatic rivers of boulders tumble down the steep slope. Follow the Ice Beds Trail from the vistas to the valley floor where you can examine the ice-filled rock crevices (even in August!) at the base of one boulder slide. Although parents must protect young children at the precipitous overlooks, this hike is highly recommended for preschoolers, preteens, and in-betweens. (And Earth Science class will never seem quite so dull again!)

From the junction of US 7 and VT-140 in Wallingford, head east on VT-140. Drive 2.1 miles and turn right onto gravel Sugar Hill Road. In 0.1 mile, at a sign for Green Mountain National Forest Picnic Area, White Rocks, turn right. Drive 0.5 mile to the substantial parking area at the end of the road.

The White Rocks Trail leads from the southwestern side of the parking area on blue blazes and quickly crosses two streams on footbridges. From here, the first White Rocks overlook is 0.25 mile away and the Ice Beds are 0.75 mile beyond the overlook. The trail snakes along a ridge under a hemlock canopy and past ledge outcroppings, climbing a stiff grade on stone steps. Although hemlock trees grow slowly, they often become very large. Have the kids hug some of the trailside hemlocks. Do their arms reach all the way around?

Five switchbacks in quick succession lead to the top of the ridge and an intersection. For now, disregard the Ice Beds Trail that turns right (west) and bear left, quickly reaching an overlook. Enjoy the tremendous

Hikers work their way up the rock slide at White Rocks Cliff.

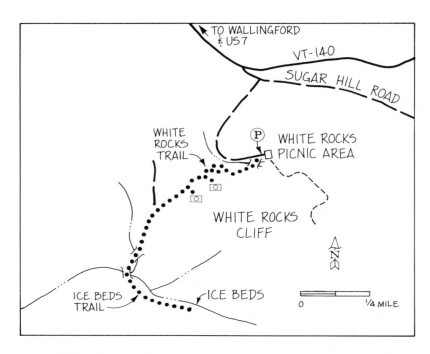

 CAUTION

 CAUTION

view of White Rocks (elevation 2662 feet) and the two boulder slides that
funnel down this sharp peak. Be sure to keep the kids well back from the
edge.

Return to the intersection and proceed straight along the Ice Beds
Trail. Climb moderately through more hemlocks, approaching the top of
a ridge. Swing behind the tallest ledge outcropping. As the trail begins a
descent, 0.4 mile from the start, bear left onto a side trail to reach another exposed ledge overlook with similar outstanding views of White
Rocks.

Do the slides seem to be close by? Put the distance in perspective by
watching the tiny climbers scaling the boulders. Pass around the binoculars so that the kids can watch these daring (crazy?) folks up close.
Spread out your picnic lunch and drink in the view. If you want to keep
younger children away from the edge while you're enjoying your sandwich, bring along a magnifying glass. Ask the kids to sit in one spot and
study the ground right in front of them. How many different colors can
they spot through the magnifying glass? Can they detect any movement
or is everything still?

Return to the Ice Beds Trail and turn left, dropping quickly down a
wooded slope with occasional stone steps to assist you. Are these hemlocks larger than the ones you hugged at the start of the hike? Put your

arms around them and see! The grade lessens at 0.55 mile; soon, a woods road joins from the right and the trail follows it southward. As you wind along the valley floor, cross a stream over railroad ties and follow the narrowing path as it twists eastward to cross another stream over a plank.

One mile from the start, you'll reach the Ice Beds at the base of the largest rock slide. According to a United States Forest Service (USFS) sign, a shattering of cheshire quartzite rock during the Ice Age probably created the rock slide. Ice and snow that accumulate within the rock crevices during the colder months are preserved throughout the year by the constant downdraft of cold air in this shaded canyon. Even in August, the kids will be able to see ice within the fissures. Straddle the small stream on a hot day and feel the blast of cold air coming off the mountain. Melting ice feeds the stream, maintaining a water temperature of 40 degrees throughout the summer months. (Big folks will be impressed, too!)

Return the way you came.

7. Mount Ascutney

Type: Dayhike or overnight
Difficulty: Challenging for children
Distance: 5.6 miles, round trip
Hiking time: 5.5 hours
High point/elevation gain: 3144 feet, 2600 feet
Hikable: May–October
Map: USGS Mount Ascutney

It's long, it's tough, it's complicated. But the hike to the Ascutney summit is worth it. In fact, with all of the intriguing distractions, the kids will probably notice neither the length of this route nor the steady climb. Numerous stream crossings near miniature waterfalls, water slides, and pools highlight the initial mile, while a series of overlooks with terrific local views characterizes the next mile or so. The frequent trail junctions allow kids to hone their map- and compass-reading skills. A trailside lean-to shelters overnight campers and the summit tower invites all to survey the landscape from a giant's perspective. An added bonus—unlike most mountain climbs, as you gain elevation, the slope eases. Your legs will appreciate that!

From I-91 in Ascutney, take Exit 8 to US 5, VT-12, and VT-131. Follow signs to US 5 North and, in 0.3 mile, turn left onto US 5 North and VT-12 North heading toward Windsor. (Signs indicate that the Mount Ascutney Ski Area is 7 miles away.) In 1.1 miles, turn left to head north on VT-44A toward Brownsville, following a sign to Ascutney State Park. Two and seven-tenths miles from US 5, watch for the sign on the right for the "Windsor Trail Parking Lot." Turn left onto a gravel drive and park in the grassy lot at the bottom of a field.

The Windsor Trail initially follows a farmer's road, skirting the left-hand side of a pasture heading southward. The road bends right (southwest) shortly, still following the edge of the field, and then veers left into the woods on white blazes. Winding under tall white pines, the road is softened by a carpet of needles. Can you walk without making a sound?

In 0.2 mile, the road rises gently along the northern rim of a deep gorge that cradles Mountain Brook. The blazes are sharp and frequent—let the kids lead the way. As the pine trees surrender to deciduous ones, the pitch gradually steepens so that it is climbing briskly just under the 0.5-mile mark. Here, loose stones underfoot make walking laborious for the little guys.

Seven-tenths of a mile from the start, the trail approaches Mountain Brook, which now rushes through a broad, shallow gulch. Look left to see the miniature twin waterfalls known as Gerry Falls. Between the falls, the water glides over smooth rocks into a peaceful pool.

Here, the woods road dissolves into a wide, rocky path. At 0.8 mile, as the brook splits into two branches, the trail crosses the right branch on a moderate ascent. Treading on ledge, the path winds between the two streams that are gradually spreading farther apart. Hugging the left branch, the trail passes another small water slide.

The trail suddenly twists right (west) and angles toward the right-hand stream. If it's time for a rest, instruct the children to pick a spot and sit very still for at least five minutes. Tell them to blend in with their natural surroundings as much as possible so that the forest creatures will begin to accept them as part of the environment. Soon, you may see birds landing nearby, squirrels scampering within a few feet of you, or rabbits hopping curiously in your direction.

Just over 1 mile from the start, the trail reaches the brook's right branch near a pretty water slide that empties into a pool. Cross the brook on stones. Who took the fewest steps? In 0.2 mile, the trail sweeps left and recrosses the stream. Soon it contemplates another crossing of the left branch but swings right (north) before reaching the bank.

At 1.25 miles, the trail has tracked far away from the brook. What types of plants does this damp soil nourish? (Look for sugar maple, white ash, yellow birch, and beech trees as well as varieties of mosses and ferns.) The trail narrows and the grade eases as you crest a shoulder. Play a survival game: If you had to live in these woods for a long time, where would you build a shelter? What would you use to build it? What would you eat?

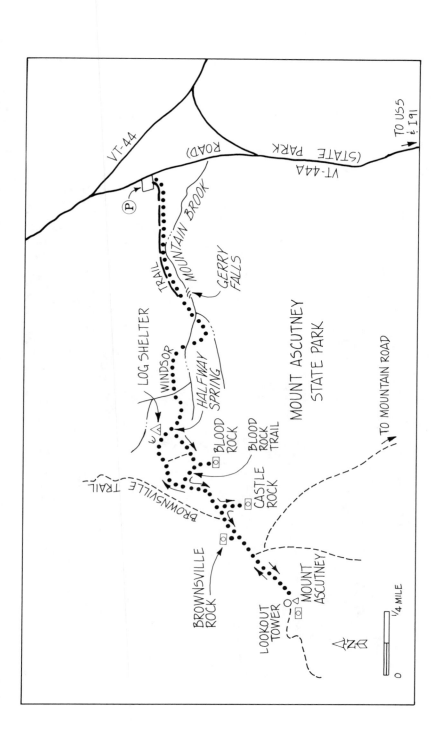

VT-44

TO US5
& I91

VT-44A
(STATE PARK ROAD)

P

MOUNTAIN BROOK

GERRY FALLS

LOG SHELTER TRAIL

WINDSOR

HALFWAY SPRING

BLOOD ROCK

BLOOD ROCK TRAIL

CASTLE ROCK

BROWNSVILLE TRAIL

BROWNSVILLE ROCK

LOOKOUT TOWER

MOUNT ASCUTNEY

MOUNT ASCUTNEY STATE PARK

TO MOUNTAIN ROAD

N

0   ¼ MILE

The stiff ascent resumes in a damp area littered with rock outcroppings. One and four-tenths miles from the start, the trail divides at a spot known as Halfway Spring; the Windsor Trail to Blood Rock Trail turns left and another branch of this trail leads right to a log shelter and running spring. Follow the left path that proceeds southward up a formidable climb. At 1.6 miles, the Windsor Trail meets the blue-blazed Blood Rock Trail.

Hikers cross River Mountain Brook near the cascades above Gerry Falls.

Bear left onto the Blood Rock Trail as the Windsor Trail departs right. Snake through an evergreen tunnel toward Blood Rock. Soon, a side trail on the left leads, in 250 feet, to the sloping ledge with dramatic views stretching well into New Hampshire.

Return to the Blood Rock Trail and turn left. This path sweeps right (west) and ends abruptly, 2 miles from the start, as it again meets the white-blazed Windsor Trail. Turn left (southwest). In 0.3 mile, turn left onto the Castle Rock spur (marked in blue) and cut through an area crowded with massive rocks and ledges. Soon, you'll emerge at Castle Rock, a dramatic overlook with eastern views stretching across the Connecticut River Valley. While the older folks rest and enjoy the vistas, let the kids climb and explore (with some supervision) on the rock outcrops farther inland.

Let the kids know that the climbing is over as you return to the Windsor Trail and turn left. The path meanders over wet areas on half-log bridges and arrives at a junction with the Brownsville Trail, 0.1 mile from Castle Rock. Continue straight (southwest) on the Windsor Trail, crossing more footbridges, and in another 0.1 mile turn right onto the side trail that leads quickly to the Brownsville Rock overlook. Enjoy stunning views over the central and northern Green Mountains. Point out the Killington peaks and Pico Peak to the north and Okemo Ski Area to the west.

Return once more to the Windsor Trail and turn right, dropping into a wet sag with more half-log bridges spanning the soggiest terrain. Avoid a left-going trail that leads to the summit parking area and, 0.3 mile from Brownsville Rock (and 2.8 miles from the start), you'll arrive at the summit.

Here, stunted spruce, birch, and fir trees have adapted to the brutal conditions and cluster around you, limiting the ground views. Climb the tower for spectacular 360-degree panoramas to the Adirondack Mountains of New York, New Hampshire's Presidential Mountains, and even Mount Monadnock (Hike 26), 60 miles away to the southeast.

To complete the hike, retrace your steps to your car.

(If you'd like to camp along the trail, return to the junction of the Windsor and Blood Rock trails and turn left, continuing on the Windsor Trail. Following "Log Shelter" signs, hike another 0.3 mile to the lean-to, nestled within a gorge near a brook and a bubbling spring. The rather dilapidated structure will accommodate three campers. In the morning, follow the white blazes of the Windsor Trail down the mountain, arriving at the Halfway Spring intersection in 0.1 mile. Turn left and follow the Windsor Trail back to your car.)

8. Mount Tom

Type: Dayhike
Difficulty: Easy for children
Distance: 3.2 miles, loop
Hiking time: 2.5 hours
High point/elevation gain: 1357 feet, 700 feet
Hikable: May–October
Maps: USGS Woodstock North and South

The paths that wind over and around Mount Tom are tame by Vermont standards. Reflecting its proximity to Woodstock, the civilized Faulkner Trail switches methodically back and forth up the side of the mountain, passing stone walls, park benches, and a stone bridge. Rather than being intrusive, these subtle human touches are an improvement to the natural landscape. The switchbacks that begin the hike were made for kids, who will delight in this zigzagging route to the summit. More adventurous tykes may prefer the return trip along the slightly wilder North Peak Trail.

From I-89, take Exit 1 to US 4, "Woodstock, Rutland." Head west on US 4 toward Quechee, Woodstock, and Rutland. Drive 10.2 miles to the intersection with VT-12 in Woodstock. Drive another 0.3 mile on US 4 and, with the Woodstock Green on your left, turn right onto Mountain Avenue. Drive through the covered bridge and, in 0.4 mile, park on the right-hand side of the road next to (unmarked) Faulkner Park.

Walk toward the northeastern side of Faulkner Park along the paved path. At the edge of the park, turn left onto the gravel, unblazed Faulkner Path and begin a series of switchbacks. Counting these hairpin turns is a good way for kids to chart their progress. As you begin on an easy grade through tall pines, look straight up to see the kaleidoscope pattern of their branches.

At the third switchback, who will be the first to spot the tree that seems to grow out of a boulder? A sign pointing right "To River Street," 0.4 mile from the start, marks switchback five as you sweep left. Beyond this turn, the trail squeezes between two boulders (you can count boulder squeezes too) and passes a stone arch bridge on the right. How many kids can fit underneath at one time?

As you round switchback nine at 0.85 mile, drag a stick across the mossy ledges that hug the trail to see if you can make an interesting sound. The first one to reach the huge old oak tree on the right wins a piggyback ride from the one who arrives last. Count another boulder squeeze on the next switchback.

View of Woodstock from the Mount Tom summit

On the eleventh, nearly 1.3 miles from the start, you'll meet the yellow-blazed Upper Link Trail, joining from the right. Can you find any acorns that are still wearing their "hats"? Pass a moss-coated boulder slide on the right and dodge an overhanging ledge near switchback twelve. Switchback thirteen is quickly followed by two more close turns. As the grade steepens, the switchbacks tighten. Who's counting boulder squeezes? Add one more at number nineteen (you should be up to three).

Pleasant views over Woodstock and the surrounding hills appear through the trees; you'll arrive at an overlook 1.5 miles from the start at switchbacks twenty-two and twenty-three. Beyond the vista, the trail dips into a minor sag and then climbs the route's only stiff grade, winding around the right side of a ledge toward the summit. A wire cable strung along the right side of the trail keeps children safely back from the edge.

Shortly, the trail emerges onto the flat, grassy Mount Tom summit. Delightful views extend in all directions, with the Killington Peak rising prominently on the northwestern horizon, Ludlow Mountain to the south, and Ottauquechee River to the east. (If you elect to head back now, your total hiking distance will be 3.2 miles.)

Follow the Bridle Trail, a carriage road that circles the top, in a clockwise direction, taking in the panoramas, then plunge into the woods heading northwestward. In 0.3 mile, leave the Bridle Trail to follow the yellow-blazed North Peak Trail right, climbing gently. Heading northward, the narrow, well-blazed trail passes through open, deciduous woods.

As a yellow trail splits left, continue straight to reach North Peak,

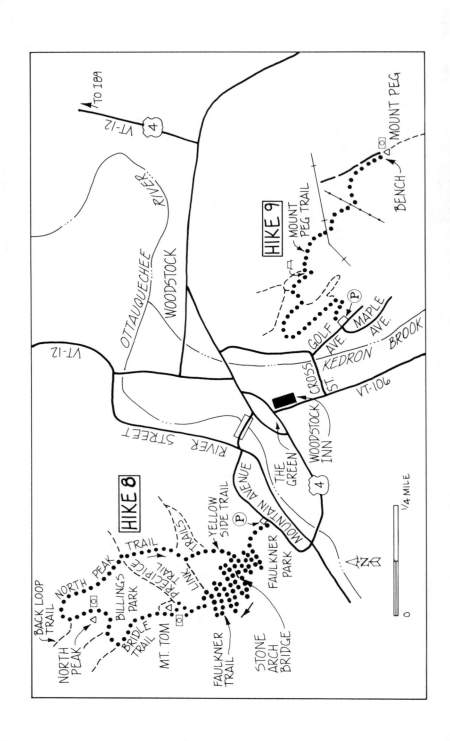

just 0.2 mile from the carriage road. The far-reaching views from this peak (over 100 feet taller than the Mount Tom summit) take in Mount Ascutney (Hike 7) to the south. After circling the summit, the path divides: The Back Loop Trail proceeds straight and the North Peak Trail heads right. Follow the North Peak Trail right (north) on a gradual-to-moderate descent. In 0.3 mile, the trail curls southeastward on a descent and drops into a rock-strewn gully.

Warn kids about the cost of whining, grumbling, or complaining: Offenders must tell three riddles or two knock-knock jokes. As you descend the steep mountainside, stone steps facilitate the drop. Leave the gully behind; soon, the Precipice Trail joins from the right, at 2.4 miles into the hike.

Shortly, turn right at another intersection, following a sign to "River Street." The trail dives into a wide, deep trench and crosses a baby stream. Catch your breath on the bench beyond the stream crossing.

At 2.6 miles, you'll reach a junction where the North Peak Trail bears left (south) on yellow blazes and the Upper Link Trail bears right (southwest). Follow the Upper Link Trail and the sign for "Mountain Avenue." Quickly, at another junction, the Upper Link Trail (marked in yellow) exits right on an ascent as you bear left, dropping gradually on the yellow Lower Link Trail.

Depart the Lower Link Trail at the next junction (2.8 miles from the start) to follow a yellow side trail straight (southeast) toward Faulkner Trail and Mountain Avenue. Hop over a second tiny stream and, in 100 yards, join the Faulkner Trail at the fifth switchback. Zigzag down the slope along the familiar path to your car.

9. Mount Peg

Type:	Dayhike
Difficulty:	Easy for children
Distance:	1.5 miles, round trip
Hiking time:	1 hour
High point/elevation gain:	1060 feet, 350 feet
Hikable:	May–October
Map:	USGS Woodstock South

Sorry, Peg. You weren't on our list. We had never even heard of you. But as we hiked up neighboring Mount Tom (Hike 8), we stopped to chat with a local woman who urged us to add this hill, one of her favorite childhood hikes. Thank goodness we took her advice! A short, pleasant woods walk leads to what we have deemed New England's most child-friendly summit. The broad, grassy expanse allows for safe exploring and offers the kinds of views that kids can appreciate. Miniature police cars and lumbering trucks wind between the tiny buildings of Woodstock far below. Whose child wouldn't love to play the part of a giant for an afternoon? You'll conquer Mount Peg in under an hour, meaning that you'll have the rest of the day to explore Woodstock, one of New England's loveliest villages.

Follow the directions to Woodstock provided for the Mount Tom hike (Hike 8). From the junction of US 4 and VT-106 in Woodstock, take VT-106 (also called School Street) south, immediately passing the Woodstock Inn. In 0.15 mile, turn left onto Cross Street. In another 0.1 mile, turn right onto Golf Avenue. Just before the intersection with Maple Avenue, park in a small, paved lot on the left.

To the left of a private residence, dive into a stand of pines at a sign for Mount Peg. Head northward on a moderate ascent. Quickly, the trail widens, bends right (east), and relaxes its climb. In 0.1 mile, switch left to head northwestward, sweeping past a small bench and an indistinct path that splits right. (Encourage the kids to practice their compass- and map-reading skills on this route.)

Two-tenths of a mile from the start, the trail curls easily to the right (east), marked occasionally by a plastic, yellow cross-country ski symbol. Who can do the best cross-country skier imitation? Winding southward, the trail drops gently to an unapparent intersection. Turn left (east), climb briefly, and crest, turning right at a T-intersection to head southeastward.

Promise the kids a short rest when you reach the picnic table. The path bends left (north) to sidestep the table at 0.4 mile. Follow the curling path for another 50 feet to where it divides: Turn right (east) and follow a red-blazed cross-country ski trail on level ground. Weave under a canopy of pines, duck under power lines, and cross a stone wall.

Seven-tenths of a mile from the start, the trail opens onto a sloping field. Although the trail appears to skirt the left side of the field, head eastward, bisecting the field, to arrive shortly at a jeep road. Turn right and climb the grassy hillside to the summit where a log bench welcomes you.

While the big people take in the lovely view over the Woodstock Valley and Mount Tom (Hike 8), the little people can play tag or somersault down the hill. Lie on your backs and find animals in the clouds. Allow enough time for frolicking and snacking and then return to your car the way you came (or let a youngster guide you along a slightly different return route using our map and a compass as guides).

10. Mount Independence

Type:	Dayhike
Difficulty:	Easy for children
Distance:	3 miles, loop
Hiking time:	2.5 hours
High point/elevation gain:	300 feet, 200 feet
Hikable:	May–October
Map:	USGS Ticonderoga (New York)

If you like to combine hiking with history lessons, Mount Independence is the place to go. A high, rocky peninsula reaching from Lake Champlain's eastern shore, Mount Independence was an essential part of our defense during the Revolutionary War, protecting American territory against a British attack from Canada. The remains of the fortifications dot the mountain and have been deemed the country's least disturbed period sites. Color-coded trails sweep across 400 acres, connecting numbered historic points, vistas, and interesting natural areas. Since

Combining hiking with history lessons at Mount Independence

you may meet up with a cow or horse (the grazing animals keep the vegetation low), you'll want to stay close to any children who would be startled by a close encounter of the farm animal kind.

 From the junction of VT-73 and VT-22A in Orwell, head west on VT-73. In 0.2 mile, continue straight (west), now on VT-73A, as VT-73 splits right. In another 2.8 miles, bear right (northwest) off VT-73A, following a sign to Mount Independence. This road becomes gravel in 1.2 miles and forks 0.4 mile later. Here, turn left onto Mount Independence Road, following a sign to Mount Independence. Drive 0.15 mile to a grassy hilltop parking area on the left.

Cross the gravel road and enter the park through a gate. Follow the grassy road for 0.25 mile through a meadow dotted with low shrubs and evergreens to the Trail Information Outpost. Here, the Orange and White trails split right and the Red and Blue trails head left. Follow the Orange Trail to the right, soon bearing left on an open hill as the White Trail diverges right. (This is a great route for the preschooler who is learning colors!) Who can spot an apple tree?

At 0.4 mile, the grassy trail reaches a log bench overlooking Lake Champlain and New York's Fort Defiance. Kids can imitate American soldiers surveying the lake for British ships. (This walk offers many opportunities for role-playing: At each marker, the kids can pretend to take part in the appropriate eighteenth-century activity.)

Beyond the vista, the trail passes through deciduous woods heading northward and then divides a field. Marker 1 identifies the site of the barracks within Star Fort, situated at the peninsula's high point. Logs illustrate the star shape of the area's stronghold. Follow the orange-blazed path as it curls left, passing an old well site at the field's western edge.

Dive into the woods, staying straight at a trail junction 0.7 mile from the start to reach the crane base (marker 2) with fine views similar to those from the log bench. Return to the junction and turn left (north), heading toward the point. Duck under tall pines and pass through a pasture near the site of the Artificers' Shops (marker 3). Blacksmiths, rope makers, wheelwrights, and shingle makers worked in this area. As each child imitates a craftsman, the others can guess whom he is acting out.

At 1 mile, the trail leaves a hardwood forest and opens onto a clearing marked with a stone memorial where a Revolutionary War flagpole once stood (marker 4). A long-ago cannon pointed northward from this spot in anticipation of enemy warships.

From the northeastern edge of the clearing, the trail drops down a wooded slope on a grassy path, reaching marker 5 at 1.1 miles. Here, a memorial marks the area where a shore battery stood guard with a row of cannons. The trail sidesteps the monument, sinking to the edge of the water at the sixth marker, 1.2 miles from the start. From this spot, a 12-foot-wide floating bridge once connected this hill to Fort Ticonderoga, visible across Lake Champlain.

Head left to wind along the shore, giving kids a good chance to ex-

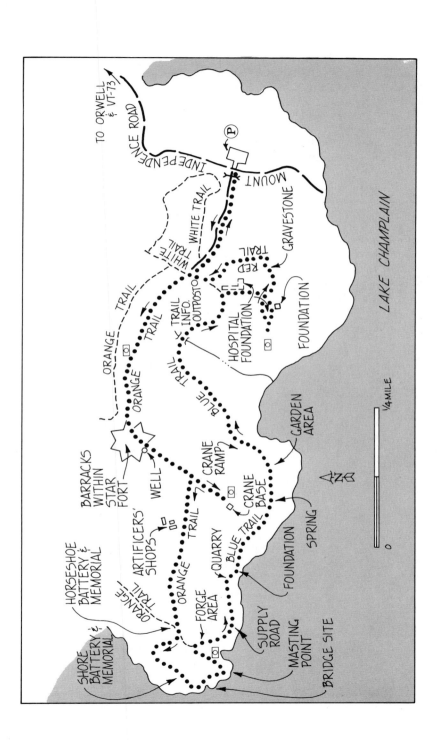

plore the water's edge. A rock outcropping (marker 7), where boat masts were once stepped, halts your walk along the water. Retrace your steps for about 50 feet, climb an embankment, and return to the Orange Trail. Turn right, passing several lovely overlooks, and then head inland.

At 1.4 miles, the Orange Trail heads left; pick up the Blue Trail that continues straight, following a Revolutionary War supply road through an overgrown meadow. Can you imagine walking along this road that connected the bridge and the hospital with a load of supplies for injured or ill soldiers?

Shortly beyond the junction, the Blue Trail passes its first marker, indicating where a forge once stood. The trail tumbles down a hill past marker 2, where you can see some of the original stonework for the supply road. You'll pass a quarry on the left (marker 3) and soon bottom out after a switchback.

At marker 4, a foundation sits in a pasture beside an old hickory tree just 50 yards from the lake. Can you see Fort Defiance? From here, the trail turns inland once more, skirting the left (east) side of a field. The trail eases into the woods to approach marker 5, where a significant spring served as the troops' major source of drinking water. Can the kids find the stone steps leading to the spring?

Curl right to cross the field, reaching the sixth marker where a vegetable garden once flourished. Look for the old drainage ditches that extend east to west across the field. Follow the trail as it curves to the left (southeast) at 1.7 miles, dividing a field fringed with birches. Blue blazes lead downhill to the remains of a crane ramp (marker 7) used to lift supplies from the base of the cliff to the top. To the right is a marshy cove.

Just under 2 miles from the start, the trail wanders southward, tumbling down a treed slope to cross a meager stream on a footbridge. The trail climbs easily through a damp, shallow ravine with a layer of loose stones underfoot. At 2.1 miles, the trail crests and bends left, reaching an intersection with the Red Trail in 0.1 mile. Turn right and follow the Red Trail past the foundation site of a hospital (marker 1) and a well-preserved foundation (marker 2). Cross a four-way intersection to an overlook of Fort Defiance and Fort Ticonderoga at the Red Trail's third marker, 2.4 miles into the hike.

Bearing left (southeast) from the overlook, the path recrosses the four-way intersection and leads past a gravestone (marker 4). As you merge right with the Blue Trail, follow red and blue blazes back to the Trail Information Outpost. Turn right to follow the grassy road back to your car.

Note: Mount Independence is open from Memorial Day through Columbus Day, Wednesday through Sunday, 9:30 a.m. to 5:30 p.m. Camping, digging, metal detecting, and artifact collecting are not permitted.

11. Rattlesnake Point and Falls of Lana

Type:	Dayhike or overnight
Difficulty:	Moderate for children
Distance:	5 miles, round trip
Hiking time:	4 hours
High point/elevation gain:	1650 feet, 1050 feet
Hikable:	May–October
Map:	USGS East Middlebury

On this trip, you and your family will wander near the picturesque Falls of Lana (named for an army general, not a beautiful woman named Lana), climb steadily through pleasant woodlands, and view Lake Dunmore, the surrounding hills, and far-off New York peaks from cliffs on Rattlesnake Point. Does a 5-mile hike seem too long? Cut the total distance by more than 3 miles by hiking to both sides of the waterfall and then returning to your car.

The trails cross Green Mountain National Forest as well as Branbury State Park property. Be sure to explore the park's swimming area, campground, and playground before you head home.

From downtown Middlebury, travel 6.7 miles on US 7 South to the junction with VT-53. Turn left (south) onto VT-53 and in 3.5 miles pass Branbury State Park and the Lake Dunmore camping and swimming areas. Drive another 0.3 mile to a sizable parking turnout on the left. A sign says "Silver Lake, Falls of Lana."

Near the northern end of the parking turnout, follow the trail that heads eastward into the woods, climbing moderately. (All park trails are blazed in blue.) Shortly, turn right onto a gravel woods road and curl left, passing a sign for the Silver Lake Recreation Area and Falls of Lana. Wander on an easy grade through mature hemlocks and stately white pines. At your first rest stop, have the kids pick out a tree and stand in such a way as to imitate its shape. Several kids can work together to "become" a tree. Notice the distinctive silhouette of each tree.

At 0.3 mile, look to the left across a cleared area crossed by a major water and power line for a pretty view of Lake Dunmore. Beyond the clearing, continue to look left to see massive, moss-covered ledge outcroppings. Soon, follow a side trail on the left to the top of the Falls of Lana. Here, watch as the water of Sucker Brook explodes through a narrow, deep canyon and spills down the rock face. Return to the gravel road and turn left, with Sucker Brook tumbling along on your left. The brook, cradled within a ravine, widens into several cool pools above the falls.

Water is always fascinating to small hikers.

At a junction 0.1 mile from the falls, near several small structures, a trail splits right (southeast), following a sign to Silver Lake. You continue straight (northeast) toward the Falls of Lana picnic and camping area, Rattlesnake Point, and North Branch Trail. Six-tenths of a mile from the start, you'll cross a substantial footbridge over Sucker Brook. (To reach a picnic and camping area and another overlook of the Falls of Lana, follow the left-hand trail just over the bridge.)

To continue to Rattlesnake Point, turn right, now on Rattlesnake Cliffs Trail, winding northeastward along Sucker Brook's left bank. At 0.7 mile, the Aunt Jennie Trail, a difficult shortcut to Rattlesnake Point, splits left as you continue to follow the Rattlesnake Cliffs Trail. The wide, level path gradually wanders farther away from Sucker Brook, entering an overgrown field at 0.8 mile. Halfway across the field, turn left (north) at an intersection following a sign to Rattlesnake Point (1.5 miles away) as the North Branch Trail heads right (east).

Follow the Rattlesnake Cliffs Trail on a moderate ascent. At 0.9 mile, recross Sucker Brook over a sturdy log bridge with a handrail. The gravel path continues to climb steadily and sidesteps an erratic boulder on the left. What do you think it's shaped like? Look around: Can you find a tree that looks like a witch? A boulder angled like a ship's hull cutting through the water? A cloud shaped like a hippopotamus?

Over a mile from the start, look left through the foliage to see the high ridge leading to Rattlesnake Point. Passing through stands of beech and birch, climb more briskly and begin a series of loose switchbacks, dodging the steepest slope. As the wide path shrinks to a foot trail, work your way over a jumble of rocks and then sweep southwestward. Who can find a leaf that has been chewed?

Two miles from the start, the Auntie Jennie Trail rises steeply to join from the left. Scale the ridge via tight switchbacks with railroad ties serving as rustic steps. Can you spot any low bush blueberries fringing the trail?

As the surrounding forest begins to open up, the trail reaches a junction, 2.3 miles from the start. Follow the trail to the left (southwest), toward Rattlesnake Cliffs, as the Oak Ridge Trail departs right for the summit of Mount Moosalamoo.

This rugged trail trips over roots and protruding ledge as it drops to a junction that forms a brief loop around Rattlesnake Point, a large rock outcrop at the southern end of Mount Moosalamoo. You can loop in either direction. If you continue straight ahead, you'll come upon Sid's Lookout at 2.5 miles, the route's best picnic spot. The waters of Lake Dunmore shimmer far below, reaching westward, it seems, to meet the Adirondack Mountains of New York. Though the two-tiered ledge provides an element of safety for curious kids, parents should still exercise caution.

Continue to follow the loop trail past a more protected overlook with similar views. Once you've returned to the beginning of the loop, kids may want to explore the various side trails that crisscross the area above the cliffs.

Retrace your steps to the car.

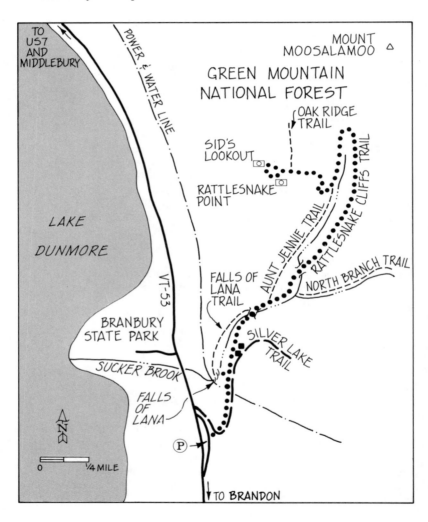

12. Red Rocks State Park

Type: Dayhike
Difficulty: Easy for children
Distance: 3 miles, loop
Hiking time: 2 hours
High point/elevation gain: 285 feet, 300 feet
Hikable: Year-round
Map: USGS Burlington

New England, natives lament, has nine months of winter and three months of darn poor sledding. And, I might add, a rather brief (albeit spectacular!) hiking season. That's what makes Red Rocks State Park such a find. A place for *all* seasons (and *all* kids), the park features a dazzling wildflower display in the spring, lifeguard-supervised swimming in the summer, stunning colors adorning the fifty-plus varieties of trees and shrubs in the fall, solitude in the winter, and fine bird-watching year-round.

Maintained by the city of South Burlington, the park offers several miles of manicured hiking trails that lead through lovely natural areas and approach a number of cliffs overlooking Lake Champlain and New York's Adirondack Mountains. (A big-wheeled stroller can navigate most of these paths.)

From I-89, take Exit 13 to I-189, Burlington and Shelburne. In less than 2 miles, I-189 ends at a traffic light; turn left onto US 7 South. Almost immediately, turn right onto Queen City Park Drive. Cross a narrow bridge over railroad tracks and turn left. Continue a short distance to the Red Rocks State Park gate. Park in the winter parking area outside the gate.

From the park entrance road, turn northward onto a wide path near the ticket house, west of the winter parking lot. Follow the gravel path as it curls left (west) to parallel the fence marking the park's border. How quietly can you walk? Imitate American Indians hunting for their dinner. . . . Would you catch your prey or scare it off with your noisy footsteps?

At a Y-intersection 0.3 mile from the start, the trail nearly merges with the park road; you stay to the right, soon passing between a massive split boulder on the left and ledge on the right. Rising gently, the trail reaches an intersection as the ledge ends. Bear left onto the more-traveled path and continue to climb, cresting at 0.5 mile and sidestepping more ledge outcroppings. Follow the right branch of the trail at a junction near the northern edge of the park (the left branch is a short-cut). Pass the East Overlook and curl left (west), rejoining the "shortcut" trail.

Drop beside the Lichen Ledges. Are the children familiar with lichens? These pioneers are often the first plants to establish themselves on a rock's barren surface. They initiate the lengthy process of converting these rocks into soil. Alga and fungus, the two plants that make up a lichen, cooperate to ensure the lichen's survival under its harsh living conditions: The alga shares food with the fungus, which provides a moist environment for the alga.

At 0.7 mile, bear right at an intersection to head northward on a pine needle carpet. Without the noise of traffic and crowds, the forest seems quiet. But is it as silent as it seems? Try this: Begin counting and stop when you hear a noise. With the chattering of squirrels, the rustling of leaves, and the calling of birds, you probably won't count past five! At 0.9 mile, the trail reaches the property boundary and curls left, from north to southwest, still weaving through stands of tall pines.

Who knows what "camouflage" means? (It actually comes from a French word that means "to disguise.") The kids can take turns running ahead and hiding just off the trail, trying to blend in with their surroundings as much as possible. How many creatures can you name that use camouflage to protect themselves from their enemies? (A polar bear's white fur blends in with the snow; the stripes on a zebra make it harder to see in tall grass; even a soldier's uniform is designed with camouflage in mind.) Can each child find a camouflaged insect?

One and two-tenths miles from the start, turn right at a junction and quickly left at another junction to open onto a cul-de-sac and overlook. From here, you have limited views of the vast waters of Lake Champlain. A narrow trail leaves the left (west) side of the cul-de-sac to wind toward the water, soon arriving atop cliffs that loom 30 to 40 feet over the water. Find level ground to enjoy a rest and snack, listening to the soothing rhythm of the waves splashing against the ledges. You may want to follow the trail eastward and westward to explore the cliffs.

Return to the cul-de-sac and turn sharply left at the first junction to wander to another lovely lake overlook at 1.4 miles. Here, parents can relax a bit more because a rail fence provides protection. Venture onto the massive flat rocks at the water's edge and pause, letting the cool lake breeze revive you. The trail loops back and returns to the junction with the first overlook trail. Head straight (east), soon passing another familiar trail that joins from the left. Next the trail skirts another vista of Lake Champlain's Shelburne Bay. Don't the Adirondacks make a lovely backdrop?

One and three-quarters miles into the hike, bear right at an intersection with the trail from the Lichen Ledges. Pass a final overlook side trail on the right and, just under 2 miles from the start, turn right at a

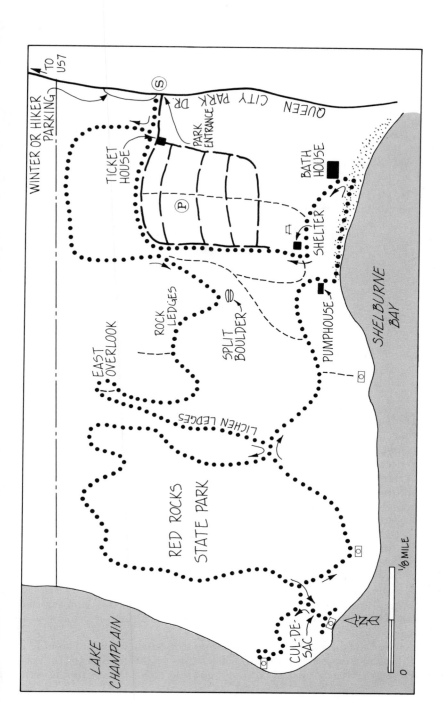

junction and quickly join a gravel path that cuts through a clearing. Drop down a set of stairs, passing to the left of a pumphouse, to arrive at the shore. Turn left a short distance to the public beach. Swim or stretch out on the sand before following the trail that leads from the bath house (with changing and rest facilities) through the picnic and cookout area to the park road. Follow the park road northward to the parking lot.

Note: A minimal parking fee is charged in season (if you park within the Red Rocks boundaries). Camping and alcoholic beverages are not permitted. Pets must be leashed.

13. Kettle Pond

Type:	Dayhike or overnight
Difficulty:	Easy for children
Distance:	3 miles, loop
Hiking time:	2.5 hours
High point/elevation gain:	1410 feet, 150 feet
Hikable:	May–October
Map:	USGS Plainfield

Water, so fascinating to children and so soothing to adults, is never far away on this hike around pristine Kettle Pond. The narrow trail winds along the gentle terrain of the pond's northern side with frequent excursions to the water and then tracks over more rugged ground along the less-accessible southern shore. The kids will enjoy a brief visit or an overnight at one of the primitive waterfront shelters (rented for a nominal fee on a "first come, first served" basis at the New Discovery Campground in Peacham, just north on VT-232). Bring along a store-bought net or a coat hanger covered with a piece of old nylon stocking to skim the water for aquatic insects. If you would like to view Kettle Pond (and the rest of the expansive Groton State Forest) from above, climb nearby Owl's Head Mountain (Hike 14).

From I-91, take Exit 17 to US 302 and US 5. Follow US 302 west for 8.2 miles. Turn right (north) onto VT-232. In 2 miles, enter Groton State Forest. Five and nine-tenths miles from US 302, pass a sign for the Kettle Pond Youth Group Area and turn left into a driveway leading to a parking area.

The blue-blazed Kettle Pond hiking loop heads westward from the parking area on level ground. In 150 feet, the trail forks; bear right. Follow the rocky, root-choked path to a clearing at 0.1 mile with a hearth

Water striders, dragonflies, tadpoles . . . what will YOU see?

and a lean-to for camping. Beyond the camping area, the trail leads quickly to a small, rocky beach at the water's edge. As you gaze at the unspoiled pond rimmed by high hills, you'll sense the vastness of this Vermont wilderness. Did you bring a net? Skim the top of the water. What did you scoop up?

The trail hugs the northern side of the pond, winding amidst moss-draped rocks and crowded hemlocks. Three-tenths of a mile from the start, the path flirts with the gentle waves that splash the rocky shore, crossing a stream where it empties into the pond. Ask the kids to describe how the plants near the water are different from those inland. Then ask them, "What do people have in common with plants?"

Dodge a wet area at 0.35 mile and soon rejoin the water. At the 0.5-mile mark, the trail opens onto a clearing near a large rock that is half-submerged in the water. If the kids have worked up a sweat, you may decide to stop here for a swim.

The tight trail hops over another stream and passes a second stone hearth at 0.8 mile. In another 0.3 mile, as you near the western tip of the pond, pass a second lean-to with an open hearth. A side trail leads 75 feet from the campsite to the water. Here, the trail begins to curl left (south).

If you notice something of interest along the trail—an insect, a bird, a plant—point it out to your young companions even if you don't know its name. Observing and enjoying nature is more important than identifying it, especially when you are trying to hold a child's attention.

As you round the pond's western side, the trail trudges over rocky terrain (warn the kids to step over rocky crevices that might trap tiny feet), squeezing between large boulders at 1.4 miles. Curling eastward, the path strays to the right of a cabin and avoids the pond's marshy shore.

Who will spot the third lean-to (part of the Kettle Pond Youth Camping Area) at 2.3 miles? With the now-distant water shimmering through the trees, the trail finds the main Youth Camping Area, strewn with lean-tos, at 2.6 miles. Follow the gravel road that leads from the camping area to the highway. Turn left onto VT-232 and hike 0.1 mile back to your car.

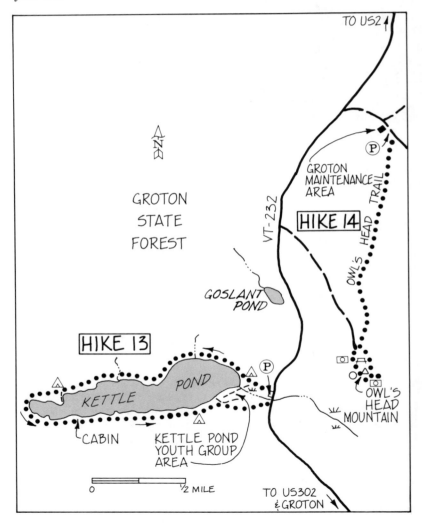

14. Owl's Head Mountain

Type: Dayhike
Difficulty: Easy for children
Distance: 2.8 miles, round trip
Hiking time: 2 hours
High point/elevation gain: 1960 feet, 300 feet
Hikable: May–September
Map: USGS Plainfield

Groton State Forest's 25,000 acres encompass mountains and lakes, forests and bogs. The area draws not only hikers but boaters, fishermen, campers, cross-country skiers, and hunters, and owes much of its current appearance to the work of the Civilian Conservation Corps. Nearly 75 years ago, this group reforested areas burned by fires, built forest roads, and erected many of the lean-tos and other structures that still stand today.

Of all of the mountaintops within the forest, Owl's Head is the most popular, due to its easy access and magnificent views. Preschoolers, teenagers—even grandparents—will want to be included on this trip.

From I-91, take exit 17 to US 302 and US 5. Follow US 302 West for 8.2 miles; turn right (north) onto VT-232. In 7.6 miles, just past the Marshfield town line, turn right onto a gravel driveway at a sign for the Groton Maintenance Area, District 4. Drive 0.3 mile and park on the left side of the road, just beyond the maintenance buildings.

Alternatively, from the junction of US 2 and VT-232, drive 4.6 miles on VT-232 South to the gravel drive on the left. Follow the directions above.

Continue eastward down the gravel road to a trail sign, where the Owl's Head Trail ducks into the woods on the right. Who's the best at role-playing? Select an animal that lives within this forest to imitate, perhaps a black bear, deer, moose, mink, beaver, or an otter. See who can maintain his or her "role" the longest.

The blue-blazed path winds southward through uncluttered hemlock and spruce woods. Though well maintained, the trail shows a few signs of heavy traffic. Let the kids take turns leading the way, guided by the frequent paint blazes.

One-half mile from the start, the trail trudges up a short hill, swerving left over squat ledge in another 0.2 mile to avoid a wet area. Hop from stone to stone over another damp section and curl left on an easy ascent. At 1.1 miles, the trail opens onto a gravel turnaround near a picnic shelter. Merge with the gravel road heading westward to reach the picnic shelter shortly.

Pause to take in the delightful views of nearby Kettle Pond (Hike 13) and Vermont's Worcester Mountains. Take a vote: Who wants to climb the remaining 0.2 mile to the Owl's Head summit the easy way? How many votes for the tough route? If easy wins, return to the gravel turnaround and bear right, following a gentle trail up the eastern side of the hill.

If the easy way was outvoted by your adventurous companions, pass the picnic shelter on the right to climb southward, then eastward, on a rugged trail over exposed granite. (We saw a rabbit family dart into the woods here.) To distract them from the rocky climb, ask the kids to guess whether "hare" is just another name for a rabbit. (No! Hares are larger and are born covered with fur, with their eyes open. Rabbits live with a group in burrows—unlike hares—and are born blind, without hair.)

The trail skirts the open edge of the summit on smooth, exposed baldface. Parents can relax as kids explore the low stone tower and romp about the mountaintop—there are no sharp drop-offs. Although spruce trees flourish here, the exposed edges offer views to the west, south, and east. From the summit's southeastern side, look for Groton Lake and New Hampshire's Mount Washington and Franconia region mountains. To the west, you'll have superb views of Camel's Hump and Mount Mansfield.

Return to the car the way you came.

A stone tower crowns Owl's Head summit.

15. Mount Hunger

Type: Dayhike
Difficulty: Challenging for children
Distance: 4.3 miles, round trip
Hiking time: 4 hours
High point/elevation gain: 3554 feet, 2200 feet
Hikable: May–October
Map: USGS Stowe

Mount Hunger's open south summit is well known for its fabulous views of notable Vermont and New Hampshire peaks. The climb is steady and relatively long, but stream crossings, cascades, and ledgy scrambles break up the trip. Inappropriate for most preschoolers, this trip will appeal to older kids who can appreciate the dizzying panoramas.

From I-89, take Exit 10 to VT-100 North. In 2.8 miles, near Waterbury Center, turn right (east) onto Howard Avenue. In 0.3 mile, turn left onto Maple Street. Drive another 0.2 mile and turn right onto Loomis Hill Road. Follow Loomis Hill Road (which turns to gravel after 2.1 miles) for 3.6 miles to a parking turnout on the right for Mount Hunger, Waterbury Trail.

The Waterbury Trail begins as a wide path heading eastward and soon curls right (southeast) and narrows to rise gently through mature, mixed woods. How about having a scavenger hunt? Tell each child to look for a feather, a seed, a berry, and a smooth rock. In 0.15 mile, the trail bisects mossy granite outcroppings. Do all types of moss feel the same?

Follow sporadic blue blazes along sweeping switchbacks. In the fall, the kids will shuffle through layers of leaves as vividly colored as a box of Crayolas. At 0.45 mile, the moderate climb eases and, in 0.2 mile, the gently rising trail crosses a stream over two 10-foot lengths of halved logs. Beyond the stream, you'll climb easily for a short distance.

Soon, the pace changes and the trail heads eastward into the slope, finding occasional log steps to assist in the moderate-to-steep ascent. At 0.8 mile, the trail curls southward and gradually relaxes its climb, nearly leveling at the 1-mile mark.

Listen for the sound of rushing water. . . . You'll reach a series of cascades 1.1 miles from the start where the water collects in random pools. On a humid day, you'll appreciate the coolness of the poolside perches. What happens to an acorn or a twig tossed into the hurrying water?

The trail climbs along the left bank of the stream, passes the cascades, and quickly turns right to cross the stream over rocks. (Count how many steps it takes you to get across.) Depart the stream on a moderate ascent, then zigzag up a steep slope.

Climb briskly (and sometimes soggily) for the next 0.5 mile. Birch trees fringe the trail at 1.3 miles as the cascading water whispers in the distance. In another 0.2 mile, the trail finds the now meager stream again, crosses to the opposite bank, and crosses back again.

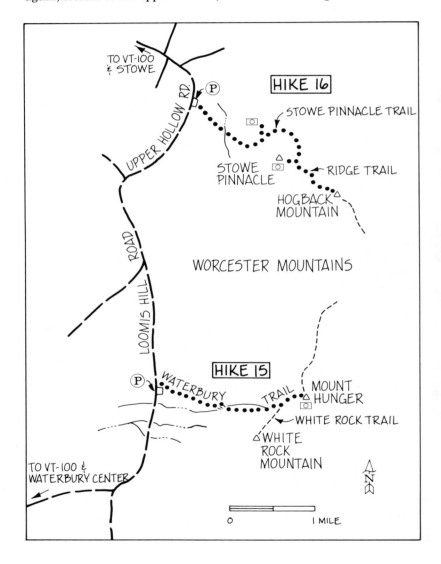

Kids, what type of trees first appear at the 1.5-mile mark? (Evergreens.) At 1.6 miles, the trail departs the stream once more, relaxing its climb as it passes through a hemlock and spruce grove 0.1 mile later. Have the children feel the needles of a spruce tree and then a hemlock. How are they different? (Spruces have sharp, square needles; hemlocks have flat, short needles.)

At 1.8 miles, the trail crosses a pair of petite streams on halved logs. In another 0.1 mile, you'll need to help the kids mount a series of steep ledges, squeezing through a crevice along the way. Stay straight (east) at an intersection at 2 miles as the White Rock Trail bears right (south).

On its final surge toward the summit, the trail breaks out onto exposed baldface littered with stunted spruce trees. The pitch eases as you approach the broad, airy mountaintop, safe for exploration by careful kids. (Seek refuge among the ledges if the wind is brisk.)

The superb panoramic views take in nearly every peak in the main range of the Green Mountains as well as many White Mountain and Adirondack peaks. To the north and south you'll see other mountains in the Worcester Range. Look west to see the distinctive shape of Camel's Hump rising to a height of over 4000 feet. Focus your binoculars across the valley to the northwest; you'll see the famous Von Trapp Family Lodge.

Reverse direction to return to your car.

Family hiking on Mount Hunger

16. Stowe Pinnacle and Hogback Mountain

Type: Dayhike
Difficulty: Challenging for children
Distance: 4.5 miles, round trip
Hiking time: 4 hours
High point/elevation gain: 3300 feet, 2300 feet
Hikable: May–October
Map: USGS Stowe

Pick your distance: a 2.6-mile "moderate" hike to and from the first overlook, a 3.2-mile "moderate" round-trip hike to Stowe Pinnacle, or a 4.5-mile "challenging" trip to and from the summit of Hogback. Since your best views will come from Stowe Pinnacle, only hardy souls who crave a challenge will push on to the wooded Hogback summit.

With two turnaround points in addition to the final destination, you can be a little generous in assessing your family's abilities. Bring the six- or seven-year-olds who've been begging to climb a "real" mountain and see how they do. Even if they poop out at the initial overlook, you'll all be able to enjoy lovely views of Mount Mansfield and other peaks in the Green Mountains before you head back to the car.

From the junction of VT-100 and VT-108 in Stowe, take VT-100 south and in 1.7 miles turn left onto Gold Brick Road. In 0.3 mile, turn left, still on Gold Brick Road. Two and one-tenth miles from VT-100, turn right onto Upper Hollow Road. In 0.5 mile, the road becomes gravel; continue on it another 0.1 mile to a parking area for the Pinnacle Trail on the left.

Enjoy the view of your destination—Stowe Pinnacle with Hogback Mountain over its right shoulder—from the parking area. The blue-blazed Stowe Pinnacle Trail leaves the back of the parking area at a sign for the Pinnacle (1.5 miles away) and heads eastward through abandoned (often damp) pasture land. Boards lead over the soggiest sections but kids will have a hard time avoiding wet feet.

At 0.2 mile, the trail ducks into the woods, still crossing over some damp terrain on planks. How many different types of trees can you identify here? The rugged path climbs briskly at 0.4 mile, with carpets of moss flourishing within the damp, shaded forest. Ask the kids to describe the living conditions of moss. Have they ever seen moss grow in a sunny location? Probably not, since coolness and moisture are critical to a moss's reproductive system. The moss plant produces male and female parts on its stem tips, and the sperm must swim to the female part.

At the 0.5-mile mark, the trail cuts left (northeast) and then swings right (east), resuming its moderate ascent through a lovely stand of white birches. Have the kids take turns acting out different forest creatures while the others try to guess the animals being imitated. (No fair using noises!)

The path meets a stream 0.6 mile from the start and wanders along its right bank, crossing to the left side in less than 0.1 mile. Can you find any curls of birch bark along the ground? Toss them into the tumbling water and pretend they are miniature birch-bark canoes.

The trail winds easily through the woods, avoiding the steepest route up the mountain until 0.9 mile from the start, when the pitch intensifies and the trail passes under exposed ledge. Kids may need a hand in another 0.2 mile as the trail picks its way through a chaos of boulders on moderate-to-steep terrain, switching back to alleviate the pitch.

As you crest a shoulder 1.2 miles from the start, the trail splits: The blue blazes lead straight as well as left, to a vista. Follow the spur trail to the left, soon arriving at an overlook on open ledges. With the Stowe val-ley spread out before you and Mount Mansfield in the distance, relax and catch your breath.

Return to the main trail and continue to head eastward on fairly level ground. Shortly, the trail bends right and drops for about 0.1 mile, curling around the mountain's eastern side and resuming its climb toward the Pinnacle. Pick your way through an area of stones and bony roots with ledge bordering on the right.

One and a half miles from the start, you'll reach another shoulder and trail junction. Follow the right-hand trail for 0.1 mile on a gradual ascent through spruce woods to the Pinnacle. There's no need for parents to be overly concerned with roving children because this is a sloping, expansive crown, rather than a summit with sheer drop-offs. The views extend to Camel's Hump, Mount Mansfield, and the Stowe valley to the west and north, the nearby Hogback summit to the south, and other Worcester Mountains to the south and east. Gobble down your lunch or just lie on your back and watch the lazy parade of clouds.

If you're up to it, return to the junction and follow the blue-blazed Ridge Trail to the right (south) toward the Hogback Mountain summit. Climb steeply through a spruce forest for 0.5 mile to the wooded peak. Though the views are limited, you'll appreciate the seclusion of this mountaintop hemlock grove. Smell the Christmas scents and peek through the trees for cropped distant views.

Retrace your steps to the car.

17. Moss Glen Falls

Type: Dayhike
Difficulty: Easy for children
Distance: 1 mile, round trip
Hiking time: 1 hour
High point/elevation gain: 950 feet, 150 feet
Hikable: April–October
Maps: USGS Mount Worcester
and Stowe

Short and sweet, the hike to Moss Glen Falls is the only one in the book that comes with this guarantee: No one in your hiking party will whine, complain, or grumble. There's just too much to see and do! Even kids who are normally unfazed by nature's marvels will stand in awe of this impressive waterfall and the chasm that carries Moss Glen Brook.

Although most youngsters have the ability to make the trip, parents should be aware of the potential dangers near the waterfall. We recommend that there be at least one adult for every two young children.

From the junction of VT-12, VT-100, and VT-15 in Morrisville, travel south on VT-100. In 5.6 miles, turn left onto paved Randolph Road. In 0.3 mile, turn right at a fork onto gravel Moss Glen Falls Road. Drive another 0.5 mile and, just before the bridge over Moss Glen Brook, park on the left in a large parking area.

Alternatively, from the junction of VT-100 and VT-108 in Stowe, drive 3 miles north on VT-100 to Randolph Road and turn right. Follow the directions above.

Follow the trail southward from the parking area through mixed woods. Let the kids lead the way across a series of boards and logs that span a mucky tract. It may be hard for the children to avoid wet feet because the ribbon of trail soon weaves through a soggy pasture alongside Moss Glen Brook. The shallow brook splashes on a pebble bed, enticing kids to explore its banks and toss in a few stones. Is there any sound more satisfying to a youngster's ears than the "kerplunk" of a rock breaking the surface of the water?

One-quarter mile from the start, the trail leaves the field and ducks back into the woods. Climbing abruptly up a series of rock steps, the path trudges steadily toward the top of Moss Glen Falls. Partway up, you'll reach an overlook where you can look to the right and see torrents of water spilling through the tight ravine. Only a mountain goat (or an extremely agile, experienced hiker and climber) would dare to inch down the gorge wall to the base of the falls. (The view from above is as good as the one from below anyway, and you won't get soaked with the spray.)

Moss Glen Falls

Continue to follow the rocky ridge high above the ravine, quickly gaining elevation as well as better views of the falls. You will want to keep young children close to you here. Pause for a look when you reach the top, but don't turn back yet. Follow the trail as it hugs the edge of the impressive 50-foot-deep chasm that cradles the swift brook. Soon, the chasm walls begin to shrink until the canyon is an unassuming river bed. Now you can drop down the bank to look into the belly of the chasm. Anyone care to return to the car by way of a barrel ride? No? Then return by the familiar route on foot.

18. Elmore Mountain and Balanced Rock

Type: Dayhike or overnight
Difficulty: Moderate for children
Distance: 4.5 miles, round trip
Hiking time: 4 hours
High point/elevation gain: 2608 feet, 1400 feet
Hikable: May–October
Map: USGS Morrisville

Elmore State Park deserves a weekend rather than an afternoon, offering swimming on the sandy shore of Lake Elmore, picnic facilities, and a camping area at the base of the trail. (In addition to the main trail, a short nature trail loops around the trailhead.) The mountaintop is easily accessed by most families via an interesting route that winds along a stream and beside moss-covered ledge.

Because Elmore stands alone at the northern end of the Worcester Mountain Range, its views are varied and extensive, taking in the nearby farming valley as well as faraway mountain ranges. And—surprise—the hike doesn't end at the summit! Continue for another 0.5 mile to Balanced Rock, a huge erratic tipped toward the mountain's steep slope.

From the junction of VT-12 and VT-100 in Morrisville, take VT-12 South. In 4.4 miles, just before the village of Lake Elmore, turn right into Elmore State Park. At the gate, pay a small per-person fee and drive 0.5 mile along the main park road to the white metal gate that marks the trailhead. A picnic pavilion and small parking area are to the right.

The Elmore Mountain Trail passes through the gate, following the gravel road southwestward. The road, lined by hemlocks and birches,

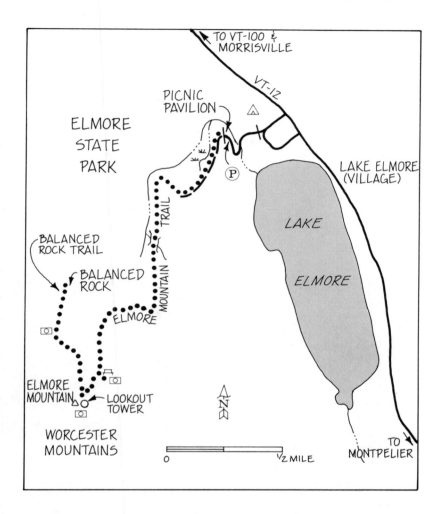

curls westward and skirts a beaver pond on the right 0.2 mile from the start. Follow the slow-moving stream that feeds the pond as it meanders alongside the trail for the next 0.1 mile. What does it sound like when a pebble is tossed into the stream? How about a bigger rock? Climb easily along the road with occasional glimpses of Lake Elmore to the east.

When the road ends at 0.5 mile, follow a wide path as it bends right (marked sporadically in blue) into mixed woods heading westward. With no rocks or roots to trip up little feet, your young hikers can dash ahead here. The foot trail flirts briefly with the wandering stream just beyond the 0.5-mile mark, then rises gradually until the pitch steepens 0.1 mile later. Climb briefly up this moderate slope and, at 0.7 mile, follow the trail as it bends left (south) and resumes its moderate ascent with occasional rock intrusions.

The trail dodges a moss-covered chunk of ledge and levels 0.8 mile from the start. What does moss feel like? Dry or damp? Soft or rough? Does all moss feel the same? In another 0.1 mile, balance on a half-log bridge over a branch of the stream and begin a gradual-to-moderate ascent, sweeping northward, then southward. At 1 mile, the stream snakes near the sheer, moss-covered walls of a gorge on the right of the trail. Soon after, the trail emerges on the eastern rim of the mountain, with the wooded slope dropping off sharply to the left.

At 1.3 miles, the trail cuts into the mountain on a brief, moderate ascent before curling back to the left (south) on more gradual ground. A picnic table set in a grassy clearing marks the 1.5-mile mark; from here, a short side trail on the left leads on open ground to exposed ledges over-

Balanced Rock on Elmore Mountain: your goal.

looking the shimmering waters of Lake Elmore, about a mile away. An old cellar hole and a chimney are all that remain of the lookout cabin that once sat here.

From this spot, 1.6 miles from the start, point out to the kids your immediate destination, the fire tower perched on top of the mountain. From the western side of the clearing, the trail resumes its climb up the mountain, trudging up a short, steep ledge. The grade soon eases as the trail rises gradually, twisting on rugged terrain surrounded by spruce groves. How does the end of a spruce needle feel? Sharp . . . or dull?

At 1.7 miles, after traveling southward on a gradual ascent, curl right (west) into the mountain and climb briskly to an intersection with the Balanced Rock Trail. Follow the Elmore Mountain Trail to the left, arriving in less than 0.1 mile at the summit tower.

Climb the rickety tower's sixty-one steps to surround yourself with views of the Green Mountains (notably Camel's Hump and Mount Mansfield) to the west and New Hampshire's Presidential Range to the east. Since Elmore is one of the lowest peaks in the Worcester range, you'll also look over the pastoral Lamoille River valley at tiny cows roaming the open meadows, patches of striped, planted fields, and red barns clinging to the hillsides. Notice the sun reflecting off the metal roofs so common in central and northern Vermont.

On most hiking trips, the summit marks the final destination and the beginning of the return trip. But on this hike, the kids have something more to look forward to. Return to the junction north of the fire tower and turn left, heading toward Balanced Rock along a narrow trail with ledge underfoot. One-tenth of a mile from the summit, the trail opens onto an exposed ledge outcropping with pretty easterly views. At the northern end of the outcropping, the trail turns left into the woods, cresting quickly. Drift through a spruce forest with a moss carpet softening the rocky terrain. Drop easily from east to west across the ridge, reaching a western overlook of Mount Mansfield and the Stowe valley 0.4 mile from the summit intersection.

Beyond the overlook, the trail cuts back to the eastern side of the ridge and passes to the right of some 20-foot ledges, falling down a gradual-to-moderate slope. After crossing baldface, look eastward for a view of Lake Elmore. As you drop back into spruce woods, let the kids lead the way to Balanced Rock, a cigar-shaped rock teetering precariously on ledge, threatening to plunge down the steep mountain slope. They'll want to examine it close-up and offer some opinions as to when the rock might take its final tumble.

NOW it's time to head back to the car, looping back over the summit to retrace your steps along the Elmore Mountain Trail.

Mount Pisgah looks impressive from the CCC Road on Burke Mountain.

19. Burke Mountain

Type:	Dayhike or overnight
Difficulty:	Moderate for children
Distance:	6 miles, round trip
Hiking time:	5 hours
High point/elevation gain:	3267 feet, 1400 feet
Hikable:	May–September
Map:	USGS Burke Mountain

You've heard that you can't judge a book by its cover, but did you know that the same thing applies to mountains? Indeed, the steep slopes of conical Burke Mountain seem to indicate a formidable trail to the summit. In reality, the grades are surprisingly easy and the walk is a pleasant one. You may even feel a little guilty enjoying such spectacular views from the lookout tower since you didn't have to work very hard to get there.

Burke doesn't cater just to hikers: downhill and cross-country ski trails crisscross the mountain, camping facilities accommodate over-nighters, and a toll road delivers motorists to the summit.

From the junction of US 5 and VT-114 in Lyndonville, head north on VT-114. In 4.6 miles, turn right following signs to Burke Mountain Ski Resort. At 2.1 miles, bear left onto the auto toll road to the summit of Burke Mountain. (Look for the sign: "Sugarhouse Store, Camping and Picnic Areas.") In 0.1 mile, park before the toll house.

Walk southward for 0.6 mile along the paved summit toll road to the "CCC Road" on the right. Turn right (southwest) at the sign onto the level, grassy CCC Road, intersecting a number of ski trails within the next 0.4 mile. From the open ski slopes, you'll have good views to the north and west of the characteristic profile of the Lake Willoughby region peaks.

Leaving the ski area behind, climb on a gentle rise, although the slope from left to right drops steeply. Water from hurrying streams spills down the wooded hillside, splashing across (or under) your path several times in the next 0.3 mile. Occasional blue diamond blazes indicate that cross-country skiers sweep across this snow-covered path in the winter. Urge tiring kids to find a sturdy walking stick to help (if only psychologically) on the climb.

At the height of the land, 1.7 miles from the start, follow the blue-blazed West Peak Trail as it splits left (southeast) to skirt a camping shelter and hearth in about 40 yards. Climbing easily, then more briskly, the narrow footpath winds up the mountainside through a birch forest. Two-tenths of a mile beyond the junction, the slope relaxes and the trail joins a seasonal stream. Who will be the first one to spot a bird's nest?

At 2.1 miles, on a moderate ascent, the trail passes through ever-green stands and dodges moss-covered ledges. Smell the spruce trees as you follow the snaking path through heavy woods. Soon, ledge intrudes underfoot; the lush moss, however, creeps across the path to soften the surface. If you find that your group has scattered with some children lagging behind and others far ahead, consider putting one adult in front with another bringing up the rear.

At 2.5 miles, the trail opens onto exposed baldface with fine views to the west and north of the Passumpsic valley and Lake Willoughby. One-tenth of a mile beyond the baldface, the trail arrives on the wooded summit of Burke's West Peak, where a lean-to camping shelter perches near a rock hearth. Follow the trail to an open area not far from the shelter that offers fine southern and western views. Here, look to the left and you'll see the nearby summit of Burke Mountain.

Drop to an intersection cradled in a sag and turn right (southwest).

Track across a level ridge through a thick spruce forest. Shortly, in a col between the West Peak and Burke Mountain summits, bear right at another trail junction.

Shortly, the trail opens onto the parking lot at the end of the auto toll road. The lookout tower looms through the woods to the east. From here, you can follow a paved access road to the summit tower or follow the unblazed Profile Trail. This distinct footpath enters the woods on the southeastern side of the parking lot, leading to the summit in 0.2 mile. You may want to be more adventurous and explore one of the interconnecting paths that splits from the Profile Trail.

More than ninety steps lead to the top of the summit tower, as high as a nine-story building. As you might expect, the views into New Hampshire and Canada are unequaled.

Return the way you came or follow the auto road back down. (Remind your weary little hikers that it's all downhill from here!)

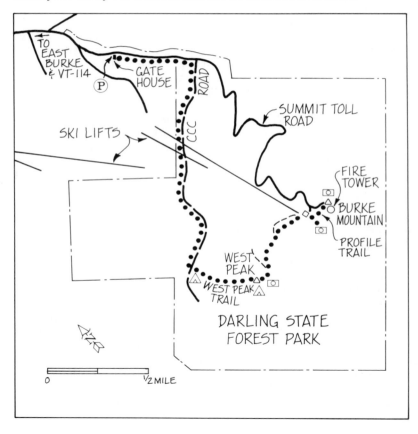

20. Mount Hor

Type:	Dayhike
Difficulty:	Moderate for children
Distance:	3 miles, round trip
Hiking time:	2.5 hours
High point/elevation gain:	2660 feet, 1000 feet
Hikable:	May–October
Map:	USGS Sutton

The three vistas encompassed by this hike take in surprisingly varied scenery. Two offer views of Lake Willoughby and the surrounding mountains while the third, just below the Mount Hor summit, takes in a mosaic of small ponds with New Hampshire mountains on the horizon. The first section of the hike is the toughest, so let kids know that once they have conquered that initial slope, the rest of the trip is a relative cinch.

Despite the precautions parents must take at the overlooks (where the hillside falls away sheer for up to 1200 feet), this is a terrific hike for youngsters. After all, looking down on things for an afternoon is a nice change for little guys.

From the junction of US 5, VT-122, and VT-114 in Lyndonville, drive 7.2 miles north on US 5 to a junction with VT-5A in West Burke. Go straight, now on VT-5A. Drive 5.6 miles and turn left (west) onto a gravel road at the parking area for Mount Pisgah. Drive through the parking lot and in 1.7 miles, park on the right, at the height of the land, in a turnout for about eight cars.

Hike along the road in a westerly direction for 50 feet to a sign on the right for the Herbert Hawkes Trail. Head northward into the woods and quickly turn right onto a wide path that climbs easily through thick, young woods. Focus the kids' attention on their surroundings: Have them try to find something sharp, something round, something squishy, and something blue.

Winding generally northward, the trail climbs more steeply at 0.3 mile as it swings left and cuts into the mountain. In another 0.1 mile, award a granola bar to the first one who reaches the spring that percolates from underground, flooding the trail. Shortly, the trail resumes its northerly course, swinging away from this steep section.

One-half mile into the hike, the trail divides: You turn right onto the east branch as the west branch heads left. Have you found all of the items on the first list? Now look for something fuzzy, something that floats, something wet, and something that doesn't belong in the woods (like a gum wrapper). Track along fairly level ground to a wet area at 0.65 mile where you'll have to balance on logs and stones to cross the damp spots. As the trail cuts through hemlock groves, worn rocks and bony roots may trip up tired little legs.

Eight-tenths of a mile from the start, continue straight along the east branch as the Wheeler Pond Trail splits left (north). Weave through deciduous woods on rolling terrain to another junction in 0.2 mile. Continue straight toward East Lookout (also called Willoughby Lookout) as the path to North Lookout veers left. (You won't want the kids to precede you here.)

Drop briefly to the sheltered lookout atop precipitous cliffs. From here, Lake Willoughby stretches before you (1200 feet below!) with the cliffs of Mount Pigsah (Hike 21) rising from the water on the opposite shore. Can you pick out tiny boats bobbing on the lake? Enjoy a snack (but save the picnic lunch) before returning to the junction with the path to North Lookout. Turn right and soon descend for 0.1 mile to another dramatic overlook that takes in the lake as well as peaks along the Canadian border. To the left of Mount Pisgah, you can see Bald Mountain.

Hike 0.7 mile back to the east branch/west branch junction and turn right to follow the seldom-traveled west branch. Climb moderately for 0.1 mile to the wooded summit of Mount Hor. Drop along the trail for a short distance through evergreens to a third overlook, Summit Lookout. Outstanding views unfold to the south of Burke Mountain (Hike 19) and New Hampshire's Mount Moosilauke and Franconia Notch area. Look westward to see the peaks of the Green Mountains. Have the kids count all of the small ponds below—among them are Bean, Wheeler, Blake, Duck, and Vail ponds. Here's the spot to spread out the picnic.

When you're done admiring, retrace your steps to the car.

21. Mount Pisgah

Type: Dayhike
Difficulty: Challenging for children
Distance: 3.6 miles, round trip
Hiking time: 3.5 hours
High point/elevation gain: 2692 feet, 1600 feet
Hikable: May–October
Map: USGS Sutton

Did a climb up Mount Hor (Hike 20) pique your interest in the Pisgah cliffs across the lake? These cliffs, plummeting more than 1000 feet to the eastern shore of Lake Willoughby, are a National Natural Landmark and offer dramatic views of local spots as well as distant peaks. Although parents with small children must exercise EXTREME caution at the overlooks (sheer drops of 500 and 1000 feet), older children who are experienced hikers will have no trouble hiking safely. Go for it!

From I-91, take Exit 23 to US 5 North. At the junction of US 5, VT-122, and VT-114 in Lyndonville, continue on US 5 North for 7.2 miles to the junction with VT-5A. Bear right onto VT-5A and, in 5.6 miles, turn left into a substantial parking area.

Cross the road to the Mount Pisgah trailhead where a sign announces that the summit is 1.7 miles away. The well-traveled trail, marked in blue, heads northeastward into the woods. Soon, cross a swampy pond outlet over a lengthy log footbridge (with a handrail) and then skirt the base of the pond across a second extended footbridge. (There's nothing like a pair of neat bridges to interest the kids in what lies ahead!)

Climb the bank of the pond and curl left, skirting the pond's eastern side. Quickly, the trail sweeps right, departing the water on an easterly track. Who will be the first to spot the third log crossing at 0.25 mile? In another 0.1 mile, follow the trail on a series of switchbacks leading to the top of the mountain ridge. The trail swings left (north) at 0.45 mile, cresting and then following the ridge, rising gently.

Enjoy your first Lake Willoughby views 0.6 mile from the start, with the cliffs of Mount Hor rising from the opposite shore. Although they'll be tempted, discourage the kids from exploring the left-going side trails. As the main trail ventures northward, the left slope steepens rapidly.

At 0.65 mile, the trail passes high above the southern tip of the lake, Vermont's deepest at over 300 feet. Trending northwestward with little change in elevation, the path flirts with the edge of the steep, wooded slope that plunges toward the highway and the lake.

Nine-tenths of a mile from the start, follow a side trail that splits left and arrives in 30 feet at Pulpit Rock. (Keep the kids right beside you on this side trip.) The ledge hangs 500 feet over Lake Willoughby and VT-5A, offering magnificent views over the rippling water to Mount Hor. Even folks who are usually immune to acrophobia may feel a few butterflies here. Fall hikers should watch for migrating hawks soaring southward.

Beyond the queasy overlook, the trail climbs moderately through mature woods, wandering away from the edge of the ridge. Here, the kids are free to take the lead. The first one to reach the erratic boulder at 1.1 miles gets to carry the pack. (Most kids consider that an honor, not a drag.) The trail continues to sweep away from the ridge on an abating grade.

After a brief descent at 1.3 miles, the gradual-to-moderate climb resumes. The trail sidesteps another boulder at the 1.5-mile mark and continues its climb to open baldface, where over-the-shoulder views of Burke Mountain (Hike 19) make a lovely backdrop for a picnic.

View from Pulpit Rock, looking over Lake Willoughby to Mount Hor

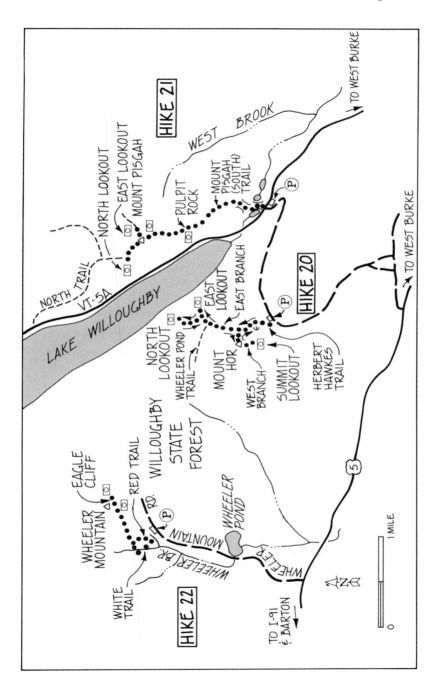

HIKE 21

TO WEST BURKE

WEST BROOK

EAST LOOKOUT
MOUNT PISGAH

NORTH LOOKOUT

PULPIT ROCK

MOUNT PISGAH (SOUTH) TRAIL

P

TO WEST BURKE

NORTH TRAIL

VT-5A

LAKE WILLOUGHBY

EAST BRANCH

EAST LOOKOUT

HIKE 20

P

NORTH LOOKOUT

WHEELER POND TRAIL

MOUNT HOR

EAST BRANCH

SUMMIT LOOKOUT

HERBERT HAWKES TRAIL

WEST BRANCH

5

TO WEST BURKE

WILLOUGHBY STATE FOREST

EAGLE CLIFF

RED TRAIL

WHEELER MOUNTAIN RD.

P

WHEELER MOUNTAIN

WHITE TRAIL

WHEELER POND

WHEELER BK.

WHEELER MOUNTAIN

HIKE 22

TO I-91 & BARTON

N

1 MILE

0

Turn the pack over to the fellow who's the first to arrive at the sign announcing the upcoming "North Trail and Lookouts." As you arrive at the treed summit of Mount Pisgah, 1.7 miles from the start, a side trail leads right to East Lookout. Drop along the side trail for 150 yards to an overlook with excellent easterly views that take in the 3300-foot Bald Mountain and southeasterly views extending to the White Mountains. Here, parents can relax and kids can safely enjoy the views.

Return to the junction and continue northward toward North Lookout. In 0.1 mile, follow a side trail to the left, once more taking care to precede the kids. From the ledge that could be called Pulpit Rock II, the world drops away at your feet as you stand 1000 feet above the ice blue water. The dizzying views encompass Jay Peak, local Wheeler Mountain (Hike 22), Mount Hor, and some Canadian peaks. With the forceful winds and tight space on this lofty ledge, you'll want to explore with extreme caution.

Retrace your steps to the car.

Note: If peregrine falcons are nesting in the area during the summer months, the state may elect to close the trails near the cliffs.

22. Eagle Cliff on Wheeler Mountain

Type: Dayhike
Difficulty: Moderate for children
Distance: 2.3 miles, round trip
Hiking time: 2.5 hours
High point/elevation gain: 2371 feet, 725 feet
Hikable: May–October
Map: USGS Sutton

Even though Wheeler is one of the lower mountains in the Lake Willoughby area (at 2371 feet), its Eagle Cliff provides magnificent, long-range views. I know, vistas keep the old folks happy, but what's in it for the kids? They'll delight in the frequent scrambles up rocky outcroppings and alongside massive ledges. And as the trail runs over lengthy, open baldface, even youngsters will appreciate the far-reaching panoramas. You won't have to worry about initial motivation—the view of Wheeler that they'll have from the car will be inspiration enough.

From the junction of US 5 and VT-5A in West Burke, travel north on US 5 for 8.3 miles. Turn right onto Wheeler Mountain Road. (Watch for a sign to Wheeler Pond Camp.) Follow this gravel road past Wheeler Pond at 0.9 mile. In another mile, beyond a pair of private homes, park in the turnout on the left.

Alternatively, from I-91 in Barton, take Exit 25 to VT-16 North. In 1.3 miles, turn right onto US 5 South. In another 4.8 miles, turn left onto gravel Wheeler Mountain Road, following the sign to Wheeler Pond Camp. Follow the directions above.

From the parking area, drop briefly through the woods to a right turn onto an old jeep road. Follow the trail northward, as it climbs easily along the right-hand side of an overgrown field. Two-thirds of the way across the field, the trail splits: Turn right onto a red-blazed alternate trail as the main white-blazed trail continues straight along the edge of the field (eventually rejoining the red trail).

As you follow the red trail, rising gently through mixed woods, play "How is it like me?" Pick anything you see—a tree, a mushroom, a squirrel—and ask the kids what that object has in common with them. Does it need water to live? Does it have a family? Does it make any noise?

How is a squirrel like me?

The pitch steepens and, at 0.25 mile, the trail meets an impressive, smooth ledge that looks like a tidal wave. Cutting beneath the "tidal wave," the trail scales a 10-foot ledge (that will give the kids no trouble) to reach its base. Guided by red blazes, cut left and begin a steep, 150-foot ascent along the left-hand side of the rock slab. Adults may need to lend a hand to youngsters; kids can repay the favor by watching for the red blazes that stray left and right.

Pause to take in views to the south, west, and east of Norris Mountain and Wheeler Pond. On top of the "tidal wave," 0.4 mile from the start, the white and red trails converge. The trail, now marked in white and red, ducks in and out of woods along the ridge leading to Eagle Cliff, opening onto baldface at 0.6 mile. Expanding views take in Burke Mountain (Hike 19) and Mount Pisgah (Hike 21).

CAUTION With spruce trees on its left, the trail climbs in the open, about 15 to 20 feet away from the cliffs that drop down Wheeler's southeastern face. As the grade levels, the commanding views extend to Lake Willoughby and Mount Mansfield, Bald Mountain, Jay Peak, and other peaks in the Green Mountains, as well as prominent peaks in the Whites. Guided by a sign for Eagle Cliff, the trail darts into the woods near the summit and is quickly swallowed by spruce trees.

Follow the rocky path with little change in elevation for 0.15 mile where it ends abruptly at spectacular Eagle Cliff. This wide ledge, high above Lake Willoughby, offers dizzying views and a choice picnic spot a comfortable distance from the edge.

On the way down, you may want to follow the white-blazed main trail for the entire distance rather than taking the alternate red trail. It's a bit longer, but not as steep.

Look up to see the pattern of the pines.

A father and son descend from Ritterbush Lookout.

23. Devil's Gulch

Type: Dayhike or overnight
Difficulty: Moderate for children
Distance: 5 miles, round trip
Hiking time: 4.5 hours
High point/elevation gain: 1670 feet, 1050 feet
Hikable: May–October
Maps: USGS Eden and Hazens Notch

When you stand amidst the boulders that line the floor of the dark, narrow Devil's Gulch, it's not hard to imagine time turning back a century or even ten centuries. This murky gorge, untouched by modern times, is almost primeval, and is sure to be the setting of ghost stories invented on the car ride home. But the Gulch isn't the only thing for kids to look forward to: Views from Ritterbush Lookout, dozens of stream crossings over stepping stones and log bridges, kid-sized waterfalls and cascades, and the Green Mountain Club's (GMC) Ritterbush Cabin will keep them excited from start to finish. Unlike most hiking routes, you will descend on the hike in and ascend on the return trip.

If you are planning to break up the hike with an overnight at the cabin, bring along a flashlight covered with red cellophane. You can take a midnight stroll to spot wildlife: Animals won't be able to see your red light, but you'll be able to see them!

From I-91, take Exit 26 to VT-58 West and US 5 North. In 0.2 mile, turn left onto VT-58 West. Travel 12.9 miles to Lowell and turn left (south) onto VT-100. After 8.7 miles, in Eden, turn right (north) onto VT-118. In 4.5 miles, a sign on the left announces the Long Trail; park on the right side of the road where there is room for about four cars.

Cross the road and enter the woods, following the white-blazed Long Trail southwestward. The well-trampled path runs along a ridge that drops off to the left. For the first 0.8 mile, the trail climbs easily through thin, mixed woods sprinkled with birch trees. Do the woods seem quiet

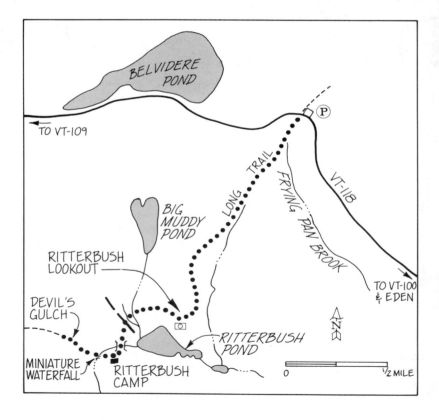

and still? Begin counting and stop when you hear a noise—you probably won't get beyond five before a bird whistles or wind rustles the leaves. How quietly can you move through the forest?

At 0.8 mile, the trail embarks on a lengthy descent to the Ritterbush Lookout and Devil's Gulch. (Remind kids to conserve their energy; it will be a long climb back to the car.) Initially, the trail drops through a gully, hopping over frequent wet spots. A stream joins from the left at 1 mile and accompanies you for 0.2 mile. Have a scavenger hunt for sounds: Listen for a bird call, an airplane, a woodpecker, and a chattering squirrel.

At 1.7 miles, the trail opens onto the safe, narrowly exposed ledge known as Ritterbush Lookout with terrific views of Ritterbush Pond and the surrounding mountain ridges. From the lookout, the trail switches right, then left, tumbling down a rocky hillside. An adult may want to lead the way to choose the best footing. You can see the pond through the trees, but the trail avoids the swampy shoreline.

After a drop of about 100 yards, the trail swings right, to circle above the pond from a distance. It drops gently to a pair of stream crossings just under 2 miles from the start. Be patient if the kids stop for a little water play. Beyond the streams, head straight across a woods road, still following the white blazes of the Long Trail.

Over the next 0.2 mile, hop over several trickling streams that feed the pond. Balance on halved logs to cross a wet area, then drop into a cool, moss-covered ravine. At 2.2 miles, cross over a hurrying brook on a log bridge. Remember "Pooh Sticks," Winnie the Pooh's favorite water game? Drop twigs off of one side of the bridge and look to the other side to see whose stick emerges first.

Climb past an overhanging rock mass and soon reach the Ritterbush Camp, a cabin maintained by the GMC that sleeps eight. (If you decide to camp here overnight, use the fire sites provided with only dead or downed wood as fuel.) From the right side of the cabin, continue 0.1 mile on the Long Trail to the bank of a racing brook. Water cascades over the jumbles of rocks and spills down miniature waterfalls. If the kids beg to stay here, promise them better things to come.

Navigate a rough section of slippery roots and moss-covered boulders to duck under a rock tunnel into Devil's Gulch. The sides of the dark, damp gorge reach steeply skyward as a maze of boulders twists across the gulch floor. Give the kids plenty of time to explore the caves and hollows before retracing your steps to the car.

NEW HAMPSHIRE

24. Little Monadnock and Rhododendron State Park

Type: Dayhike
Difficulty: Easy for children
Distance: 3.3 miles, round trip
Hiking time: 2.5 hours
High point/elevation gain: 1780 feet, 600 feet
Hikable: April–November
Map: USGS Monadnock

The only Monadnock that exists for most out-of-staters is the "Grand" one, though local hikers have discovered that Little Monadnock in Fitzwilliam has as much to offer—albeit on a smaller scale—as its big brother. Visit in mid- to late July when 16 acres of wild rhododendrons (one of the largest colonies in the Northeast) are in full bloom with generous, pink flowers. July is also the month when the mountain's blueberry bushes will be loaded down and ready for picking. Put the kids, camera, and berry buckets in the car and head over!

 From the junction of NH-12 and NH-119 in Fitzwilliam, drive 1 mile on NH-119 heading west. Turn right onto Rhododendron Road at a sign

for Rhododendron State Park. In 2 miles, turn right onto the gravel
Rockwood Pond Road and into Rhododendron State Park. Immediately
bear left at a fork and park near the information bulletin board.

To the left of the information board, squeeze between two granite
posts to head northward on the wide Rhododendron Loop Trail. Soon, as
the park name promises, lush rhododendron bushes border the path. The
Laurel Trail splits left as you follow the Rhododendron Loop Trail
straight to cross a footbridge over a dribbling stream. Can the kids spot
any newts or salamanders? (Friends of ours counted more than thirty
while hiking this trail after a rainstorm!)

At 0.2 mile, the trail divides again; head right on the white-blazed
Little Monadnock Trail, rising gently toward the summit of Little Monadnock. Look for red squirrel "middens": piles of scales from pine and
spruce cones. Squirrels scrape off the scales to get at the cone's small inner seeds.

At 0.6 mile, you'll leave the boundary of Rhododendron State Park
and pass through a stone wall. Soon, climb on all fours up a squat ledge.
At the top, the white trail turns right but a more trodden path veers left.
Follow the worn trail on the left, which shortly rejoins the white-blazed

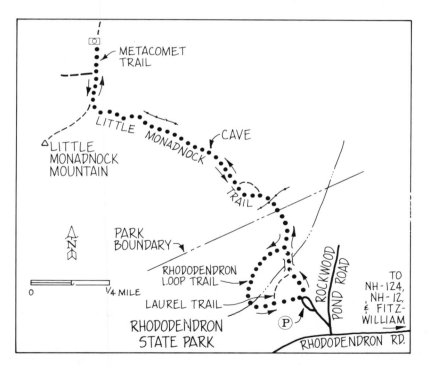

trail. Turn left, dipping in and out of a gully. As you work your way up a hillside, look right at 0.8 mile for the kid-sized cave formed by a random settling of rocks.

If you've come too early to admire the rhododendrons in bloom, perhaps the wildflowers that edge this section of trail will be showing off their blossoms. The trail climbs briskly to the left of a stone wall through mixed conifers. What will the kids notice first: the signs or the sounds of woodpeckers? (If you see sawdust at the base of a tree, you'll probably see woodpecker holes farther up the trunk. Sawdust may mean gnawing insects and insects usually attract hungry woodpeckers.)

Near the summit on exposed granite, the Little Monadnock Trail and the white-blazed Metacomet Trail converge. Grand Monadnock (Hike 26) looms on the eastern horizon. Although you could head left (west) to the treed summit of Little Monadnock Mountain, we recommend you bear right (north), now following the Metacomet Trail. The kids can begin to scan the ground for wild blueberry bushes. A logging road branches left in 0.1 mile; you continue straight for another 0.1 mile to an exposed area with superb 180-degree views. To the east, Grand Monadnock broods over southwestern New Hampshire, while Mount Sunapee (Hike 30) and Mount Kearsarge rise over the local hills to the north. The northwestern horizon is consumed by the mountains of Vermont, notably Mount Ascutney (Hike 7).

Relax, snack, and then return along the Metacomet Trail to the Little Monadnock Trail and back to Rhododendron State Park, where you bear right at the first intersection to complete the Rhododendron Loop Trail. From that junction, your car is 0.4 mile away.

Cresting the summit of Little Monadnock

Peering into the brook that flows through Chesterfield Gorge

25. Chesterfield Gorge

Type:	Dayhike
Difficulty:	Easy for children
Distance:	0.8 mile, loop
Hiking time:	45 minutes
High point/elevation gain:	850 feet, 125 feet
Hikable:	April–November
Map:	USGS Keene

Pick a sunny, spring day to visit Chesterfield Gorge—you'll want to witness the runoff swelling this narrow ravine. The gorge is a terrific place to evaluate inexperienced hikers—the route is short, easy, and consistently appealing. If kids lose interest or wear out here, it may be a sign that they're not quite ready for family hiking. If they prance around the gorge and beg for more, turn the page!

From I-91 in Brattleboro, Vermont, take Exit 3 for US 9 East toward Keene, New Hampshire. In 9.6 miles, turn left into a large, paved parking lot at a sign that says "Chesterfield Gorge State Wayside, A Geological Park."

From the northern side of the parking area, signs direct you to "Gorge Trail" or "Toilets" (where you can also get information about the gorge). The gorge trail, wide and well traveled, sweeps left and drops on rustic steps along Partridge Brook. In 0.1 mile, the path turns right and spans the stream on a wooden footbridge without railings—keep an eye on preschoolers. Climb the bank of the gorge and head northwest; here, sturdy railings and fences guard the edge. Walk along the level trail for 0.2 mile as the water races through the ravine 20 to 50 feet below.

Soon, the trail sinks gently toward the western end of the gorge where you cross back over the stream on a second footbridge. Kids may want to take their time here because the bridge offers a great spot from which to examine the tumbling stream close-up. The trail switches back to climb the opposite bank and then snakes along the edge of this rim heading eastward. You'll soon return to the first stream crossing; retrace the initial route to the parking area.

26. Mount (Grand) Monadnock

Type: Dayhike
Difficulty: Challenging for children
Distance: 4.5 miles, round trip
Hiking time: 4 hours
High point/elevation gain: 3165 feet, 2000 feet
Hikable: May–October
Map: USGS Monadnock

Mount Monadnock is to central New England what Mount Washington is to northern New England, and it has the dubious honor of being one of the most visited peaks in the Northeast. Tens of thousands of hikers are drawn to the Grand Monadnock each year for many of the same reasons that Henry David Thoreau and Ralph Waldo Emerson were attracted in the nineteenth century: The sculpted mountain, capped with a barren summit, is the unchallenged ruler of the low, surrounding hills that stretch west to Vermont and east to the Atlantic.

The 20 miles of hiking trails within Mount Monadnock State Park include paths that snake to the mountaintop from all sides. The route we've chosen is one of the least traveled, with views emerging early in the route. The mountain is at its best in autumn, but because most people know that, a fall hike feels a lot like standing in line for a movie. To stack the "solitude" odds in your favor, visit in early summer.

From the junction of NH-101 and NH-124 in Marlboro, drive 5.1

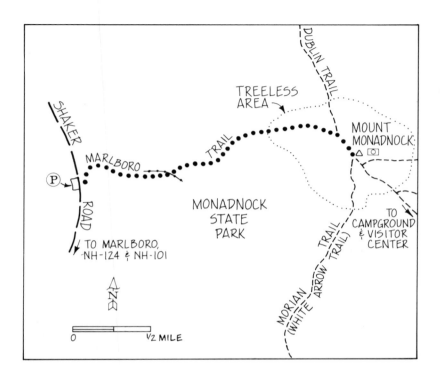

miles on NH-124. Turn left onto Shaker Road and, in 0.7 mile, turn left into a parking area for Monadnock hikers.

From the parking area, head east across the gravel road to the trail information bulletin board. The wide, white-blazed Marlboro Trail begins to the left (northeast) of the trail sign, initially on level ground. Traveling through hemlocks and hardwoods, the trail begins a gradual climb at 0.15 mile over rocky terrain. (Our preschooler enjoyed jumping from rock to rock here.) Kids who run ahead can wait for the others at the great, smooth boulder on the left, 0.3 mile from the start. Who can find the first rock painted with an "M"? (Put the youngest hiker in charge of counting "M" rocks.)

The path hugs and then divides a stone wall at 0.5 mile. A moderate-to-steep ascent up rock steps quickly leads to relatively open baldface. From here to the summit, the trail offers nearly constant views over the southern New Hampshire valley and to the exposed peak ahead. (Be sure to keep a careful eye on the weather because there is little shelter from the elements on this route.) As the trail rises in and out of sturdy evergreen clusters, kids may find a few blueberry bushes amidst the low shrubs. Sweeping across more exposed terrain, the trail follows cairns and white blazes on a gradual ascent that conceals the elevation you are gaining. The gentle slope and consistently smooth ledge underfoot mean that kids can quickly and effortlessly cover a significant distance.

Patches of young vegetation and barren slopes testify to the harsh conditions this mountain has withstood in recent history: logging and land clearing in the 1700s and 1800s, the great hurricanes of 1815 and 1938, and several large-scale fires, the most recent one in 1953.

One mile from the start, the trail cuts through a groove between two chunks of ledge and, over the next 0.4 mile, climbs on a moderate-to-steep grade over some formidable ledges (be prepared to lend a hand to young hikers). At 1.8 miles, the trail surmounts another exposed shoulder where hikers have a clear view of the treeless summit. In 0.2 mile, the Dublin Trail merges from the left (north) to join the Marlboro Trail. After scaling several short ledges and rising gently toward the peak, the Marlboro and Dublin trails meet the Morian Trail (also called the White Arrow Trail), which joins from the right. Together they march toward the massive, open summit with its weathered ledges that invite kids to climb and explore.

The most devastating of the recent fires was the 1820 blaze that stripped the summit cone of all vegetation and soil; it will be thousands of years before enough soil accumulates to support tree roots once again. Farmers reportedly set the mountain on fire in an attempt to kill wolves that had attacked nearby flocks of sheep. The outstanding panoramic view extends westward to Vermont's Green Mountains, northward to the White Mountains, and southwestward to the Berkshires. The Grand Monadnock towers 885 feet over its eastern neighbor, Pack, that bears the same last name. All other monadnocks were named after the Grand one; "monadnock" has come to stand for an isolated mountain that has resisted erosion.

After sharing stories with the other hikers gathered at the summit, reverse direction to complete the hike. (Remember: The great majority of hiking accidents occur on the descent, so choose your footing carefully and rest whenever you need it.)

Note: Camping and fires are permitted in the state park campground at the base of White Dot Trail. The visitor center and state park headquarters are located in the same area.

27. Pack Monadnock/Miller State Park

Type: Dayhike
Difficulty: Moderate for children
Distance: 3.2 miles, loop
Hiking time: 3 hours
High point/elevation gain: 2285 feet, 1000 feet
Hikable: April–November
Map: USGS Peterborough South

Pack (South Pack, to be specific) doesn't attract as many hikers as its formidable neighbor Grand Monadnock (Hike 26), though a steady stream of cars chugs up the summit road in season. From the mountaintop on a clear day you can see—if not forever—at least to Boston and to the White Mountains. While you'll share these panoramic views with the tourists, you'll find solitude along the Wapack Trail, which winds for nearly 1.5 miles through heavy woodlands to the summit. This rugged footpath challenges young hikers with just enough rock scrambles and steady climbing to make things interesting, but not overwhelming.

From Milford, travel west on NH-101; from Peterborough, travel east on NH-101. The entrance to Pack Monadnock and Miller State Park is on the northern side of NH-101 across from Temple Mountain Ski Area, near the Temple/Peterborough town line.

Before the hike, you may want to study the trail information board at the northeastern side of the parking lot near the auto road. The foot trail ducks into the woods to the right of the board following yellow and blue triangular blazes. In less than 100 feet, the trail divides; bear left on the yellow-blazed Wapack Trail. (You will return by way of the blue trail, the former Wapack Trail.) Within 0.1 mile, the trail crosses the paved auto road and reenters the woods, ascending briskly.

For the next 0.3 mile, the trail rises along rocky, rugged terrain with ledges on the right and left; young hikers may need a hand along particularly challenging sections. "Pack" is an Indian word meaning "little"; at this point in the hike, the kids might consider the name quite inappropriate. As the trail winds along the mountain's western side, it frequently emerges onto open ledge with marvelous views of southwestern New Hampshire, predominantly Temple Mountain to the south and Grand Monadnock to the west.

At 0.6 mile, the trail leaves the rim of the mountain and turns inland to climb at a consistent pace toward the summit. Any grumblers? Get silly: If you were a tree, what kind would you be? Why? Get serious:

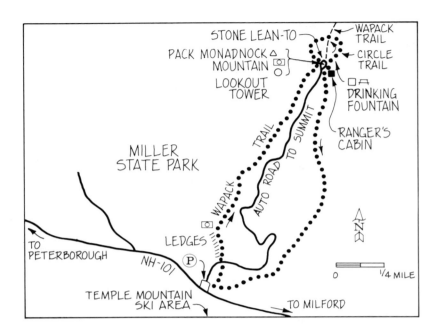

How do deciduous trees benefit by shedding their leaves each fall? (Once the leaves have fallen off, the tree's interior is sealed off from the frost and snow. Also, less snow accumulates on bare branches, thus fewer branches break off.)

Near the summit, about 1.2 miles from the start, the trail dips into a ravine (saturated though passable in the spring). The path struggles out of the gulch to resume its northerly climb through a dense hemlock forest and then opens onto the auto road just below the summit. Yellow arrows guide you to the right as the road splits to circle the peak. Beyond this fork is the ranger's cabin, a drinking fountain, restrooms, and picnic tables. (When the summit road is open, you may have to pay a small fee here.)

Dismiss the acrophobia and climb to the top of the lookout tower. The 360-degree view takes in Grand Monadnock to the west and North Pack and Crotched Mountain (Hike 28) to the north. Temple Mountain is directly to the south, and beyond it, Wachusett Mountain. The distinctive Boston skyline defines the southeastern horizon and the peaks of the White Mountains, nearly 100 miles away, outline the northern one.

Leave the auto tourists in the parking lot and follow the blue-blazed Circle Trail, which starts near the ranger's cabin. This trail runs along the northern rim of South Pack, providing stunning views to the north and west, and returns you in 0.4 mile to the summit parking area.

Spread out a picnic lunch on one of the tables and savor the spectacular panoramas.

To descend, return to the fork in the road and head left into the woods on the blue-blazed trail. Drop moderately through dense woodlands for 1.4 miles to return to the parking area at the base of the mountain.

28. Crotched Mountain

Type:	Dayhike
Difficulty:	Easy to moderate for children
Distance:	2.5 miles, round trip
Hiking time:	2 hours
High point/elevation gain:	2066 feet, 700 feet
Hikable:	April–November
Map:	USGS Peterborough North and Greenfield

If you have your heart set on viewing the peaks of the White Mountains but the kids can't endure another two hours in the car, consider a march to the top of Crotched Mountain. The summit is not as high as those of its mighty neighbors, but its strategic location in central New England allows for some fine viewing to the north and south. Although three trails climb to the peak, the Bennington Trail is the best choice for families since it is not too long and the trek is broken up by a flowing spring at 0.5 mile, rock outcroppings for climbing or resting on, a scenic lookout and mountaintop blueberry picking close to the summit. If you hike during blueberry season in late July and early August, be sure to bring along appropriate containers.

From the intersection of US 202, NH-47, and NH-31 in Bennington, turn south onto NH-47 and NH-31. In 0.3 mile, as NH-47 and NH-31 divide, turn right onto NH-31 toward Greenfield (a sign directs you toward "Crotched Mountain Center"). In 1.6 miles, turn left onto MTn [sic] Road (a sign at the corner announces "Bennington Trail"). In 0.4 mile, the road turns to gravel and forks; a "TRAIL" sign indicates that you bear right. One-tenth of a mile later, the road becomes less passable. Park here on the right-hand side across from a private residence.

Walk along the gravel road to a fork in 0.1 mile. Bear right on the more overgrown road, guided by a "TRAIL" sign and circular orange blazes. Immediately, the Bennington Trail skirts the right-hand side of a clearing, then ducks into the woods and ascends a moderate grade. Initially, the thick underbrush makes the trail a little difficult to follow, but frequent blazes should keep you on the path.

Soon the trail wanders along a wide, rocky stream bed that carries runoff waters in the spring or after a heavy rain. Here, the climb is more gradual. Within the first 0.3 mile, the trail crosses two streams by way of crude log bridges. You may want to lend a hand to preschoolers as they practice their balancing skills.

After a steep, brief, uphill trek, pass through a break in a weary stone wall and follow it left (north) for a short distance. Ask the youngest member of the family to count the number of stream crossings. After the third crossing, have the kids look for Taylor's Spring, a small pipe poking out of the ground spouting water into a brook below.

After everyone enjoys a cold drink, follow the trail as it sweeps right (east) and climbs moderately through a birch forest. Climbing can get a bit monotonous—even for adults. Try a game of "Who will be the first one to see...": a stone wall, a mushroom, a tree stump, a rock bigger than a car—think up some of your own.

When the trail reaches a flat clearing 0.8 mile from the start, the Greenfield Trail joins from the right and you bear left. These two trails merge for the final ascent to the summit along a well-worn, rocky, and root-choked stream bed. As you approach the height of Crotched, the forest is consumed by hemlocks. Warn kids that the needles underfoot can make for slippery going, especially when wet.

A terrific climbing rock looms on the left—just in time to revive the kids' interest in this adventure. Beyond it, a sign points to a side trail that leads right to a scenic view. As you hike this side trail, panoramas unfold to the south and west, taking in all the monadnocks: Pack, Grand, and Little (Hikes 27, 26, and 24). Here, in season, the wild blueberry

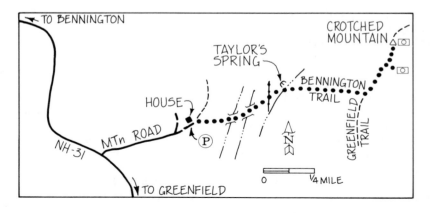

bushes offer an abundant crop to those willing to spend a few minutes searching among the leaves. (This is a better choice than the summit for a picnic site.)

Return to the main trail and climb the final 100 yards to the rugged summit, marked by the rusted footings to an old fire tower. Broken glass and other signs of human disrespect suggest that there is a way other than the hiking trails to access the summit. (Indeed, beyond the crest, a deteriorating stairway leads to an access road which, in 0.5 mile, enters the mountain's ski area.) From the wooded summit, point out the peaks of the White Mountains 80 miles away.

To complete the hike, return as you came.

Blueberry picking on Crotched Mountain

29. Odiorne Point

Type: Dayhike
Difficulty: Easy for children
Distance: 2.2 miles, loop
Hiking time: 2 hours
High point/elevation gain: 60 feet, 100 feet
Hikable: May–October
Map: USGS Kittery (Maine)

Odiorne Point State Park's 137 acres include two miles of seashore, the largest undeveloped coastal tract in New Hampshire. Extending from Odiorne Point to the Witch Creek salt marsh, the park is an ironic blend of serene, natural beach, once called "Pannaway" by Native Americans, and concrete casements from the long abandoned World War II coastal defense installation known as Fort Dearborn.

This land was farmed and fished by ten generations of Odiornes beginning in the 1600s, and it eventually attracted wealthy families who built oceanfront estates with fountained, formal gardens. These turn-of-the-century "summer cottages" and the Sagamore House, a seaside resort, were demolished in the early 1940s to erect a military fortification that was to protect Portsmouth Harbor's naval shipyard in the event of enemy attack. Twenty years later, the state of New Hampshire purchased the parcel for $91,000. Today, the state park offers rugged beach trails as well as lovely woodland paths that curl gracefully around the ghosts of the seaside mansions.

You'll want to visit at low tide so that the kids can explore Odiorne Point's tide pools and Pebble Beach's "strandline," the ribbon of shells, seaweed, driftwood, and smooth stones left by the retreating sea. (Check the local paper for a tide chart or ask at the library or police station.) Bring sneakers or rubber-soled shoes, a magnifying glass, binoculars, a sturdy net, a waterproof flashlight or camera, and a picnic lunch to spread out on one of the seaside picnic tables.

 From the junction of US 1 and NH-1A in Portsmouth, drive on NH-1A South. Pass the Odiorne State Park boat launching area on the left at 3.1 miles and drive another 0.75 mile to the Odiorne Point Fort Dearborn Site entrance on the left. Turn here and follow the entrance road to the right. Park in the lot near the visitor center.

Stop in at the Russell B. Tobey Visitor Center to look at exhibits, visit the bookstore, and talk with staff members. Head toward the south-western end of the park along a paved sidewalk that winds between rest facilities on the left and playground equipment on the right. Follow the path to the edge of a cove known as the Sunken Forest where, at low tide, you may see clusters of stumps. Thousands of years ago, this area was a pine forest.

What causes the sea to rise and retreat twice a day? Explain to the kids that although the earth's gravity keeps the water on earth, the seas are also affected by the weaker gravitational pulls of the moon and sun. These pulls change as the earth rotates, causing the tides. As the waters recede on our coast, they advance on a faraway shore, like water sloshing back and forth slowly in a giant bathtub.

Walk along the shore heading eastward toward Odiorne Point, where the kids can join the sea gulls that prowl the expansive, rocky shore at low tide. (Warn the children that seaweed-covered rocks are

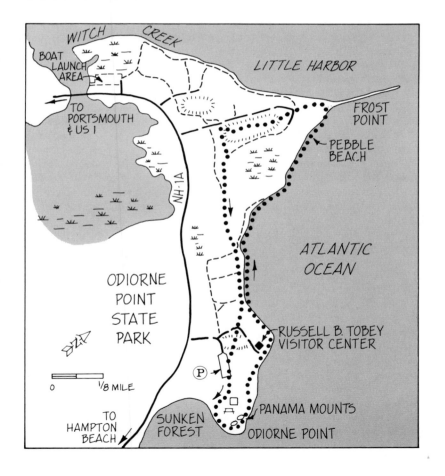

slippery.) In shallow pools where barnacles are at rest, youngsters can gently splash the water to imitate an incoming tide. A barnacle may open the hole at the top of its shell and stick out its feathery feet, trying to kick plankton and other food into its mouth. If the kids try to pull a barnacle off a rock or shell, they'll discover what most ship owners already know: The limestone "cement" that a barnacle makes to anchor itself to another object is stronger than many man-made adhesives.

Can the children find any sponges attached to tide pool rocks? How about green crabs? These creatures, which are actually green and black, are quite common along the New Hampshire and Maine coasts. Advise kids not to pick them up, though, since they have powerful pincers; it's safer to watch them from a distance as they scurry about sideways.

When you're done exploring the rocky tidal area, rejoin the paved path near the "Panama Mounts" where cannons once rested, solemn reminders of this area's diverse history. As the paved path turns left, you continue straight on a gravel trail, walking through a picnic area and then traveling along the water's edge.

For the next 0.75 mile, follow the shoreline toward Pebble Beach and Frost Point, passing the visitor center and several side trails splitting left. Along the way, the kids can look for large brown seaweeds known as wracks and kelps that sprawl on the beach, pieces of dead sponges, starfish, gull feathers, or the pincushionlike shells of sea urchins. Most of the sea urchins' spines will be gone, but you'll be able to see the perfect rows of bumps where the spines were attached.

You'll probably find signs of human activity, too. We found a colorful lobster buoy that had washed up on shore. Did you know that lobster buoys are almost as individual as fingerprints? Each lobsterman has his own special markings so that he can identify the buoys that are tied to his traps.

As you hike along Pebble Beach, a freshwater marsh lies to your left, separated by about 100 feet from the salty ocean waters. After you pass some low sand dunes, a grassy path leads to Frost Point and the jetty that reaches into Little Harbor. From here, the wide trail turns inland and the kids will turn from beachcombers into history buffs.

Shortly, at an intersection at 1.2 miles, where roads split right and left, continue straight (southwest) to climb a knoll that offers lovely views to the open Atlantic and the Isle of Shoals to the southeast. The man-made hill on which you are standing housed an underground command center during World War II. This hill and the one behind the visitor center were landscaped to camouflage the military operations. A decaying cement bunker hides among the pines on the knoll and, to the south, a weary turret sits idle.

As you begin to drop down the hill, turn left (south) at a trail junction 1.4 miles from the start, heading through white pines. At the bottom of the hill, turn left (east) at another intersection. As a wide, grassy path cuts across the trail, turn right (south) to follow this path that runs parallel to the shore trail. Ignore the side trails that split left and right, continuing straight for 0.5 mile until you see the visitor center.

Climb the second hill (to the right of the center) and descend on a flight of stairs to the parking lot and your car. The earth-covered structure you just scaled houses thirteen rooms and is protected with enough concrete and steel to withstand direct aerial and naval bombardment. Two 6-inch guns placed 210 feet apart had a range of 15 miles. (You can still see their circular concrete bases.) Take time to read the signs near the parking area describing Odiorne Point's fascinating and varied history.

Note: Odiorne State Park is open seven days a week, 8:00 a.m. to 8:00 p.m., from mid-May to mid-October. A small park entrance fee is charged. The Russell B. Tobey Visitor Center is open Tuesday through Sunday, 10:00 a.m. to 4:00 p.m., from late June through August. Fall weekend hours are 10:00 a.m. to 4:00 p.m. Entrance to the visitor center is free. Hunting between Seavey Creek and the Frost Point breakwater is permitted during waterfowl season.

30. Mount Sunapee and Lake Solitude

Type: Dayhike
Difficulty: Challenging for children
Distance: 4.8 miles, round trip
Hiking time: 4.5 hours
High point/elevation gain: 2743 feet, 1510 feet
Hikable: May–October
Map: USGS Sunapee

What do you think of when someone mentions Mount Sunapee? Skiing, right? But when the slopes are green and the skiers are sailing or swimming, Sunapee is a wonderful place to bring the family for a smorgasbord-type hike. You'll climb briskly under the dormant chair lift to the Sunapee summit, snake through the woods to the top of White Cliffs, and drop to the remote, rocky shoreline of Lake Solitude. With something just around the corner at any given moment, kids won't have time to poke each other with sticks or stuff leaves down one another's jackets.

Stretch your calves before you start; you'll feel the muscles working

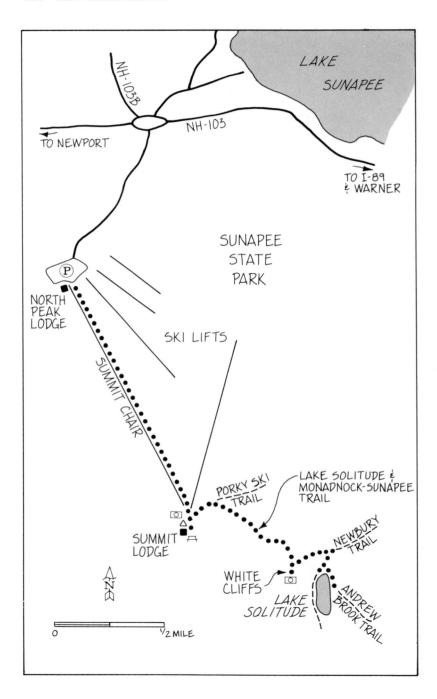

as you hike up the steep slope. (If you visit on a weekend during foliage season, you'll be able to take the chair lift to the summit for a moderate per-person fee; children under six are delivered to the top for free. This cuts 2.5 miles from the total hike and drops it from a challenging to an easy-to-moderate rating.)

From I-89 in Warner, take Exit 9 to NH-103 West. Travel about 12.5 miles to the junction with NH-103A. Continue another 2.3 miles on NH-103 to a rotary. Circle the rotary and turn right into Sunapee State Park. Drive 0.7 mile to the main Mount Sunapee Ski Area parking lot and leave your car near the North Peak Lodge.

Behind the North Peak Lodge, begin your climb up the mountain (heading southward) under the Summit Chair ski lift. The "trail" is actually the open, grassy ski slope, a change from the rugged mountain paths hikers usually encounter. To make the steep ascent easier on little legs, follow a route where the grass has been packed down by vehicles or previous hikers.

Distant, over-the-shoulder views emerge immediately and improve with each step. The steady and straight upward climb means that vertical feet are gained quickly, but not easily. To ward off complaining, play follow the leader, sing songs with the word "up" in them, and try to stump each other with silly riddles. When you stop for a breather, kids can turn around and imagine what it must be like to plummet down this snowy hill on skis.

Little hikers will need help negotiating two water lines for snow-making as you approach the summit. At the top of the lift, 1.25 miles from the start, look 50 feet to the left (east) for a sign nailed to a birch tree that points toward the orange-blazed Lake Solitude Trail and the white-blazed Monadnock-Sunapee Trail.

Relax (or snack) at the picnic table beyond the summit lodge overlooking impressive Mount Monadnock (Hike 26) before returning to the top of the chair lift. Here, join the white-blazed trail that heads southeastward down Porky Ski Trail, overlooking Lake Sunapee and Mount Kearsarge. Pass under a chair lift and, about 0.25 mile from the summit, you turn right into the woods as the Porky Ski Trail turns left (north) down the mountain.

Guided by orange and white blazes, follow the Lake Solitude and Monadnock-Sunapee Trail through mixed woods dotted with white birch. Sturdy roots spread underfoot.

Soon, 0.4 mile from the summit, the trail twists up a rocky slope to level off 0.2 mile later. Peek through the evergreens for a glimpse of the distant Lake Solitude. Just under 1 mile from the summit, a painted arrow points toward a short side trail that leads right (south) to a view of Lake Solitude. Take this trail to the overlook atop White Cliffs for a lovely view of the aptly named lake. If you decide to stop here for an energy break, you're likely to catch sight of deer, moose, or other creatures visiting the water.

From atop White Cliffs, isolated Lake Solitude seems to live up to its name.

Return to the main trail and turn right (east) following a sign for Lake Solitude. The trail drops moderately off the White Cliffs along stone steps. Partway down the descent, as the Newbury Trail merges from the left, bend right with the main trail. Shortly, you'll arrive at the northern bank of Lake Solitude. Here, the trail divides: The Andrews Brook Trail heads left on orange blazing and the Monadnock-Sunapee Trail departs right marked with white. Head left on the Andrews Brook Trail, soon emerging on the rocky shore.

If you didn't enjoy a picnic or snack atop Sunapee or the White Cliffs, settle down here. Who can point out the overlook on White Cliffs from which you just admired the lake? Retrace your steps to the car. (You may be tempted to follow what looks like a surefire shortcut, but trust us when we tell you—from experience—that the fastest way back is the way you came.)

Note: Camping is not permitted at Lake Solitude.

31. Blue Job Mountain

Type:	Dayhike
Difficulty:	Easy for children
Distance:	1.75 miles, loop
Hiking time:	1.5 hours
High point/elevation gain:	1357 feet, 400 feet
Hikable:	April–November
Map:	USGS Baxter Lake

The hike to Blue Job's fire tower is a popular one with local families. An easy, appealing climb leads to an open summit with views that stretch to Boston, the Atlantic, and the White Mountains. What more can you ask of a mountain? Since the views make the hike, save Blue Job for a cloudless, sunny day.

From the junction of US 202, NH-9, and NH-202A in Northwood, drive north on NH-202A. In 10.9 miles, turn left (west) onto First Crown Point Road. Turn right into the gravel parking area (large enough for six cars) in 5.4 miles.

Alternatively, from the junction of NH-11 and NH-202A in Rochester, follow NH-202A west for 4.3 miles. Turn right onto First Crown Point Road and drive 5.4 miles to the parking area on the right.

From the northeastern side of the parking lot, head east on a wide, well-worn path, skirting the right side of an overgrown meadow. At first glance, the world of field and forest seems limited to greens and browns. But ask the kids to look for reds, yellows, pinks, and blues, and you'll all be surprised at how colorful nature is.

The initially level path begins a gentle climb at 0.15 mile, stumbling over rocks and roots and gliding across granite. Soon, the chaos of boulders submits, forming steps to assist hikers. Cradled by boulders and ledge, the trail continues up the southern side of the mountain. Pause to let the kids flex their rock-climbing muscles. The trail crosses exposed ledge and, at 0.3 mile, bends left (north), squeezing through denser woods.

You'll arrive at the open summit crowned with a fire lookout tower 0.5 mile from the start. Climb the tower and take out your binoculars. Can you spot these landmarks: Rochester's drive-in movie screen, the former Pease Air Force Base, Boston's Hancock Tower, Mount Washington, the Atlantic Ocean? Although at 1365 feet this is hardly a high peak, the isolated Blue Job soars over the neighboring hills and offers magnificent, long-range views.

From the tower, begin a gradual, northeasterly descent through sparse pines and across open baldface. One-tenth of a mile from the summit, the trail cuts through a stone wall and comes upon an overgrown gravel operation. You are headed for the opposite ridge, 0.25 mile away.

Drop to the floor of the gravel pit, cross a gravel road and sidestep a small pond. Climb out of the pit to the open, expansive ledges that make a safe natural playground for the kids. Big folks can relax and take in the lovely local views.

To head back to your car (0.5 mile away), return to the gravel road

Surveying the central New Hampshire countryside from the Blue Job's fire lookout tower

near the pond at the bottom of the sag; turn right. Almost immediately, bear left onto an unmarked trail that leaves the road, heading westward. Follow this distinct trail as it drops through airy, mature evergreens and crosses a stream 1.4 miles from the start.

On the ascent, the kids looked for colors. As they descend and hike back to the car, they can survey their surroundings for shapes: A hole in a tree may be shaped like a circle, a leaf like an oval, a rock like a triangle. The trail widens into a gravel road and cuts across the field you initially skirted, leading shortly to the parking area and your car.

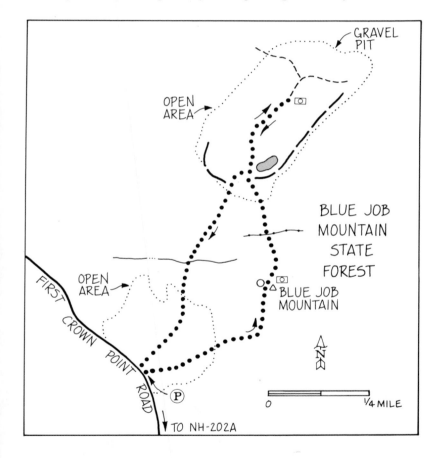

32. Mount Major

Type: Dayhike
Difficulty: Moderate for children
Distance: 4 miles, round trip
Hiking time: 3.5 hours
High point/elevation gain: 1786 feet, 1200 feet
Hikable: April–October
Map: USGS West Alton

From May to October, Lake Winnipesaukee draws tourists by the bus-full. Mount Major, rising prominently over Winnipesaukee's Alton Bay and accessed from a major New Hampshire highway, is often crowded with hiking vacationers. Try to visit during the week. But even if you have to elbow your way through the Saturday crowds, you'll be glad you did. Lake Winnipesaukee, 25 miles long, stretches before you, broken up by islands and peninsulas and dotted with dozens of boats. Look for the quaint town of Wolfeboro, nestled on the lake's eastern

A group of young hikers shares stories and the views from the Mount Major summit.

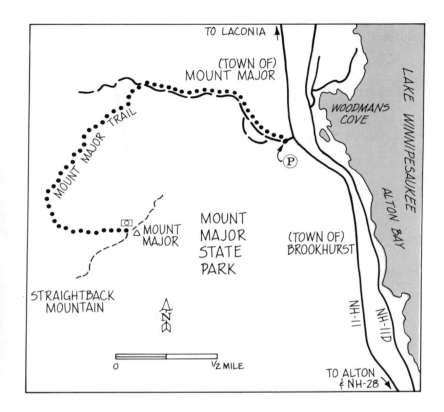

TO LACONIA

(TOWN OF)
MOUNT MAJOR

MOUNT MAJOR TRAIL

LAKE WINNIPESAUKEE

WOODMANS
COVE

ALTON BAY

P

MOUNT
MAJOR

MOUNT
MAJOR
STATE
PARK

(TOWN OF)
BROOKHURST

STRAIGHTBACK
MOUNTAIN

N

NH-11

NH-11D

0   ½ MILE

TO ALTON
& NH-28

shore; it's worth exploring after the hike. Kids don't always appreciate views, but they always appreciate water. They'll love this one.

From the junction of NH-28 and NH-11 in Alton, travel on NH-11 west past Alton Bay. In 5.7 miles, turn left into the expansive, well-marked parking area for the Mount Major Trail.

Climb gently along a wide gravel road that leaves the western side of the parking lot. The road leads through a shady grove of hemlocks, maples, and oaks. Kids can look for acorns dropped by the oak trees, pine cones shed from the hemlocks, and the winged fruits (called "samaras") that spin out of maple trees like miniature helicopters!

At 0.25 mile, the road splits; head right, though the roads merge 0.2 mile later. (Who will spot the cellar hole off to the right?) The grade levels soon after the roads rejoin and, just shy of the 1-mile mark, you turn left (west) onto a foot trail as the gravel road continues straight (north).

Guided by blue arrows and blazes, the rocky Mount Major Trail ascends stiffly, relaxes briefly at 1.3 miles, and resumes a moderate-to-steep climb at 1.5 miles. As the trail sweeps across ledge and bald-face, enjoy easterly views to Alton Bay on Lake Winnipesaukee. Formidable scrambling brings you to a shoulder, just under 2 miles from the start, where you can catch your breath as you survey the open summit and the lake.

A final surge over exposed granite leads to the expansive, flat peak, at just over 2 miles. Even though you may have shared the trail with other hikers, the summit is so broad that everyone who wishes to relax in private can find a solitary spot. Enjoy the panoramic views that take in the mosaic of water and islands, the Ossipee range, and even the White Mountains. Watch for the *Mount Washington,* a tourist liner that cruises the lake. To the west you'll see the Gunstock Ski area and Belknap Mountain (Hike 33). Kids can roam safely (with buckets for collecting blueberries) as parents relax.

Hike back to your car along the same route.

33. Belknap Mountain

Type: Dayhike
Difficulty: Difficult for children
Distance: 5 miles, round trip
Hiking time: 5 hours
High point/elevation gain: 2382 feet, 1500 feet
Hikable: May–October
Maps: USGS West Alton and Laconia

Whenever we've asked kids what features they appreciate most on a hike, "water" is what we have heard again and again. And why not? It's pretty to look at, fun to play in, and home to a great many interesting creatures. Round Pond is a secluded pool where the frogs far outnumber the people and the tracks on the shore belong to raccoons, not dogs. You'll travel to the pond along a lengthy route that leads over the summit of Belknap Mountain (a neighbor of the more crowded Mount Major) offering views that stretch for miles in every direction. Don't forget to bring your compass along; sections of the trail are overgrown and hard to follow.

 From the junction of NH-11 and NH-11A in West Alton, drive west on NH-11A. In Gilford, at the 7.6-mile mark, turn left onto Belknap

Mountain Road. Bear right at a fork in 1.3 miles; 1 mile later, turn left following a sign to Belknap Mountain (the gate is closed from 6:00 p.m. to 9:00 a.m.). The road turns to gravel and ends at a large parking area 3.9 miles from NH-11A.

Alternatively, from the junction of US 3 and NH-11A in Gilford, follow NH-11A west for 2.5 miles. Turn right onto Belknap Mountain Road and follow the above directions.

Although your instincts will point you toward the mountain trail, ignore them and walk back down the access road. Cross a stream in 0.15 mile and duck into the woods on the left (south), following the sharp, white blazes of the Piper Trail. Climb moderately along a root-choked path fringed with stately white birch trees, then briefly follow a dry stream bed on a gentler ascent.

Resting on the Belknap summit

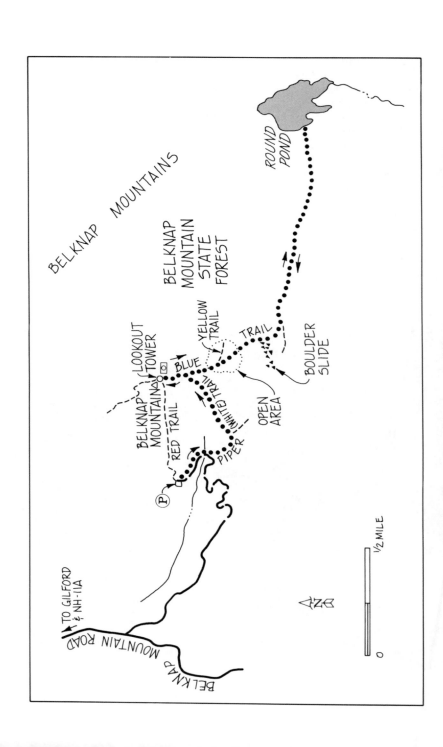

Three-tenths of a mile from the start, turn left (east), continuing on white blazes as a blue-blazed path maintained by a local Boy Scout troop heads straight (southeast). Quickly, the trail rises on a steep grade, passing formidable ledge outcroppings. From here, the grade moderates and follows cairns as well as blazes for the next 0.4 mile, climbing in and out of woods with limited views.

As you cut through groves of spruce, have the kids determine whether these are red or white spruces by studying the needles. Red ones have needles that are shiny and dark green, while white spruces produce whitish green needles that smell "skunky" when crushed.

The path crests at 0.7 mile and, 0.1 mile later, it joins the yellow-and blue-blazed trail (from Round Pond) at a large cairn. Turn left and follow the mixed blazes, continuing to curl left (north) past transmission equipment.

At 1.1 miles, you'll see the fire lookout tower. (When you climb the tower, ask the ranger to point out Round Pond, your eventual destination.) Panoramic views encompass the White Mountains, Gunstock Mountain, and Lake Winnipesaukee. Are any young hikers interested in pursuing careers as forest rangers? (To complete a 2-mile loop, follow the red-blazed trail northward then westward back to the parking area.)

To continue the 5-mile (total) hike to Round Pond, return to the intersection of the yellow, blue, and white trails, 0.1 mile south of the summit. Drop gently southwestward on the yellow and blue trail, guided once more by blazes and cairns.

One-tenth of a mile from the intersection, the yellow trail splits left (southeast) as you follow the blue trail right (south). The somewhat indistinct trail drops with the slope of the land over open baldface, cutting through a section of forest burned by an arsonist in 1989. Just before the trail bottoms out, it struggles across the left side (eastern end) of a boulder slide. The river of man-sized boulders cascades westward as you dive into dense, deciduous woods on a faint trail.

As the grade levels, turn left at a trail junction toward Round Pond. (The right-hand trail eventually leads to the Piper Trail, but has not been reconstructed since the fire.) The blazes are sharp, but the path is not well traveled, and for that reason it is hard to follow. Kids can be a real help here as they scan the trees for the blue marks. The path rambles along rolling terrain for 1 mile toward the remote Round Pond. Count mushrooms or tree stumps or moss-covered rocks along the way.

Once you reach the rugged shore, the kids will have a ball scouting for tadpoles, frogs, fish, or turtles. Remind turtle hunters that a turtle's shell is not its "house" as many people assume, but it is actually part of the turtle itself. Be gentle! Enjoy a picnic lunch with the secluded pond as a backdrop and return to your car the way you came. (Watch carefully for the blue-blazed trail that turns right and ascends the boulder field 1 mile from Round Pond.)

"Look what I caught!"

34. Mount Cardigan

Type:	Dayhike or overnight
Difficulty:	Difficult for children
Distance:	3.2 miles, loop
Hiking time:	3 hours
High point/elevation gain:	3155 feet, 1800 feet
Hikable:	April–October
Map:	USGS Mount Cardigan

The *AMC* (Appalachian Mountain Club) *White Mountain Guide* calls Cardigan the "traditional first big mountain climb for children." (You may also decide to make this the first overnight for your children with a campout at the Hermitage Shelter, 1 mile from the parking area.) We chose a well-maintained, easy-to-follow route that also encompasses the sheltered South Peak, where blueberry bushes abound and the dizzying views rival those from Cardigan's exposed summit. Frequent trail signs (despite several conflicting mileages) help kids gauge their progress.

Most of the mountain falls within a 5000-acre state park that is adjacent to the AMC's Cardigan Reservation. The club's Cardigan Lodge includes a main building, cottage, campground, and "Hi-Cabin," where hikers are fed and lodged in the summer. (For reservations, call the manager of the lodge at 603-744-8011.)

Take Exit 17 off of I-89. Drive 11.2 miles east on US 4 to the junction with NH-118 in Canaan. Turn left (north) on NH-118 following signs to Cardigan State Park. In 0.5 mile, turn right onto an unmarked road following another sign to Cardigan State Park. At a fork 2.6 miles from NH-118, bear right as the road turns to gravel. Drive another 0.7 mile and bear left at a second intersection. Continue for 0.6 mile to Cardigan State Park's parking and picnic area.

Study the wooden trail map near the parking lot. The red-blazed West Ridge Trail leaves the eastern side of the picnic area and begins a climb through mixed woods dominated by hemlocks and birches. The hard-packed and well-maintained path hops up stone steps at 0.1 mile and crosses a dribbling stream in another 0.1 mile. Tell the children to watch for changes in the vegetation as you climb toward the summit.

Shortly, an unblazed skimobile trail crosses your path, one of many such unmarked trails that crisscross the mountain. At 0.4 mile, a sign marks the intersection with the South Ridge Trail. Here, continue to follow the more heavily traveled West Ridge Trail as it heads left (east).

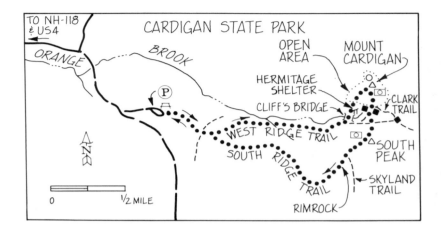

(You'll return along the South Ridge Trail.) At the frequent trail signs that include mileages, test your older children's math skills by asking them questions like "How much longer is the hike to the summit on this trail than on the South Ridge Trail?" (0.2 mile).

Rise moderately with rocks and roots underfoot to a stream crossing at 0.75 mile. If the climb is wearing thin on little hikers, play a game: Name all of the animals you can think of whose names begin with A, then B, C, and so on. One mile from the start, you'll scramble over a hemlock-shaded ledge to wind along a cascading brook. Soon, cross the brook over "Cliff's Bridge" as a side trail splits right. (Kids will want to pause on the bridge to examine the tumbling water up close.) One hundred feet beyond this sturdy footbridge along the West Ridge Trail sits Hermitage Shelter, a lean-to for overnight camping.

As you continue beyond the shelter, the red blazes and stone cairns lead onto baldface, marking your final approach to the windswept Cardigan summit. Western views stretch to Ascutney (Hike 7) and other Vermont peaks while Kearsarge looms to the south. Climb the final 0.1 mile on exposed granite with the fire tower in view. Continue straight at a marked trail junction with the Clark Trail to the rounded peak. Parents can enjoy the 360-degree view while little ones safely explore. You may need to find a cozy nook or cranny to escape the wind if you plan on spending any time here. (South Peak is probably a better choice for a picnic.)

Return to the intersection with the Clark Trail just below the summit and turn left, heading for South Ridge Trail and the warden's cabins. Follow paint blazes southward, sliding down a barren slope for 0.2 mile. The cabins and outhouse mark the boundary between the stark mountaintop and the edge of the forest. Just before the larger cabin the trail divides: The Clark Trail splits left while you continue straight on the

South Ridge Trail. In another 0.1 mile, turn left at a junction (still on South Ridge Trail) on your way to the Skyland Trail.

Drop through the woods on yellow blazing heading southward. Continue straight at a four-way intersection with orange- and white-blazed trails, guided by the familiar yellow markings of the South Ridge Trail. After rolling in and out of a damp sag, the trail crests on exposed South Peak, with commanding views that include the Cardigan summit. (You'll have better luck finding a picnic spot here since the winds are less severe than on Cardigan.)

Hike easily for 0.2 mile along the South Peak ridge. Shortly a trail sign at a junction steers you straight, still on the South Ridge Trail, toward the parking area 1.4 miles away. (The Skyland Trail turns left.) Drop moderately down a hemlock-forested slope.

Ledge intrusions define an area known as Rimrock (0.6 mile from the Cardigan summit) and provide the most challenging terrain so far. The kids will most likely need assistance here. Soon, deciduous trees dominate and, 1 mile from South Peak, the rugged South Ridge Trail joins the West Ridge Trail and turns left to arrive in 0.4 mile at the parking area.

35. Paradise Point

Type:	Dayhike
Difficulty:	Easy for children
Distance:	1.8 miles, loop
Hiking time:	1 hour
High point/elevation gain:	600 feet, 75 feet
Hikable:	Year-round
Map:	USGS Cardigan

The bear may have gone over the mountain, but your four-year-old refuses to. Save the high peaks for future years and plan a visit to lovely Paradise Point with its tame, well-marked trails perfectly suited to preschoolers. This 43-acre Audubon-managed natural area supports a nature center with a host of hands-on and live exhibits, as well as a resource library and nature store. Lovely trails wind through marsh areas and forests and follow the rugged shoreline to The Point, where you'll enjoy spectacular views of Newfound Lake. Urge grandparents to guide the little ones on this hike.

From I-93 in Plymouth, take Exit 26 to Tenney Mountain Highway,

NH-25 North, and NH-3A South. Drive 3.6 miles to the junction of NH-25 and NH-3A at a rotary in Plymouth. Head south on NH-3A. In 4.8 miles, turn right onto North Shore Road. Look for the Audubon Center sign in 1 mile; turn left onto a gravel driveway leading to a parking area.

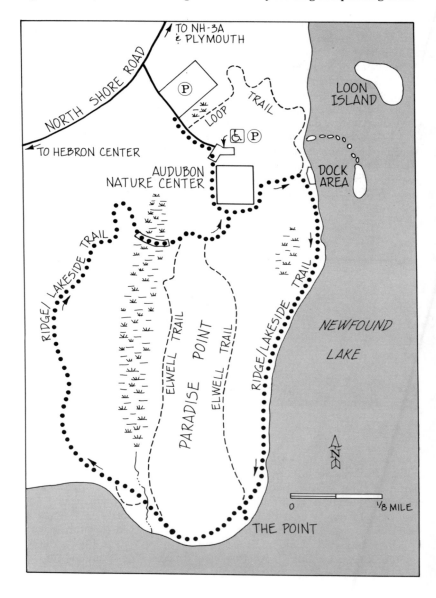

From the parking lot, walk southeastward down the gravel road, arriving in 0.1 mile at the Audubon Paradise Point Nature Center. Here, you can pick up a map or chat with one of the naturalists. From the building, head eastward on a path that leads in less than 0.1 mile to the dock area on Newfound Lake. A child-sized peninsula reaches into the water to the left of the docks. As kids peer into the water from this promontory, adults will take in the larger picture, looking out over the clear waters of the Newfound Lake inlet.

Follow the yellow-blazed Ridge/Lakeside Trail southward, winding along the rugged shoreline. Can you hear the call of the common loon? As you approach Paradise Point's southern shore, the trail rises above the lake with the rocky, tree-edged beach 30 feet below. On an open knoll 0.7 mile from the start, the red-blazed Elwell Trail joins from the right.

Turn left (south) onto a red-blazed side trail that leads quickly to a rock ledge, known as The Point, that juts into the water. Newfound Lake stretches before you, melting into the distant mountains. Reaching a depth of 180 feet in some places, the glacial lake is well known for the purity of its water (said to turn over several times a year). Enjoy the delightful concert of the sun's warming rays and the cool breezes sweeping inland.

Return to the knoll and trail junction, turning left (southwest) guided by red and yellow trail markings. Have the kids keep an eye out for tracks of the red fox. Rounding the southern tip of Paradise Point, the red Elwell Trail branches off to the right as you stay left, now heading northwestward on the yellow trail across a rough and rocky tract. Can the kids find any signs of animal homes? A porcupine's boulder den, perhaps? As you leave the water behind, ask your young companions to describe how the inland vegetation differs from the shoreline trees and plants.

Drop moderately eastward through a hardwood forest to a swamp, 1.5 miles from the start. Home to no one's favorite insect, the mosquito, the swamp also nurtures varieties of frogs and salamanders. (See if the kids can spot the brightly colored red eft salamander.) In the spring, the kids can look for frog and salamander eggs floating in the water.

Cross the marsh on a plank walk and emerge from the woods. Follow yellow and red blazes to the nature center building. From here, your car is a short walk up the gravel drive.

Note: Paradise Point Nature Center is open from 10:00 a.m. to 5:00 p.m., seven days a week, from late June through Labor Day, as well as some spring and fall weekends. Smoking, swimming, camping, fires, and bicycles are prohibited. Picnicking is allowed with the prior permission of a staff member. Donations are appreciated.

At Paradise Point, look close at hand for nature's smaller marvels.

36. Three Ponds Trail

Type: Dayhike or overnight
Difficulty: Moderate for children
Distance: 5.4 miles, loop
Hiking time: 4.5 hours
High point/elevation gain: 1800 feet, 700 feet
Hikable: May–October
Map: USGS Mount Kineo

You and your family will have a far better time visiting the Three Ponds area than John Stinson did. Nearly 250 years ago, Stinson (for whom the nearby lake and mountain were named) was captured and scalped here by a tribe of St. Francis Indians. Thankfully, your only pursuers will be springtime black flies. Before the hike, take the kids to the library and study up on the types of vegetation (like hobblebush and marsh fern) that grow in damp, boggy areas. As you hike, see how many of these species you encounter. Notice how the active beavers have affected the vegetation growth by rerouting water. If you enjoyed exploring Lake Solitude (Hike 30), you're sure to appreciate the remote beauty of Three Ponds (actually, there are four ponds). Waterproof footgear will make the soggy going more fun.

From I-93 in Plymouth, take Exit 26 to Tenney Mountain Highway, NH-25 North, and NH-3A South. Drive 3.6 miles to the junction of NH-3A and NH-25 at a rotary in Plymouth. Continue north on NH-25 for 3.4 miles; turn right onto Main Street in Rumney (at the second blinking light). Travel 6.8 miles on Main Street to a gravel driveway and large parking area for hikers on the left. (Look for the sign: "Three Ponds Trail, Mount Kineo Trail, Carr Mountain Trail.")

From the northern side of the parking area, the well-worn Three Ponds Trail heads through a damp area in mixed woods. Fun-to-cross plank walks span the wettest terrain. At 0.1 mile, the Mount Kineo Trail branches right (northeast); follow the Three Ponds Trail straight (northwest) on yellow blazing. The trail sweeps easily up a hill, then levels.

At 0.4 mile, cross the first of many streams that trickle through the area. Water always delights children, and water that moves holds a special fascination. In another 0.1 mile, the Carr Mountain Trail splits left (west) as you continue straight (northwest). Surrounded by a bog (0.7 mile from the start), the Three Ponds Trail weaves across the wettest spots on single logs. At bog's end, cross another stream and drop gently down a wooded slope.

Between the 0.8- and 1-mile marks, cross streams three times, once by way of a footbridge. After the third crossing, the trail meets an overgrown jeep road. Turn right onto the road, still heading in a northwesterly direction, to follow the bank of Sucker Brook. After crossing a tributary, sparse blazes lead uphill as the boisterous brook approaches the trail. At the crest, Sucker Brook turns from right to left and you head straight to cross two shallow sections of the brook on stones.

With Sucker Brook now on its left, the trail rises gradually to hop over the water two more times. The kids can scan the ground for partridgeberry, a plant whose leaves were used by colonial women to make a pain-relieving tea. At 2 miles, you'll come upon a lovely, remote pond, cradled by forested slopes. Soon a trail diverges right, heading uphill toward the Three Ponds Shelter, a three-sided building that sleeps six. To the south of the shelter lies the smallest of the ponds.

The main trail follows the edge of the large pond for 0.2 mile, leaving the water just before a trail junction with Donkey Hill Cutoff. For now, turn left to continue on Three Ponds Trail, immediately crossing a beaver dam. In another 0.3 mile, a side trail on the right brings you to a campsite near the upper pond where water-side rocks make a wonderful place to set out a picnic lunch. (From here, the Three Ponds Trail continues northward, passing Foxglove Pond in 0.5 mile and reaching NH-118 in 4.5 miles.)

Return to the Donkey Hill Cutoff intersection and turn left to continue the loop. The trail follows the right (southern) side of a swamp created when beavers flooded the land. What signs of beaver activity can the children find? Tracks? Gnawed tree stumps? Abandoned dams? For the next 0.5 mile, the trail rolls easily through marsh areas, then

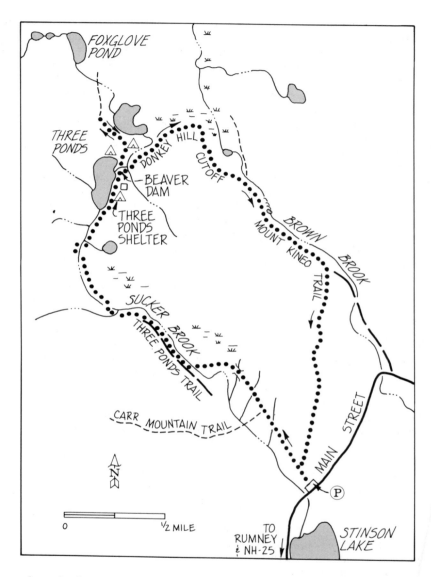

abruptly changes character as it cuts into a ridge and tracks across rocks and roots for another 0.5 mile.

Donkey Hill Cutoff ends 3.7 miles from the start of the hike at the junction with the Mount Kineo Trail. Turn right and follow the path (marked occasionally in yellow) along the engaging Brown Brook. Stay on the western side and, in 0.2 mile, you'll pass within 50 feet of a series of cascades that tumbles into a wide pool. Adults can relax while the kids explore. From here, the trail widens to become a woods road, dropping gradually along the splashing brook.

Seven-tenths of a mile from the junction with the Donkey Hill Cutoff, yellow blazes steer you onto a footpath, away from the brook and the woods road. Heading southward, the narrow path snakes through deciduous woods to meet the Three Ponds Trail. Turn left onto the familiar Three Ponds Trail and hike the final 0.1 mile to your car.

37. Georgiana and Harvard Falls

Type: Dayhike
Difficulty: Moderate for children
Distance: 2.3 miles, round trip
Hiking time: 2 hours
High point/elevation gain: 1600 feet, 700 feet
Hikable: May–October
Map: USGS Lincoln

There's never a dull moment along the trail to Georgiana and Harvard Falls. Warm up with an easy jaunt on a wide woods road, then hike on a footpath that snakes beside Harvard Brook, and finally scramble up the boulders that fringe the cascading Georgiana Falls. Although the last 0.4 mile from Georgiana to Harvard Falls is quite steep and probably not appropriate for preschoolers or adults backpacking small children, youngsters will find the initial 0.8 mile (to the turnaround point) delightful. Bring bathing suits or shoes for wading—nothing but winter weather will keep kids out of the water.

From I-93 in Lincoln, take Exit 33 for US 3 North. In 0.3 mile (just before the Longhorn Palace Restaurant and Gift Shop), turn left onto Hanson Farm Road. Drive 0.1 mile to the end of the road and park in the wide gravel area on the right before the barricade.

Head westward on a gravel road past the barricade. Walk through a tunnel underneath I-93's northbound lane and immediately turn right with the gravel road as an overgrown path continues straight. Quickly, the road sweeps left and passes under the highway's southbound lane. The noise of rushing cars fades as you head into the woods and, 0.2 mile from the start, you'll hear the soothing whispers of the distant Harvard Brook.

The gravel road rises gently to a clearing where it bends right. Follow the bend briefly and then turn left into the woods onto a red-blazed trail that leads to the bank of Harvard Brook. Though not officially maintained (since it crosses private property), the path is distinct, worn down by regular foot traffic. The path heads north, hugging the bank of the wide, shallow brook that spills through a maze of moss-covered boulders. Since a sinkful of tap water will keep most kids amused on a rainy afternoon, imagine how many games your young hikers will invent on the banks of this delightful brook!

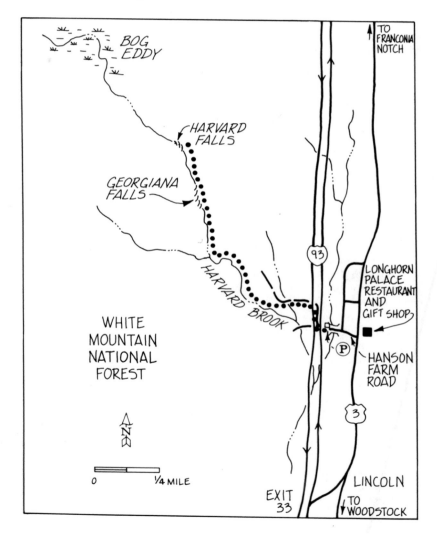

Spectacular Harvard Falls, with Franconia Notch in the distance

At 0.7 mile, you'll come upon Georgiana Falls, a spectacular cascade that tumbles into a series of deep pools. Daring young hikers will want to climb the rocks lining the falls, while more conservative youngsters will probably track through the woods. We recommend that adults hiking with or backpacking small children end the hike here for a total hiking distance of 1.6 miles.

Toward the top of the falls, the trail turns right, away from the water, to duck under a canopy of hemlocks on a moderate ascent. Soon, as the pitch steepens, the terrain becomes soft and slippery, forcing hikers to grasp at trees and sturdy bushes for help. At 1 mile, the trail sweeps along a ledge 30 feet above the brook and Harvard Falls comes into view.

The trail tapers off to end near the thundering 30-foot waterfall. Enjoy the breathtaking view of the gorge carved by Harvard Brook far below and distant White Mountain peaks. Set out your picnic lunch on one of the rocks overlooking the falls, but don't expect to enjoy polite conversation with your meal—you'll have to shout to be heard over the water!

Return to your car the way you came.

38. Greeley Ponds

Type: Dayhike
Difficulty: Easy to moderate for children
Distance: 4 miles, round trip
Hiking time: 3 hours
High point/elevation gain: 2245 feet, 350 feet
Hikable: May–October
Map: USGS Mount Osceola

It's not panoramic views that excite most kids, but plank walks and bridges, frog-filled ponds and rivers. The 4-mile hike to and from Greeley Ponds includes all these favorites and covers relatively level terrain, making it a great walk for the entire family. Gravelly beaches border the two wilderness ponds and allow ample room for exploring the shore or stretching out under the sun. This is a popular route, so expect to have company.

From I-93 in North Woodstock, take Exit 32 for North Woodstock, Lincoln, and the Kancamagus Highway (NH-112). Travel east on the Kancamagus Highway through Lincoln for 9.7 miles. Turn right into a substantial parking area with a sign for "Greeley Ponds Trail, White Mountain National Forest."

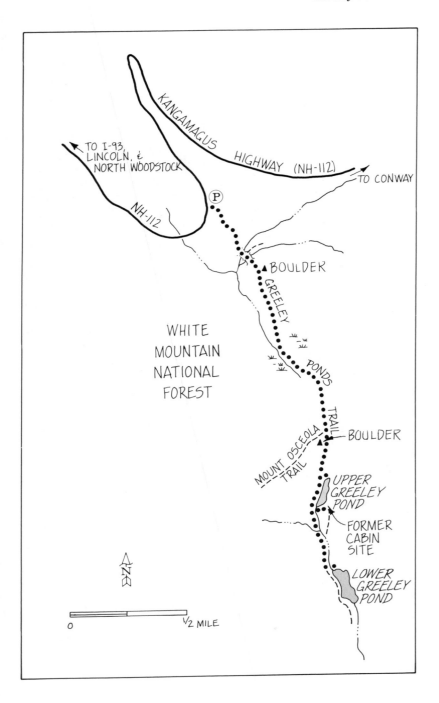

Rest stop beside Lower Greeley Pond

The worn, yellow-blazed trail leaves the southern side of the parking area to climb gradually through dense woodlands, tripping over exposed roots. Remind children to watch in front of them and to pick up their feet. In 0.1 mile, footbridges carry hikers over damp gullies and dribbling streams and, 0.2 mile later, a pair of long, well-constructed footbridges spans two branches of a brook. (Ignore the side trail that splits left after the first bridge.)

Shortly after crossing a fifth bridge at 0.35 mile, the trail dodges right to avoid a titanic boulder sustaining several trees. Kids, how does a tree grow out of a rock? One-half mile from the start, as you pass through stands of hemlocks, remember Christmas by rolling a few needles between your fingers and sniffing. Soon, log trestles and planks stretch about 100 feet across a marshy area. (Here, we startled a moose who left his spot in the swamp and crashed through the woods to get away!) Over the next 0.5 mile, you'll continue to traverse wetlands and streams by way of footbridges and split logs. The trail bends left (southeast) at 1 mile to begin a mild ascent.

After two more stream crossings, 1.3 miles from the start, the trail divides: The Mount Osceola Trail heads right (southwest) toward Mount Osceola via East Peak. Continue straight (south), still following the infrequent yellow blazing of the Greeley Ponds Trail. One-tenth of a mile from the trail junction, you'll pass to the left of another errant boulder. What would you name this boulder? (Don't you think the rock's top looks like a hat?)

Who will be the first to see the upper Greeley Pond, 1.6 miles from the start? The main trail avoids the shore, tracking about 15 feet above the western side of the pond, but a side trail outlets to a sandy beach at the pond's northern end. The jagged cliffs of Mad River Notch rise abruptly out of the water and provide a lovely backdrop for your picnic or energy break. Back on the Greeley Ponds Trail, hike to the pond's southern shore where a side trail splits left for the site of the former AMC (Appalachian Mountain Club) Greeley Pond Cabin and another natural, sandy beach. (Overuse of this camping area threatened to change the character of the wilderness ponds, so the cabin was dismantled.)

Return to the main trail, descending steadily southward on a less-traveled path toward the lower pond. Cross a plank walk to reach the edge of the lower pond, more rugged than the first, with a swampy shore that appeals more to moose and deer than to human visitors. Encourage the children to sit quietly (they probably need a rest) and watch for beavers and swallows, dragonflies and speckled trout (they'll emerge from the water to gobble up hatching flies).

On the way back, between the upper and lower ponds, you'll notice a trail junction that was not obvious on the hike in (due to the angle at which the path joined Greeley Ponds Trail). Stay left as this side trail splits right leading to the former camping site on the upper pond. Return along the familiar Greeley Ponds Trail.

39. Boulder Loop Trail

Type: Dayhike
Difficulty: Moderate for children
Distance: 3.1 miles, loop
Hiking time: 2.5 hours
High point/elevation gain: 1954 feet, 1100 feet
Hikable: May–October
Map: USGS North Conway West

As you hike the Boulder Loop, you'll feel as if you have your very own naturalist along. Equipped with a Forest Service interpretive leaflet (available at the trailhead or at the White Mountain National Forest Information Center, Passaconaway) that is keyed to numbered "STOPS" along the route, you will gain a better understanding of such common trailside phenomena as lichens, felled trees, and fallen boulders. Looking for the various stations will keep kids moving and will mark their progress in an understandable way.

Don't be fooled into thinking that this is just a tame nature walk, though. Halfway through the loop, you'll climb onto a set of sheer cliffs with tremendous views over the Passaconaway Valley. Call it a nature walk with punch.

From NH-16 in Conway, head west on the Kancamagus Highway (NH-112). In 6.5 miles, turn right onto Dugway Road. Pass through the covered bridge and drive 0.1 mile to a parking area on the right.

The yellow trail leaves the northern side of Dugway Road, quickly curves right (east), and splits 0.1 mile from the start. Head left and begin a 1.4-mile climb to the overlooks on the southwestern spur of the Moat Range. As you pass along a sheer 30-foot cliff, you'll come upon the first stop described in the leaflet. Here, lichens, one of the first plants to cover bare earth and rock, flourish on nearby boulders.

Send the kids ahead to find STOP 2, marking the boundary between a deciduous forest and mixed woods that now include conifers. (Explain to children the difference between coniferous and deciduous trees: conifers, or evergreens, have cones and don't lose their needles all at once while deciduous trees lose their foliage in autumn.) The trail winds moderately up a wooded slope and passes STOP 3, an area hit hard by a "nor'easter." What do these toppled trees have in common? (They've all fallen in the same direction, blown by the storm's powerful winds.) At STOP 4, look for young red spruce trees. Red spruces have scaly bark, dark green needles, and pinecone scales with rounded edges.

Before reaching STOP 5, the grade lessens to give hikers a reprieve as they look out over the Swift River and the Kancamagus Highway winding through the Passaconaway Valley hundreds of feet below. Who will be the first to spot STOP 6? Here you'll see "sheet joints," fractures near the surface of rocks that result from expansion within the granite mass. If you look to the left (east), you'll see the ledge overlooks, your destination.

STOP 8 features the decaying trunk of an old hemlock. Can the kids guess what might have caused its demise? (The brochure suggests drought, lightning, disease, wind, insects, or a combination of these forces.) Between STOPS 9 and 10, the trail leaves the moist, shady woods and crawls to a dry ledgy area. Hemlock and birch trees flourish in the moister soil while on the rock outcroppings the red oak has little competition from other varieties of trees.

STOP 11, 1.2 miles into the hike, ushers you toward the overlook. Turn right here onto a side trail that travels for 0.2 mile along the sheer cliffs with dramatic views to the south, east, and west over Mount Passaconaway, Mount Chocorua, and Middle Sister. Children should be warned to stay well back from the edge. A yellow "X" marks the end of

A covered bridge spanning the Swift River

the ledges (and the best views); return to the trail junction at STOP 11 and turn right to continue the loop.

Dropping steadily, the trail curls westward past STOP 13, 0.4 mile from the ledge overlook. You'll notice that trees have been selectively cut as part of the Forest Service's timber management program. Descending more steeply after a brief respite, the trail reaches STOP 14 near an impressive hemlock. Hemlocks, capable of surviving under the shaded canopy of the forest, thrive once they are exposed to more direct sunlight. At STOP 15, the boulders that were so frequent at the start of the hike are once again numerous.

Cross a tributary to the Swift River at STOP 16. The Swift River flows into the Saco River in Conway, which eventually feeds into the Atlantic Ocean. Huge boulders seem to block the trail and create a tunnel at STOP 17. These boulders split from the ledges above many years ago. Trees and plants have since grown to accommodate this chaos of rocks. At the final stop, number 18, look for stumps that are all that remain of trees felled 50 years ago for timber. Continue to the trail junction marking the end of the loop and go straight (west). Walk the 0.1 mile back to Dugway Road and your car.

40. The Basin and Lonesome Lake

Type:	Dayhike or overnight
Difficulty:	Challenging for children
Distance:	5 miles, round trip
Hiking time:	4.5 hours
High point/elevation gain:	2760 feet, 1300 feet
Hikable:	June–October
Maps:	USGS Franconia and Lincoln

This is one of the most popular White Mountain National Forest hiking routes—and for good reason. The trail departs the Basin, an always-crowded tourist attraction, to travel beside the Cascade Brook for 2.5 miles to the remote shores of Lonesome Lake. Here, you can spend the night at the Lonesome Lake Hut, which accommodates 46 and is open to the public from mid-June to mid-September. (Tents are not permitted near the hut or the lake.) For information and schedules, contact the Reservation Secretary by writing to Pinkham Notch Camp, Box 298, Gorham, NH-03581, or by calling (603) 466-2727.

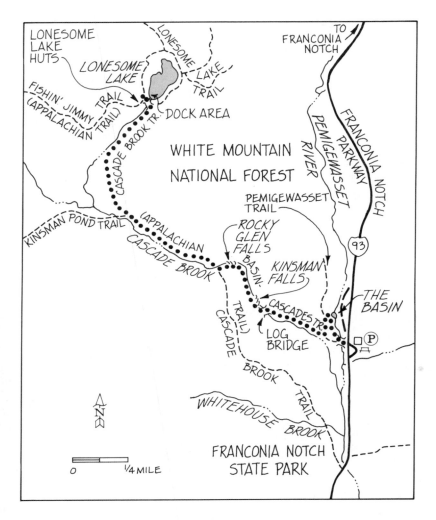

The trail's "challenging" rating stems from the length and rugged condition of the trail, not the elevation gain. Since the path travels through numerous wet areas, waterproof footgear is recommended.

In Lincoln, just north of the 106 mile marker on I-93 North (here, also called the "Franconia Notch Parkway"), exit the highway at a sign that says "The Basin, 0.5 mile." Follow signs to the Basin and park in the ample, paved parking area.

From the parking area (with restrooms and picnic tables), follow the signs to the Basin that lead under I-93 on the paved bike and footpath.

Beyond the underpass, as directed by the Basin sign, cross the Pemigewasset (an Abenaki Indian name meaning "swift") River on a metal bridge. Follow the landscaped gravel path (actually, it is the unmarked Basin-Cascades Trail) for 0.1 mile to the Basin, a magnificent pothole created by the swirling waters of the Pemigewasset River. Adults as well as kids will be mesmerized by this dramatic natural masterpiece.

After admiring the Basin, leave the busloads of tourists behind and follow the Basin-Cascades Trail (unmarked and unblazed) heading westward. Soon, as the Pemigewasset Trail splits right, you bear left, continuing southwestward to a sign for the Basin-Cascades Trail at a junction 0.2 mile from the start. Turn right. (Ignore the mileages on these signs; many are incorrect.) The trail heads westward, departing the Pemigewasset River and joining the tumbling Cascade Brook. The worn, root-choked path snakes uphill along the brook's northern bank under lofty hemlocks. Who will notice the National Forest Boundary at 0.3 mile?

The Basin, a magnificent pothole along the Pemigewasset River, receives thousands of visitors each year.

The hurrying brook that rushes alongside the trail for nearly 2 miles is an entertaining, delightfully noisy playmate for the kids. Nearly 0.5 mile into the hike, children will need help (actually, parents will need help too) crossing the river on a single, springy log several feet above the water. On the southern bank (yea, you made it!), the trail rises above the brook and passes the delightful cascades known as Kinsman Falls. Here, the pitch lessens but the trail may still be tough on little legs because it is very rooty and often soggy.

At the 1-mile mark, granite walls embrace the fierce Rocky Glen Falls, which spills 15 feet through a canyon. The Basin-Cascades Trail ends just beyond the waterfall at a junction with the combined Cascade Brook Trail and Appalachian Trail (AT). Here, you cross from the southern to the northern riverbank over a jumble of boulders as you head westward on the white-blazed AT.

The rugged trail leaves the bank of Cascade Brook and climbs easily in and out of damp sections. Ask the kids to hike with all of their senses: What can they see, hear, touch, smell? At 1.6 miles, the Kinsman Pond Trail branches left (southwest) as you continue straight. From here, Lonesome Lake and the huts are just under 1 mile away.

If you have anything that appeals to them, hiking friends tell us, you may entice the familiar Canada jays to eat right out of your hand. Slippery logs span more damp spots as the trail swings northward away from the brook. On steeper grades, stones create welcome steps. The trail rejoins the brook at 2 miles. How has the character of the brook changed since you last saw it?

Nearly 2.5 miles from the start, you'll arrive at a trail junction near the outlet to Lonesome Lake. Turn left onto the Fishin' Jimmy Trail (which has merged with the AT) and skirt the southern end of the lake over a footbridge. In 0.1 mile, look for the dock area and huts on the lake's western shore that mark the end of your trip in. Here, you can go for a swim, enjoy the lovely views of the Franconia range, chat with other hikers, or prepare for an overnight stay. (By the way, who can figure out how supplies are brought to huts like this one?)

On the return trip, kids can race with the Cascade Brook all the way back to the Basin.

Hikers admire Bridal Veil Falls.

41. Bridal Veil Falls

Type:	Dayhike or overnight
Difficulty:	Moderate for children
Distance:	4.8 miles, round trip
Hiking time:	4 hours
High point/elevation gain:	2100 feet, 1000 feet
Hikable:	May–October
Maps:	USGS Franconia and Sugar Hill

Bridal Veil Falls, one of the more captivating waterfalls in the White Mountain National Forest (WMNF), tumbles down Coppermine Brook in the ravine between Cannon Mountain and the Cannon Balls. The Coppermine Trail leads gradually uphill for 2.4 miles to the falls. With the brook as a delightful companion, the miles will pass quickly for kids. And on a steamy summer day, youngsters will be attracted to the frequent wading pools like pigs to mud puddles. Plan to spend the night in the WMNF Coppermine Shelter near the falls.

 From I-93 in Franconia, take Exit 38. Drive south for 0.1 mile to the junction of NH-18 and NH-116 (Church Street). Continue straight on

NH-116 and, in 3.4 miles, turn left onto Coppermine Road. Park on the road's right-hand shoulder.

Begin walking eastward on Coppermine Road. (If you prefer, you can drive along Coppermine Road until it becomes too rough.) In 0.3 mile, the pavement ends and the gravel road divides; bear left at a trail sign following yellow blazes. Can you hear the hollow drumming of the woodpecker? Follow the sound to its source and you'll see a bird climbing up the side of a tree using its claws to grip the bark and its tail feathers for balance. Woodpeckers eat the insects that live under the bark.

At a fork 0.6 mile from the start, continue straight, guided by an arrow for the Coppermine Trail, as an unmarked woods road bears right. Ascend easily along the rugged gravel road. (Who will be the first to hear the Coppermine Brook?) One mile from the start, you can listen for the rushing water to the right; in another 0.1 mile you'll be able to see it.

The trail briefly hugs the brook's northern bank at 1.4 miles, departs it on a moderate ascent, and returns to the water's edge. This pattern repeats over the next 0.5 mile as the relatively straight path travels beside the weaving river. Since no one seems to know how Coppermine Brook got its name, take turns making up silly stories. Here's a start: "Legend has it that 100 years ago, George Copper and Tom Mine went fishing . . . ."

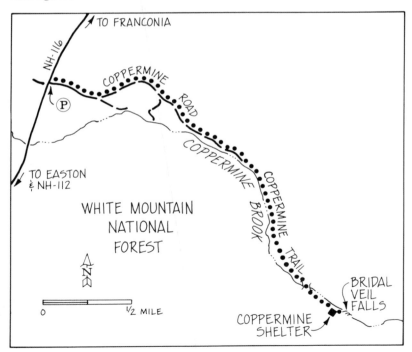

Nearly 2 miles from the start, the trail narrows and rises above the brook on a short, moderate ascent, leaving the riverbank for 0.25 mile. The kids can run ahead and wait for the adults where the trail rejoins the brook near a sturdy footbridge. Have a splashing contest: Drop acorns, pebbles, pinecones, and twigs from the bridge to see what will make the best splash.

After crossing the brook, travel along the southwestern bank for 0.1 mile to the WMNF Coppermine Shelter, nestled between rock ledges and a pool. Travel another 0.1 mile to the cascading Bridal Veil Falls, crossing the brook at the base for the best views. Let the kids splash in the pools before retracing your steps to the car or setting up camp.

42. Artist Bluff

Type:	Dayhike
Difficulty:	Moderate for children
Distance:	1.8 miles, loop
Hiking time:	1.5 hours
High point/elevation gain:	2320 feet, 550 feet
Hikable:	May–October
Map:	USGS Franconia

Artist Bluff is not just another pretty face. Although it soars magnificently over NH-18 and I-93, dotted on most nice days with dozens of rock climbers, it does more than catch your eye from the highway. It offers you a chance to take in terrific views for very little effort and to escape the tourists that congregate at Profile Lake, the Flume, and the Basin. The trip to Artist Bluff via Bald Mountain will take less than 2 hours, making it a great hike to combine with other local activities.

From I-93 (here, also called the "Franconia Notch Parkway") in Franconia Notch, take Exit 3 to NH-18, Echo Lake Beach and Ski Area. Travel 0.8 mile north on NH-18. Just beyond the Cannon Mountain Peabody Slopes parking area, park on the right-hand side of the road near the entrance to a gravel pit. A sign says "Hiker Parking."

Cross the expansive gravel pit diagonally left (northeast) to the edge of the woods. Put the kids in charge of locating the trailhead (look for the "TRAIL" sign and the red blazes). As you climb moderately up the rocky path through deciduous woods, play animal charades. Who does the best frog, tiger, elephant, or snake?

A snack on top of Artist Bluff

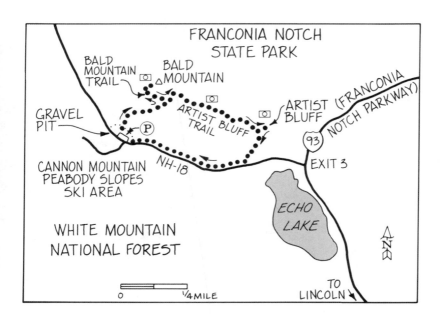

At 0.3 mile, the Bald Mountain Trail splits left (west) as the Artist Bluff Trail continues straight (north). For now, head left (still on red) and work your way up the steep, rocky hillside to the open summit of Bald Mountain. You are rewarded for your brief effort with tremendous views of the Franconia area: 5300-foot Mount Lafayette looms to the south and the ski slopes sweep down the side of Cannon Mountain to the southwest. Look right (west) to see the peaks of Vermont and the tips of the Adirondacks.

Return to the trail junction and swing left, rejoining the Artist Bluff Trail on an ascent. Can the kids find the trailside spruce trees with trunks scarred by lightning? Two-tenths of a mile beyond the junction, the trail levels before making a final surge to an overlook with dramatic views of Cannon's crisscrossing ski trails. As we relaxed here for a few minutes, we saw several gliders drifting above the valley.

Hike along gently rolling terrain for the next 0.1 mile to another vista, beyond which the trail slides steeply down the mountainside. Partway down, the trail drops into a gully. At the head of this gully, a side trail branches left and leads quickly to the exposed ledges of Artist

Bluff. While there is plenty of room to explore here, the ledges form sheer cliffs and parents should warn kids to stay back from the edge. As you unpack your picnic lunch, you'll be able to watch rock climbers scaling (or clinging to, depending on their capabilities) these cliffs. Look southward across Echo Lake to Eagle Cliff and Mount Lafayette.

After a pleasant rest on the bluff, return to the main trail and bear left (south). The trail falls steeply down the gully for 0.25 mile to NH-18. Turn right (west) and follow the highway for 0.5 mile back to your car.

The Old Man in the Mountain surveys Franconia Notch.

43. Zealand Pond and Zealand Falls

Type:	Dayhike or overnight
Difficulty:	Moderate for children
Distance:	5.4 miles, round trip
Hiking time:	4.5 hours
High point/elevation gain:	2637 feet, 650 feet
Hikable:	May–September
Map:	USGS Crawford Notch

Water, water, water! We know kids love it, so we included this trail on the Twin-Zealand Range, which encompasses a river, bog, pond, and waterfall. Just under 3 miles from the start, you'll come to the AMC (Appalachian Mountain Club) hut near Zealand Falls, at the northern end of Zealand Notch. Here, you can spend the night or just relax for a few hours and trade stories with other hiking families. Since the grade is gradual, this hike is well within the capabilities of most children, especially if you break it up with an overnight. For information about the hut, call the AMC at (603) 466-2727.

Lengthy log bridges span soggy swampland on the way to Zealand Pond.

From the junction of US 3 and US 302 in Twin Mountain, travel east on US 302. In 2.1 miles, turn right at a sign for Zealand Road, White Mountain National Forest Recreation Area. Follow Zealand Road for 3.4 miles to its conclusion at a gate and the start of the Zealand Trail.

The blue-blazed Zealand Trail leaves the southern side of the parking area, initially a wide path lined with young hemlocks. Soon the trail's complexion changes as it scales a knoll over rugged terrain. As you drop off the hill, a solid footbridge carries you over a brook, 0.3 mile from the start. (Although the trail parallels the Zealand River for its length, the two are separated by 100 yards or so for the first 0.7 mile.)

Rising gradually, the wide path now follows a former railroad bed. Anyone getting restless? Ask each other some animal trivia questions: How far can an adult kangaroo jump? (Twenty-seven feet!) How many of its legs does a spider use when it walks? (All eight.) In what two ways might an animal's coat change in preparation for winter? (It may turn white or become thicker.) Do porcupines shoot their quills? (No.)

Seven-tenths of a mile from the start, the trail approaches the Zealand River and weaves along the western bank through mixed woods. At 1.5 miles, cross a series of tributaries over sturdy footbridges and stepping stones. (Since the kids will most likely want to play a few water games, plan to take an extended energy break here.)

As you continue, your first distant mountain views emerge. Skirt a bog on the left and soon cross this soggy swampland over lengthy log bridges. After fording another stream at 2.2 miles, the trail divides: As the A-Z Trail bears left (east) toward Crawford Notch, you continue straight and shortly cross the outlet to Zealand Pond.

This pond is unusual because, since it's at the height of the land in Zealand Notch, it has an outlet at each end. Kids, do you realize that if you could turn yourself into a tiny boat and float down the Zealand River, you would eventually end up in the Atlantic Ocean?

As you hike along the eastern shore of Zealand Pond, look right (west) to see the distant falls. The Zealand Trail ends at a junction near the southern tip of the pond (2.5 miles from the start), where the Ethan Pond Trail continues straight. You swing right (west) onto the white-blazed Twinway Trail, skirting the southern end of the pond. Kids, do you see any beaver dams?

After briefly heading northward, the trail again marches westward, nearing the final, steep ascent that leads to the AMC hut. Halfway up the climb, a side trail splits left (south) for Zealand Falls, a cascade that tumbles down a series of square-edged rock steps. The Twinway Trail continues to the hut, 0.2 mile from the end of the Zealand Trail. From here, the views down the valley toward Mount Carrigain are magnificent.

Built in 1932 to accommodate 36 guests, the Zealand Falls Hut sits near the bank of the Whitewall Brook. It is open to the public during the summer and fall and on a caretaker basis in the winter. Spend the night or just a pleasant afternoon before retracing your steps to the car.

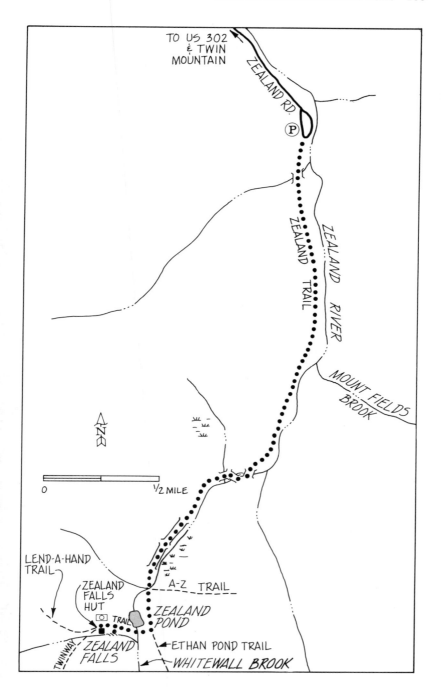

44. Arethusa Falls and Frankenstein Cliff

Type:	Dayhike
Difficulty:	Challenging for children
Distance:	4.3 miles, loop
Hiking time:	4 hours
High point/elevation gain:	2510 feet, 1500 feet
Hikable:	May–October
Maps:	USGS Stairs Mountain and Crawford Notch

Take it to a vote: Who wants to visit the state's highest waterfall? Now, who wants to climb to the top of some 600-foot cliffs? Guess what? On this hike, everyone wins! The trip to Frankenstein Cliff by way of Bemis Brook and Arethusa Falls will satisfy water-lovers as well as view-lovers.

The 2.4-mile round-trip hike to the spectacular falls, however, may be enough for adults hiking with preschoolers. The continuation of the loop hike to Frankenstein Cliff (named for a local artist, not the fellow with bolts in his neck) is demanding and the cliffs are not appropriate for unchaperoned exploring. So, alter the route to suit your needs.

 From the junction of NH-16 and US 302 in Bartlett, travel west on US 302 for approximately 15 miles. After a sign announces the nearby Arethusa Falls, turn left onto an access road. In 0.1 mile, park on the left in a lot near the private residence still known as Willey House Post Office.

Alternatively, from the junction of US 3 and US 302 in Twin Mountain, travel east on US 302 for approximately 14 miles to the access road on the right. Follow the above directions.

Cross the railroad tracks, bearing left toward the Arethusa Falls Trail. The yellow-blazed path dives into woods dotted with birch trees, heading southwestward. On the left, Bemis Brook spills raucously down the mountainside through a deep gorge. Soon, the trampled trail veers right, away from the brook. At 0.15 mile, the blue-blazed Bemis Brook Trail splits left (to visit pools and minor falls), rejoining 0.3 mile later. At all junctions, continue straight on the Arethusa Falls Trail.

Some people believe that the trail and the falls were named for the orchid arethusa that once grew in the area. Can you guess why flowers are so pretty and fragrant? Flowers must attract the insects that will help bring pollen grains and "plant eggs" together to make new plants.

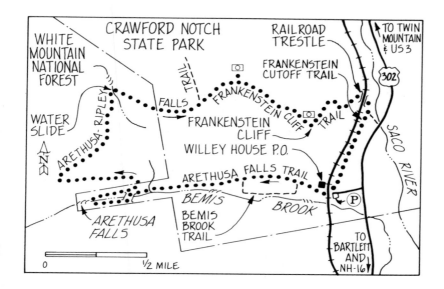

Climb moderately on the rocky trail beside the stately white birch trees. One-half mile from the start, the pitch eases as the narrow trail cuts deeper into the ridge. To your left, the hill plummets into the gorge carved by Bemis Brook. At 0.7 mile, you can look down at the water tumbling over the rust-colored stones and spilling into frequent pools.

Soon the lofty trail approaches the brook and, in another 0.1 mile, the brook responds, rising to join the path. Cross a substantial tributary and continue to follow the muddy, northern bank. Here, the root-crossed trail is likely to be slippery. Use your imagination: What do the roots look like as they twist across the trail? Dozens of slithering snakes, perhaps?

As the trail struggles to follow the water's edge, the rugged terrain forces it to rise and fall near the bank. Just over 1 mile from the start, follow the blazes to cross from the right (north) to the left (south) side of the brook over a log bridge. (Kids may opt to cross on the less slippery stones.) Shortly, you'll reach the base of Arethusa Falls, the highest waterfall in New Hampshire. Ribbonlike streams of water plunge more than 200 feet to the rugged rocks below. Here, appropriately, the Arethusa Falls Trail ends. If accompanied by preschoolers, you may want to turn around here and return the way you came for a total hike of 2.4 miles. If you continue, save your picnic lunch for Frankenstein Cliff, where there is more room to spread out.

Lend a hand to kids as you cross the brook at the base of the falls. The blue-blazed Arethusa-Ripley Falls Trail originates on the northern bank of Bemis Brook and heads eastward up a steep ridge away from the water. The trail cuts across a wooded hillside and shortly switches back to head westward at the top of the ridge. Soon, after curling northward, the trail winds along a fairly level ridge for nearly 1 mile, crossing several streams. (At 1.8 miles, kids will beg for a chance to pause near the stream that splashes down a water slide.)

Just over 1 mile from the falls, the Arethusa-Ripley Falls Trail intersects with the Frankenstein Cliff Trail. Turn right (southeast) onto the Frankenstein Cliff Trail as the Arethusa-Ripley Falls Trail continues left (north). Follow the trail as it dips and rises; soon, turn left onto a short side trail that leads to an overlook with pretty views of the Crawford Notch area.

The main trail begins a solid descent 0.5 mile from the junction with the Arethusa-Ripley Falls Trail. Dive through thick evergreens for 0.2 mile to the edge of a precipitous drop-off with fine southerly views down into Crawford Notch. You will not want the children to precede you here, since in another 0.1 mile you'll arrive atop the sheer Frankenstein Cliff. The kids can count the tiny cars speeding along the highway 600 feet below as adults take in the larger view that includes Moat Mountain, and Mounts Paugus, Passaconaway, and Crawford.

After enjoying a picnic lunch with the impressive Notch views as a backdrop, follow the trail as it ducks into the woods, heading northeastward. Ask the kids for their help in following the blue blazes along an initially twisted route. Two-tenths of a mile beyond the cliffs, the trail switches back right (south) on a steep descent, wrapping around a ledge outcropping. Pick your way through a skimpy boulder field and then approach the base of the cliffs. Kids who like to spin around until they are stumbling and dizzy can achieve a similar feeling by standing close to the cliffs and looking straight up at the rock face.

From here, the blue markings lead hikers across the slope to wind generally eastward to the bottom of the grade. Head under a 70-foot-high railroad trestle and then turn right (south) at a trail junction to join the Frankenstein Cutoff Trail. Enjoy a pleasant 0.5-mile stroll through the woods back to the parking area. The kids have earned a few dozen pats on the back!

45. Kearsarge North

Type: Dayhike
Difficulty: Challenging for children
Distance: 6 miles, round trip
Hiking time: 5.5 hours
High point/elevation gain: 3268 feet, 2700 feet
Hikable: May–October
Map: USGS North Conway East

Kearsarge North (called "Pequawket" in colonial times) isn't part of the White Mountain huddle. It sits just far enough beyond the principal ranges to provide an expansive view incorporating all of the prominent peaks. Kids who are up to a 6-mile hike will end this day with a real feeling of accomplishment. Take home a souvenir of your hike—such as a topographical map or photograph from the summit—so that your kids will be able to share this experience with their classmates.

Just north of North Conway on NH-16 (beyond the "Rest Area, Scenic Overlook and Information Center" on the left), turn right onto Hurricane Mountain Road. Drive 1.4 miles to a small parking area on the left.

The unblazed Mount Kearsarge North Trail leaves the parking area heading north; the summit of North Kearsarge is 3 miles away. Duck under a stand of tall pines and, at 0.15 mile, cross a dribbling stream. As an unmarked trail splits left (west) at 0.4 mile, you continue straight and soon begin a moderate ascent through a hemlock and pine forest.

Who will notice the first yellow blaze? Climb in a northeasterly direction along a hard-packed trail. A restless child can pretend to be an Indian hunting for food or an explorer walking uncharted land.

Just under 1 mile from the start, you'll have a brief reprieve as the trail swings right (southeast) onto a shoulder. But soon the path curves northwestward and then northward, resuming its steady climb and passing several large boulders. Weary little hikers can be recharged with a game: Imitate bird calls, with prizes for the best chickadee, bobwhite, or crow. First Prize: a 5-minute piggyback ride.

One and a half miles from the start, granite breaks through the soil underfoot. Shortly, the trail opens onto exposed baldface cluttered with pitch pines. Frequent yellow blazes splashed on the granite and an occasional cairn lead hikers across this open area. At 1.8 miles, look for the distant summit peering through the pine trees. In another 0.2 mile, southern and western views emerge as the trail struggles up a steep slope in and out of woods.

The trail avoids a direct route to the summit, ascending and cresting the northwest ridge. Nearing your destination, the trail strays northward, then cuts right (southeast) over ledge. What holiday are you reminded of when you smell the hemlock and spruce trees? With less than 0.1 mile to go, the first panoramic views envelop you as the trail breaks onto open ground.

Soon, you'll reach the wide, flat summit. Climb the fire tower (evi-

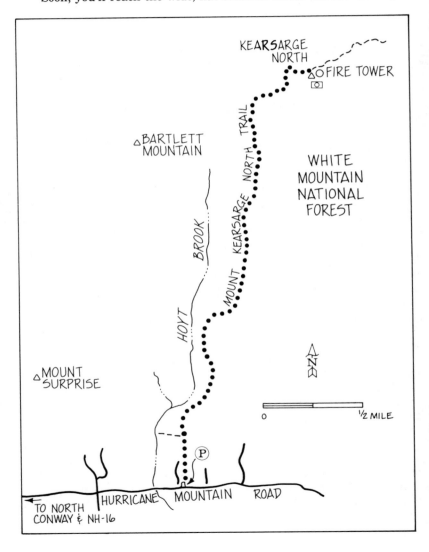

dence of relatively easy access and the commanding views) to look at Mount Washington with its crown of clouds and the other mountains in the Whites. Do you hear anything but the blowing wind? See if the kids can locate the massive anchor bolts on the summit, all that remains of the two hotels that once sat grandly on this mountaintop. They were both destroyed during severe storms.

Retrace your steps to the car.

46. North Doublehead

Type: Dayhike or overnight
Difficulty: Challenging for children
Distance: 3.5 miles, round trip
Hiking time: 3.5 hours
High point/elevation gain: 3053 feet, 1750 feet
Hikable: May–October
Map: USGS Jackson

You've hiked The Roost (Hike 62), Mount Agamenticus (Hike 53), and Mount Peg (Hike 9). Now you and the kids are ready to tackle a real mountain (and you're even considering an overnight). North Doublehead is the mountain for you. With a White Mountain National Forest (WMNF) cabin at the summit, you can spend a relaxing evening miles from the nearest television or lawnmower. There's no appropriate turnaround point along this route, so it would be something of a letdown if the group had to head back before reaching the summit. To avoid disappointment, make sure everyone (and everyone's gear) is up to a steep mountain climb. Allow yourselves enough time for frequent rests and energy breaks.

From the junction of US 302 and NH-16 in Bartlett, head north on NH-16. In 2 miles, turn right onto NH-16A ("to NH-16B, Jackson Village") and cross a covered bridge. In 0.3 mile, bear right onto NH-16B as NH-16A heads left. Drive another 1.6 miles to the Black Mountain Ski Area, where you bear right onto Dundee Road as NH-16B bears left. Seven-tenths of a mile later, turn left into a gravel driveway that leads to a parking area for several cars. (A sign announces the Doublehead Ski Trail.)

From the parking area, the wide Doublehead Ski Trail heads in an easterly direction toward the summit of Doublehead. At a junction in 100 yards, follow the well-worn cross-country ski trail to the right on blue diamond blazes as a logging road heads straight.

The trail, rising initially on a gradual grade, steepens at 0.2 mile. A stream briefly visits on the left and, just under 0.5 mile from the start, the trail trudges up a grassy hillside and hops over another stream. At the 0.6-mile mark, follow the narrow Old Path straight (east) as the ski trail veers left. Hike through mature deciduous woods up a moderate grade that steepens 0.1 mile beyond the junction.

Over the next 0.6 mile, the trail winds steadily up the mountainside on a moderate-to-steep grade. Make sure the kids know the rule: Whiners must walk backwards for 30 paces! If fussiness threatens to become contagious, play "Simon Says." "Simon says 'Hop like a bunny!' " "Simon says 'Wave a leaf in the air like a flag!' " "Gallop like a horse!" (You're out! I didn't say "Simon says!")

The trail splits 1.35 miles from the start: As one branch turns right toward South Doublehead, you turn left (northeast) on the path that leads to North Doublehead. A gradual ascent through hemlocks gives everyone a much-needed rest. The respite soon ends as the trail works its way up a steep boulder slide. Play follow the leader up the rock steps. (Appoint the pokiest one as the leader to spur him or her on!)

At 1.6 miles, a side trail drifts left and drops for 100 yards to high ledges with westerly views over Jackson Village and the White Moun-

Doublehead Cabin at the summit of North Doublehead

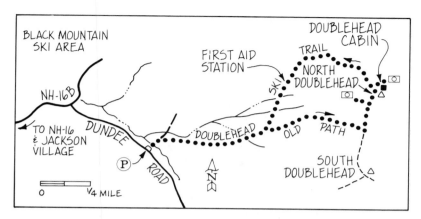

tain ranges. These views are better than those from the sheltered summit, making it the choice spot for an extended rest or picnic.

Back on the main trail, climb steeply under a hemlock canopy to reach the wooded summit and the WMNF Doublehead Cabin 1.7 miles from the start. The cabin, nestled in a spruce grove, has eight bunks, gas lights, and a stove (but no water). Behind the cabin, a short path leads to an overlook with views to the east of the Mountain Pond area, Kezar Lake, the Royces (Hike 61) and North Baldface.

Prepare for dinner and an overnight stay, or find the blue diamond cross-country ski trail to the west of the cabin to return to your car. Drop on a moderate-to-steep grade off the mountain with occasional views to the southwest. A WMNF first-aid station (0.85 mile from the summit) offers medical supplies to injured hikers.

One mile from the cabin, the trail crosses a pair of streams (the hike's only reliable water source) and in another 0.2 mile reaches the intersection with Old Path. Bear right to follow the cross-country ski trail back to your car.

47. Glen Boulder

Type: Dayhike
Difficulty: Challenging for children
Distance: 3 miles, round trip
Hiking time: 3.5 hours
High point/elevation gain: 3650 feet, 1900 feet
Hikable: June–September
Map: USGS Stairs Mountain

The hike to Glen Boulder is, without a doubt, the toughest hike in this book. Are you still reading? Good for you! (You're either in excellent physical condition or you're my mother, who reads everything I write.) Since 1905, hikers have been struggling up the eastern spur of Mount Washington (known as Boott Spur) to admire this famous landmark. And what a landmark! As you drive on NH-16, look for the truck-sized boulder perched on the exposed mountainside. You'd better visit soon; it looks juuust about ready to go. . . .

From the junction of US 302 and NH-16 in Bartlett, drive north on NH-16. In 10.6 miles, turn left into the parking area for Glen Ellis Falls.

From the southern end of the parking area, head southwestward on a gravel road toward Glen Boulder, 1.5 miles away. Pass restrooms on the left and turn northwestward onto the blue-blazed Glen Boulder foot trail. The trail quickly curls left (southwest) and rises gently through deciduous woods peppered with conifers.

Looking north through Pinkham Notch from Glen Boulder

After crossing a dainty stream at 0.15 mile, the path climbs steeply on stone steps for 0.1 mile. The grade relaxes briefly, then resumes once again within a rock channel built to prevent erosion. This is a steadily tough climb and children will need to be distracted from sore legs. Older ones can try to name U.S. presidents or state capitals; younger ones can play "Opposites" (you say "up," they say "down") or name words that rhyme with "go" or "play." A mixed group can play "Keep the Story Going," in which someone begins a story and each person in turn adds a sentence.

At 0.4 mile, the trail turns right (north) at an indistinct junction onto Chimney Bypass following signs for the Glen Boulder Trail. (This route circumvents the demanding Chimney portion of Glen Boulder Trail.) Soon, turn left at a junction where the Direttissima Trail heads right (north) for the Pinkham Notch Camp, 1 mile away. Follow the level though rugged trail heading generally west/southwest, soon rejoining Glen Boulder Trail above the detoured section.

A stream crossing at 0.55 mile marks the start of a moderate ascent. Soon, you'll squeeze beside a 15-foot cliff. Over the next 0.2 mile, the trail hops over two streams and struggles up steep boulder slides. After crossing the Avalanche Brook Ski Trail at 0.8 mile, the Glen Boulder Trail marches westward toward a cascading brook. Still climbing moderately up the rocky slope, the trail steps over a tributary and, at 1 mile, crosses the lively main branch of the brook on stones. (This may be a good spot to take an energy break. The kids can splash in the water.)

The gradual ascent becomes steep at 1.1 miles as the trail rises stiffly up the eastern side of Boott Spur. Ask the children what changes they notice in the vegetation as you approach the tree line. At 1.15 miles, look eastward to see the Wildcat Mountain peaks. After a scramble up a formidable ledge 1.25 miles from the start, you'll leave the trees behind. Put one child in charge of finding blue paint blazes and make another responsible for spotting cairns. A third can keep an eye out for Glen Boulder, which will soon be visible on the horizon.

The trail sweeps left (southwest) over ledges, heading toward the boulder. Dive into a thicket of spruce and scrub as you near the 1.5-mile mark and exit on a steep ascent, reaching the boulder 0.1 mile later. (We made our first snowball of the year here—in September!)

As the kids approach the boulder, they'll realize that "awesome" doesn't apply only to skateboard tricks and music videos. Adults can take in the vast panoramas, looking southeastward toward North Doublehead (Hike 46) and Kearsarge North (Hike 45), eastward to see Wildcat, and northward for Mount Washington and the smoke stacks of Berlin, New Hampshire. Hard as it may be to believe, the summit of Boott Spur is another 1850 vertical feet above you!

After you've properly admired the boulder, return the way you came, exercising caution as you descend the ledges.

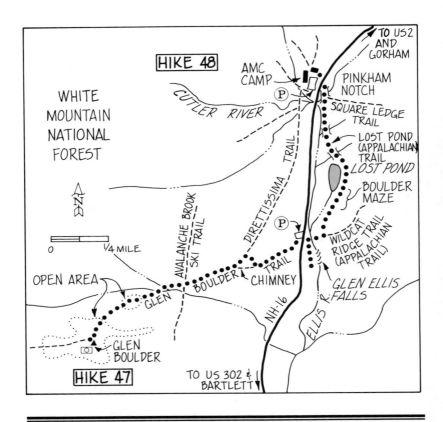

48. Glen Ellis Falls

Type: Dayhike
Difficulty: Easy for children
Distance: 2.2 miles, round trip
Hiking time: 2 hours
High point/elevation gain: 2050 feet, 150 feet
Hikable: June–October
Maps: USGS Stairs Mountain, Carter Dome, and Mount Washington

On the hike to Glen Ellis Falls, you will see water at its most peaceful and its most powerful. Follow the hurrying Ellis River to the shores of tranquil Lost Pond. From here, negotiate a boulder maze to rejoin the river and arrive at the waterfall just over 1 mile from the start. While you'll find solitude along the trail, expect crowds at the impressive falls. This is a terrific hike for the entire family—it's within the capabilities of most preschoolers, yet varied enough to entertain a twelve-year-old. (One rather tricky river crossing makes this a poor choice for springtime or after a heavy rain.)

From the junction of US 302 and NH-16 in Bartlett, drive north on NH-16. In 11.3 miles, turn left into the parking area for the AMC (Appalachian Mountain Club) Pinkham Notch Camp.

Cross NH-16 and walk southward on the highway for 50 yards to the Lost Pond trailhead. Heading eastward, cross the Ellis River on log footbridges. Do the kids know where this water comes from and where it is going? The river begins as a trickle on the eastern slope of Mount Washington (6288 feet above sea level), joins the Saco River near Glen, New Hampshire, and winds through Maine to the Atlantic Ocean.

Beyond the bridges, turn right (south) onto the white-blazed Lost Pond Trail and Appalachian Trail (AT). Immediately the Square Ledge Trail heads left as you continue straight (south) on the wide Lost Pond Trail. As you follow along the eastern bank of the Ellis River (soon joined by the Cutler River), the cascading water and the highway traffic compete for your attention. Which little hiker does the best tow truck, motorcycle, or train imitation?

The trail crosses a tributary over a footbridge 0.25 mile from the start and continues to wind southward through an evergreen forest. At 0.4 mile, the trail curls left (southeast) away from the river, shortly crossing a third footbridge over a stream that originates on Wildcat Mountain. Rising gently, the trail hops over wet sections on logs and stones.

You'll arrive at the rugged northern shore of Lost Pond 0.5 mile from the start. Follow the shoreline and, in less than 0.1 mile, rocks offer you front-row seats to a postcard-perfect view of Mount Washington. (On the way back, stop here for a picnic lunch far from the crowds that gather at the falls.)

Departing the shore, the blazes lead hikers through a 0.2-mile boulder maze with overhangs and caves that will entice little explorers. At 0.8 mile, the trail plunges down a rock-strewn hill (you'll have a scramble on the way back) and balances on logs to cross a stream and weave through more boulders.

The Lost Pond Trail ends 0.9 mile from the start at a junction with the blue-blazed Wildcat Ridge Trail. Here, the AT leaves you to bear left (east), joining the Wildcat Ridge Trail. You turn right (west) onto the Wildcat Ridge Trail (toward Ellis River and NH-16). In 0.1 mile, the trail arrives at the bank of the wide, shallow river. Though this stone-to-stone crossing is hairy in the spring and after heavy rains, at other times of the year it is not hard to make it across with dry boots.

Follow the western riverbank southward for 75 feet and join the

Pausing to admire Glen Ellis Falls

tourists flocking toward the falls. With stairs and guardrails to assist you, drop to the base of the falls for an impressive view. The water explodes over the cliff and crashes 64 feet to the pool at the base. As placards near the falls explain, within seconds, enough water spills over the escarpment to serve a city of 25,000 for a full day.

Retrace your steps along the peaceful Lost Pond Trail to your car.

49. Imp Face

Type: Dayhike
Difficulty: Challenging for children
Distance: 6.5 miles, loop
Hiking time: 5.5 hours
High point/elevation gain: 3290 feet, 2100 feet
Hikable: June–September
Map: USGS Carter Dome

The trail to Imp Face is a lot like the gangster "Baby Face" Nelson—a cute name belies a tough character. You'll gain more than 2000 feet and cover nearly 6.5 miles as you climb to the Imp Face summit and loop back along an easily followed route. With the only suitable turnaround point at the 2.2-mile mark, you'll want to be sure that you and your family are up to at least 4 hours worth of strenuous hiking. Although you'll encounter a number of brooks and streams, the highlight of the trip is the dizzying panorama from atop Imp Face. Gather together a fit group of view-lovers and go!

From the junction of NH-16 and the Mount Washington Auto Road, drive 1.2 miles north on NH-16. Turn right into a parking turnout large enough for four cars.

From the parking area, head eastward guided by a sign that tells hikers that the "Imp" is 2.2 miles away. The Imp Trail, marked in yellow, rises gently through a stand of mature hemlocks, leveling 0.35 mile from the start. To the left of the path, a shallow ravine cradles Imp Brook. Let the kids run ahead, waiting for you beside the giant trailside boulder 0.5 mile from the start that is covered with a web of tree roots.

At 0.65 mile, the path curls left (northeast), crosses the cascading Imp Brook over stepping stones, and begins a moderate ascent. In another 0.1 mile, the pitch steepens, with stone steps and logs to facilitate the tougher grades. Just under 1 mile from the start, the trail crests a shoulder and hops over another stream but quickly resumes a moderate ascent. This is a good hike for children to lead: The trail is hard-packed and wide with few rocks or roots.

At 1.25 miles, climb briskly, aided by wooden steps. As you near the 1.4-mile mark, weary kids can look ahead for a cluster of birches bordering the path that marks the easing of the grade.

At 1.75 miles, the trail heads steeply up the slope in a southwesterly direction. Urge kids to imitate rabbits: Since rabbits have longer hindlegs than forelegs, they run faster uphill than downhill. Play chase the rabbits: Assign one child to chase the others, the "rabbits," and tell the

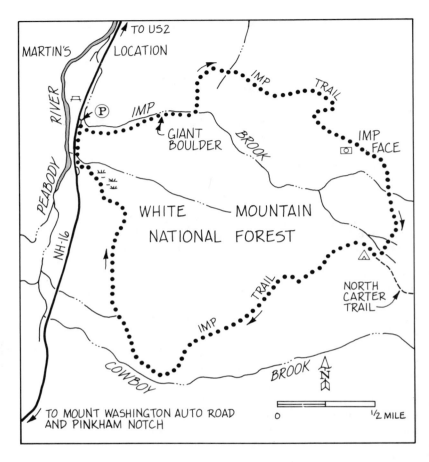

kids how real rabbits escape. They crisscross their tracks and take giant leaps to confuse animals following their scent. They also stamp the ground with their hind feet to warn one another of danger.

As the trail bends southeastward at the 2-mile mark, notice the intrusion of granite, heralding the baldface ahead. On the final approach to the summit, veer eastward and zigzig up the steep slope, arriving at the high, exposed Imp ledges 2.2 miles from the start. Even younger children will be delighted with these panoramas across the Presidentials. The sharp peaks of Adams and Jefferson reach for the clouds beside the always-impressive Mount Washington. Look southward across the Imp Brook valley to the adjoining ridge; you will circle the valley and return along this ridge.

After you have admired the layers of impressive mountains, drop off

Imp Face through a hemlock grove on a short, steep descent. Continue on rolling terrain with sweeping views across the valley. At 2.5 miles, the trail leads over a stream, the first of many within the next mile. Assign a child to keep count.

The yellow blazes lead generally southward, with cropped views of the Presidentials persisting. Cross a second and then a more substantial third stream at 2.8 miles. The trail rolls through more hemlock stands, leading across streams four and five. (What holiday are you reminded of as you sniff the hemlock trees?)

At 3.1 miles (just under 1 mile from the summit), the trail arrives at a junction. The North Carter Trail heads left on blue blazes as you turn right (west), heading toward NH-16, 3.1 miles away. Continue to follow the yellow blazes of the Imp Trail, passing an ideal tent site on the left in 100 yards. The trail leads northward, dropping easily along the bank of the stream you recently crossed, and soon swings westward. At 3.4 miles, balance on a split-log bridge over a wet area and then race with the brook that follows the trail for 0.1 mile.

The now-rocky trail drops first within a dry stream bed heading southwestward and then to an old logging road 4 miles from the start. At 5 miles, you'll hear the whispers of water in the distance as the trail tumbles down a series of brief, steep pitches with stone steps. In another 0.5 mile, cut across the left-hand side of an open area that has been seeded by the Forest Service. Cross a swampy section at 5.8 miles on logs as the descent eases and levels.

A final drop at 6 miles leads to the bank of a stream 0.1 mile later. Exit the woods at 6.2 miles and turn right (north) onto NH-16. You'll return to your car in 0.3 mile. Whew! Exchange pats on the back and find an ice-cream stand!

50. Giant Falls

Type: Dayhike
Difficulty: Moderate for children
Distance: 2.8 miles, round trip
Hiking time: 2 hours
High point/elevation gain: 1550 feet, 800 feet
Hikable: May–September
Map: USGS Shelburne (NH-Maine)

Most visitors to the White Mountains have only one complaint: the other visitors. Where can a hiker escape the crowds in such a popular area? The Peabody Brook Trail. Although it begins as a logging road in a residential area, it soon narrows to follow an overgrown path that leads along the bank of Peabody Brook to Giant Falls. You and the kids will feel like pioneers as you stomp through the brush in these remote woods. The anticipation of a dramatic waterfall at the end of the route is enough to keep most kids (and adults) motivated. (But remember—Giant Falls is our little secret!)

From the junction of US 2 and NH-16 in Gorham, drive east on US 2. In 3.3 miles, turn left (north) onto North Road. Cross the Androscoggin River and watch for the trailhead on the left, 1.25 miles from US 2 (just before a dense stand of white birches in the yard of a stone house). Park on the right-hand shoulder of the road. (Overnight parking is not permitted at the base of this trail.)

The blue-blazed Peabody Brook Trail heads northward on an old logging road. Squeeze between two yards, watching for the "TRAIL" sign on a post. (Although it is potentially passable, a gate prevents motor vehicles from using the road.) Bear right (north) at an intersection with the Sinclair Trail in 0.1 mile. Quickly, the trail curves right, crosses the wide, shallow Peabody Brook in about seven steps, and turns left to follow the eastern bank on a gradual ascent.

As the brook cuts through a deep ravine at the 0.2-mile mark, the trail rises moderately beside it, soon leveling. The trail and the brook bend briefly northeastward at 0.3 mile; 0.1 mile later, a logging road departs left and continues on the other side of the brook. You continue straight, still following the Peabody Brook Trail on a gentle slope. One child can be an Indian, hunting for his dinner, while the others pretend to be bears, rabbits, or deer trying to escape him.

At 0.45 mile, the trail has wandered northeastward away from the brook. In another 0.15 mile, the logging road turns right as you continue straight, rising gradually along the Peabody Brook Trail (now a foot-

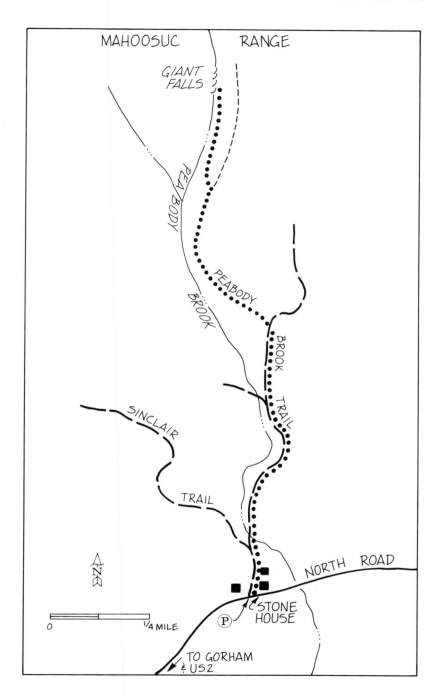

MAHOOSUC   RANGE

GIANT
FALLS

PEABODY

PEABODY

BROOK

BROOK

TRAIL

SINCLAIR

TRAIL

NORTH   ROAD

N

0   ¼ MILE

P   STONE
HOUSE

TO GORHAM
& US 2

path). Climb stiffly from 0.7 to 0.9 mile with high ledges on the right. At 1 mile, the trail splits: the Peabody Brook Trail goes straight (northeast) as you follow the sign that points left (northwest) to Giant Falls.

Drop gently along this lightly traveled side trail. Who will be the first to hear the cascading water? As the trail begins to taper off, stay as close to the right (west) bank as you can. It will be easy for children to pretend that they are explorers—it seems as if no one has been here before.

About 1.2 miles from the start, you'll come upon a wading pool that will lure the kids into its shallow waters. In another 0.1 mile, you'll see the water of Giant Falls spilling 150 feet down the rock tiers. The trail ends here, though some daring hikers have blazed a trail up the steep left-hand side of the falls. Enjoy a solitary picnic on the rocks near the base and return the way you came.

51. North Sugarloaf

Type:	Dayhike
Difficulty:	Moderate for children
Distance:	2.6 miles, round trip
Hiking time:	2 hours
High point/elevation gain:	2310 feet, 700 feet
Hikable:	May–October
Map:	USGS Whitefield

You've probably changed since the last time you hiked to North Sugarloaf. Larger family? Newer car? A little more wisdom to go along with the gray hairs? Well, North Sugarloaf has undergone a few changes too! Volunteers have made major improvements along the trail and on the summit. Rustic steps facilitate the ascent and water bars fight the effects of erosion. Mountaintop trees have been cut to improve the views. The "new and improved" North Sugarloaf is worth another visit!

From the junction of US 3 and US 302 in Twin Mountain, drive 2.1 miles east on US 302. Turn right at a sign for Zealand Pond, White Mountain National Forest Recreation Area. Follow Zealand Road for 1 mile and park on the right, just before the bridge over Zealand Brook.

Follow Zealand Road over Zealand Brook to the Tressle and Sugarloaf trailheads. Turn right (northwest) into the woods following yellow blazes. Wind along the brook for 0.15 mile to a fork. The Tressle Trail continues to hug the riverbank as you turn left (northwest) on the Sugarloaf Trail, departing the river on level terrain. In less than 0.1 mile, cross a grassy road and a skimobile trail.

As the trail begins to climb 0.25 mile into the hike, it dodges left to avoid a split boulder and then sidesteps a second boulder. (You can pause to let the kids try a little rock climbing.) Now climbing moderately, march past a row of tall white birches that guard the trail. This stiff ascent continues for 0.25 mile, relaxes briefly, then resumes on a slope fitted with log and rock steps. (Can the kids keep a count of the steps?)

Shortly, the trail crests and splits, heading for North and South Sugarloaf. Turn right (north) toward North Sugarloaf and hike on level ground along the top of a ridge. Soon the trail swings left and drops briefly, wrapping around the northern side of the mountain in search of a gentler approach to the summit.

As the trail swerves southeastward, a final surge will bring you to the top, 0.3 mile beyond the North/South Sugarloaf junction. The summit offers patches of trees to escape the wind and large expanses of open baldface to take in views of all the Presidentials, particularly Mount Washington, to the east. Follow the yellow blazes that lead across this expansive summit to take in panoramic views. Did the kids notice the intricate patterns created by logging operations on the adjoining ridge of Mount Oscar? Find a cozy nook for a picnic and then hike back to your car the way you came.

Most toddlers are quite content to do their hiking in a backpack.

MAINE

52. Vaughan Woods Memorial

Type: Dayhike
Difficulty: Easy for children
Distance: 2.5 miles, loop
Hiking time: 1.5 hours
High point/elevation gain: 160 feet, 200 feet
Hikable: March–November
Map: USGS Dover East
(New Hampshire)

Take this easy jaunt along the east bank of the Salmon Falls River almost anytime—even when the gate is closed during the colder months, you can park along Old Field's Street and hike 0.25 mile to the trailhead. The generally level path follows the riverbank for just over 1 mile, then loops back to the parking area through airy woodlands. At least one major trail is suitable for strollers.

From the junction of ME-236 and ME-4 in South Berwick, travel east on ME-236 for 1 mile. Turn right onto Brattle Street, following a sign to Vaughan Woods. At 0.8 mile, at a junction with Old South Road, continue straight, now on Old Field's Street. In 0.2 mile, turn right into Vaughan Woods Memorial. Drive 0.25 mile down the driveway to the parking area.

The trail, originating at the northern side of the parking and picnic area, heads westward along the wire fence on the property's border and soon drops to the mouth of a stream flowing into the Salmon Falls River. Cross the footbridge on the left and walk along the bank of the river, heading southward on the upper path (suitable for wheelchairs and strollers) or the more rugged River Run. Mobile kids will prefer River Run, which wanders through a hemlock and spruce forest along the sloping riverbank. For the next mile, ignore the numerous white-blazed side trails (with cheerful names like Shady Stroll, Porcupine Path and Windy Walk) that split left (east) away from the river.

At 0.2 mile, adults can relax on a bench overlooking the river at Oak Point while kids explore the water's edge. Ask the youngest hikers how squirrels help to propagate oak forests. (They bury acorns in the fall to retrieve in the winter, but sometimes their memory or sense of smell fails them and they miss some of their caches. With the warm spring weather, some of the forgotten acorns begin to grow into oak trees!) Beyond a second bench at a river overlook is a huge white birch surrounded by hemlocks. Can the kids guess what the Indians made from birch trees? (Give them a hint: The tree is also called "canoe birch.")

The trail crosses a second footbridge 0.55 mile from the start, followed quickly by a half dozen more bridges over dry gullies. After crossing the fourth dry gully (just before the white-blazed "Old Gate Trail" side trail branches left), the kids can imitate Winnie the Pooh in search of honey. They will find a bee tree that Pooh Bear would sigh for by looking for the large white pine on the left side of the trail with a hole 3 inches in diameter and about 15 feet from the ground. Perhaps they'll spot the bees entering or exiting their hive through this opening.

Salmon Falls River at Vaughan Woods Memorial

More footbridges will bring you to the head of Cow's Cove at 1 mile, so named because the first cows to arrive in this part of Maine landed here in 1634. Just past the cove, the trail splits; take the right path over the ninth footbridge, arriving at a peninsula. Here, at 1.2 miles, the River Run Trail ends and Bridle Path heads left (east) passing through stands of spruce and hemlock. The trail gradually curls north and passes the site of the 1656 Warren homestead, reduced to a cellar hole and some crumbling gravestones. Once again, disregard the white-blazed side trails that depart left from Bridle Path (shortcuts to River Run). After passing the intersection with Shady Stroll, turn right onto a smooth gravel path to cross the tenth bridge. Continue on this path to the picnic and parking area.

53. Mount Agamenticus

Type: Dayhike
Difficulty: Easy for children
Distance: 1 mile, loop
Hiking time: 1 hour
High point/elevation gain: 691 feet, 350 feet
Hikable: April–October
Map: USGS York Harbor

At nearly 700 feet above sea level, Mount Agamenticus looms over the seacoast of southern York County. For the younger ones who can't handle a lengthy climb up a mountainside, this route offers a 0.5-mile ascent to a broad, grassy summit with impressive views. The nonhikers in the family can drive to the summit via the auto road and enjoy the same panoramas.

 Take Exit 1 off I-95 in York, heading west on Chases Pond Road. Soon the road swings sharply right to head north. In 3.8 miles, Chases Pond Road merges with Mountain Road. Bear left to travel west on Mountain Road for 2.6 miles to the gravel parking area on the right-hand side of the road (just before a right-hand turn onto the summit road).

From the parking lot, enter the logged woods at a tree farm sign, heading north on a woods road that parallels the auto road. Almost immediately, the road splits. Bear left and, in less than 0.1 mile, turn right

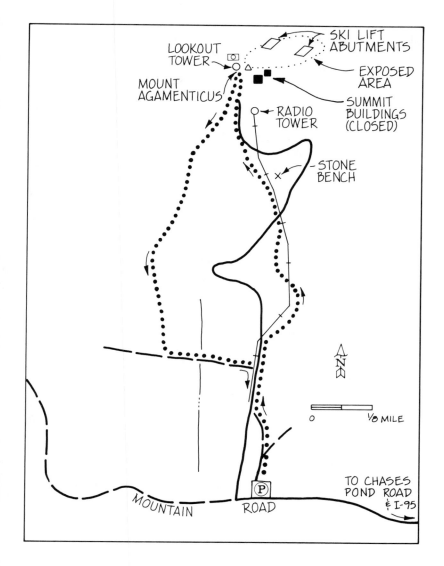

onto the paved auto road. Follow the road for 0.1 mile, turning right (back into the woods) as utility lines cross the road from left to right. On a trail pinched by pines, continue directly below the power lines. Can the kids imitate or recognize some of the bird calls they are hearing? Did you know that birds have "accents" just like people do? Even though a bird's ability to sing is instinctive (as opposed to learned), a bird living in one part of the world sounds different from the same kind of bird living in another part, just like a person from Georgia might speak differently than a person from Boston.

Soon, the trail widens as it climbs briskly northward over granite. (Warn the kids that the granite underfoot is slippery after a rainstorm.) At 0.35 mile, cross the auto road carefully, watching for cars, and continue moderately uphill on a rocky, wide trail under the power lines. In the mixed woods dotted with small white pines, hemlocks, and oaks, ask young hikers to feel the bark on different trees and guess what uses people have for bark. Any child who guesses that some spices (like cinnamon), certain medicines, and commercial cork come from bark wins a piggyback ride for thirty paces. To the right of the trail is a small stone bench: who will spot it first? Bear left away from the power lines and soon join the auto road within sight of the transmission tower; the fire lookout tower (a radar observation post during World War II) looms not far beyond.

The broad, grassy summit is a terrific place for kids to run and to explore the remains of the defunct ski operation—on the northeast side of the mountaintop are abutments that once supported the ski lift mechanism. A ski lodge and other summit buildings are closed to the public. Climb the fire tower's sixty-eight steps for expansive views to the east/northeast over the coastline, Casco Bay, and the Atlantic Ocean; look north/northwest to see Ossipee Hill (Hike 54). Mountains interrupt the northern and western horizons; on a clear day, you'll spot Mount Washington and other major peaks in the White Mountains.

To return to your car, head south from the fire tower along the edge of the woods. The trail plunges into the forest near a tree trunk that bends at a 90-degree angle. After dropping through stands of hemlocks, the path crosses a south-sloping meadow. One-quarter mile from the summit, the trail intersects a tote road; turn left (east) onto the road and quickly cross a loitering brook. You'll cross under power lines shortly before reaching the summit road. Turn right and in 100 yards reenter the woods on the left, heading downhill on the familiar woods road near the base of the mountain. In 0.1 mile, you'll see your car.

54. Ossipee Hill

Type: Dayhike
Difficulty: Easy for children
Distance: 3 miles, round trip
Hiking time: 2 hours
High point/elevation gain: 1302 feet, 700 feet
Hikable: April–October
Map: USGS Waterboro

Ossipee Hill has one of the few accessible summits that offers spectacular views of both the White Mountains and the Atlantic Ocean. This is a perfect first hike for little ones who will easily manage the trip along gently climbing woods roads. Older kids can put their imaginations to work as they explore the cellar holes, snaking stone walls, and other signs of the forest's former inhabitants. Try to visit when the fire tower is open (usually in summer and early fall).

From the junction of ME-4, ME-202, and ME-5 in East Waterboro, travel north on ME-5 for 1.5 miles to Waterboro Center. Turn left (southwest) onto Ossipee Hill Road, pass the fire station on the right, and immediately turn right (west) onto unmarked McLucas Road. In 0.1 mile, the road turns to gravel. At 1 mile (with an abandoned house on the right and a field on the left), park off the road. (If you wish to shorten the hike, you can drive another 0.7 mile over a rougher section of road to an intersection. Park on the right.)

If you've parked at the 1-mile mark, walk along the increasingly rugged road on a gradual ascent, heading westward. You may want to pause to examine the headstones in the old cemetery on the right. Have the kids ever done gravestone rubbings? Use large sheets of paper to cover the raised letters and then rub the paper with charcoal or any thick writing implement to make your own copy of the inscription.

The road levels at 0.4 mile and divides 0.3 mile later; the main gravel road turns left (southwest) as the less-traveled McLucas Road continues straight. Turn left to climb moderately through a hardwood forest for 0.15 mile before the pitch lessens and the road swings southward. Here, an old stone wall borders the right-hand side of the road. Kids may become restless along this initial stretch through the woods. Play forest bingo: See who will be the first to spot a bird's nest, a spider's web, animal tracks, or a mushroom. Or play the alphabet game: begin with "A" and take turns naming things you see along the trail that begin with the

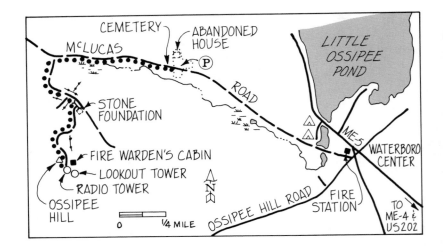

letters of the alphabet. Not only do such games make the time pass more pleasantly, they also make children more aware of their surroundings.

At 0.9 mile, pass a narrow dirt road bordered by stone walls that splits right. The weary stone walls that crisscross the area mark the boundaries of long-ago country neighbors. Can the kids see any cellar holes on either side of the road? It's fun to poke around for old bottles and other artifacts near cellar holes—just warn the kids that the wells near former homesteads may be uncovered and still filled with water.

At an intersection 1 mile from the start, turn right (southwest) onto another woods road, sidestepping a yellow metal gate. (A stone foundation sits to the left of the gate.) Ascending easily, the road snakes through the woods. At the 1.25-mile mark, you'll have your first glimpse of distant mountains to the left (northeast). As the trail levels and crosses a hunk of exposed granite, watch for your first ocean view. You'll pass the fire warden's cabin on the left and climb a final hill to the exposed granite summit and the fire lookout tower.

The wooden tower crowned with antennas is open during fire season and will support three visitors at a time. Even if the tower is closed when you arrive, climb the steps as high as you can for super 360-degree views to the Atlantic easterly and the White Mountains to the northwest. To the west of the summit, an area of outcroppings offers kids a safe place to explore before the group begins its return trip to the car, retracing the earlier route.

55. Bates Morse Mountain Coastal Research Area

Type: Dayhike
Difficulty: Moderate for children
Distance: 6 miles, round trip
Hiking time: 4.5 hours
High point/elevation gain: 210 feet, 400 feet
Hikable: Year-round
Map: USGS Small Point

You'll want to explore the unspoiled coastline, marshlands, and hills of this 600-acre preserve more than once because each time you come it will look different. Water and wind tirelessly sculpt the dunes and the beach sands; currents and waves erode once prominent islands. Try to visit just after a winter storm—that's one of the best times to hunt for treasures that have been tossed from the sea. Many seaside hikes involve lengthy and arduous stretches on loose sand, which can be especially frustrating for children. Here, you'll travel to the beach along a private paved and gravel road that allows Bates College students access for environmental studies and leads to the private homes of the St. John family (who entrusted the area to the Nature Conservancy and Bates College in 1977). Bird-watchers as well as beachcombers flock here; well over 100 different species of birds have been spotted near the marsh. You're sure to see marsh hawks, kingfishers, and herring gulls. In the spring and fall, you won't be able to turn the pages of your guidebook fast enough—this is a popular resting spot for migrating birds.

From the junction of US 1 and ME-209 in Bath (at a sign for "ME-209 to Phillipsburg"), take ME-209 south for 12 miles. As ME-209 heads left to Popham Beach, continue straight (now on ME-216) for just under 1 mile. Turn left onto a narrow paved road that leads to a small parking area. (If the lot is full, you can park along ME-216.)

Head east on the driveway up a short, shallow grade. In 0.1 mile, you'll pass a private driveway on the left. Soon, head through a metal gate to begin dropping easily toward the lush marsh that surrounds the Sprague River. The marsh extends fingerlike from Sewall Beach along the western side of Morse Mountain. Though it may look as if marsh vegetation is uniform and unvaried, many different plants thrive side by side in salt marshes like this one: reed grass, saltmarsh bulrush, salt-meadow cordgrass, spike grass, and seaside goldenrod. Travel across the narrow "second knuckle" of the marsh, crossing a wooden bridge over the river on the far side. Notice that the eastern bank of the marsh is flanked with evergreens while the western bank, particularly on the southern end, nourishes deciduous trees. Climb moderately among fir and spruce trees to level at 0.4 mile with sandstone ledges approaching the trail on the right.

After passing a boat storage building, the trail climbs gradually and at 0.6 mile, at a fork, signs point left to the beach. For now, go right to loop counterclockwise around the summit of Morse Mountain with emerging views of the Sprague River and vast marshland, Sewall Beach, and the Atlantic Ocean. Look northeastward to see Campbell Island and

Winter beachcombers with their trophy, on Sewall Beach

Popham Beach. The buildings you pass as you circle the tiny summit were used in World War II as observation posts. At the southeastern end of the loop, a footpath leads through a pitch pine forest to a rocky overlook of Fox Island and Popham Beach, Seguin Island and its lighthouse, and the Morse River estuary.

Return to the intersection and turn right, following signs to the beach on a gradual descent. Pass a private home on the left at the 1.6-mile mark. At 1.8 miles, the marsh encroaches on the trail's western side, causing soggy walking. The road forks 0.2 mile later on Morse Hill; continue straight (right fork), guided by beach signs. The gravel road dissolves into sand as you begin to hear the sounds of waves crashing on the

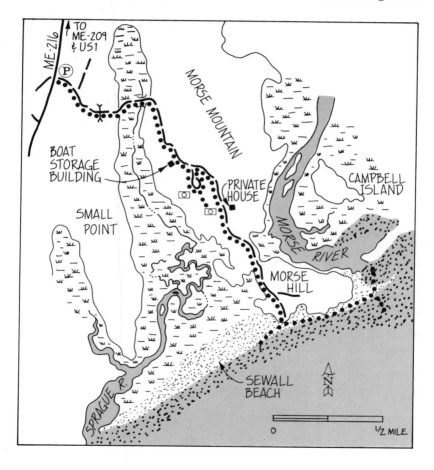

sandy shore. Soon the trail opens onto expansive Sewall Beach. What stories can the beach tell children who stop to examine marks in the fine sand? Has a man walked his dog here recently? Has a child run along the beach dragging a stick? Have shorebirds marched along the sand watching for potential predators? These are fleeting stories; soon the waves and the wind will erase every trace.

Explain to children why it is important to stay away from the nearby nesting areas of the least terns and piping plovers. The least tern, a white bird with black wingtips, lays its eggs on the sand rather than in a nest, leaving them vulnerable to destructive or ignorant trespassers. Numbering just over 100, the least tern is one of Maine's rarest birds and is an endangered species. Children must also avoid stepping on the fragile dunes. As the posted sign explains, the zone between high and low tides—the preferred place for kids to explore—is very resilient, but the other areas of the beach are easily harmed by human activity.

To the right, the sandy beach stretches for over 1 mile, ending where the Sprague River joins the ocean. Approaching the mouth of the river at low tide, you may be able to see the exposed remains of the *Hanover,* a ship wrecked during a severe storm in November 1849. Although the ship's dog survived, the twenty-four men on board did not and are believed to be buried in the marsh.

We recommend you turn left (northeast) to explore the 0.25 mile of tidal beach zone. The large rocks that are unseen or appear as islands when the tide is in are exposed and explorable at low tide. Kids will crouch endlessly over the tide pools teeming with sea creatures that were stranded by the receding tidal waters. Because these animals cannot bury themselves in sand, they are easier for children to identify and to examine. They may find barnacles or sea urchins, mussels or starfish. If you pick up and gently turn a starfish over, you'll see the hundreds of tiny suction cups that it uses to hold food or to move. What do you think that small circle is at the center of the underside? (Its mouth!) It's just as likely that they will find signs of human activity here: broken lobster buoys, bits of rope, pieces of old lobster traps.

Continue walking northeastward to the mouth of the Morse River, which is, like the Sprague River, surrounded by a windswept marsh. Across this tidal marsh is Popham Beach State Park. Looking out over the ocean, the mosaic of rock islands stretches to the Seguin Lighthouse. Explore until *you're* exhausted (because the possibilities never will be) and return to your car as you came.

Casco Bay from along the trail at Wolf Neck Woods State Park

56. Wolf Neck Woods

Type: Dayhike
Difficulty: Easy for children
Distance: 2 miles, loop
Hiking time: 1.5 hours
High point/elevation gain: 60 feet, 100 feet
Hikable: Year-round
Map: USGS Freeport

At Wolf Neck Woods, no waterfalls explode over cliffs, no panoramic views stretch over mountaintops to far horizons. This hike is not intended to bombard your senses; the rewards here are far more subtle. Watch spiders silently spinning webs, smell the salt on the ocean breeze, study the sea gulls swooping over Casco Bay and the pattern made by a cluster of trailside ferns. Kids will appreciate the numerous split-log bridges, the two encounters with water, and the abundance of knee-high

natural treasures along the level trail. Adults will emerge from this preserve relaxed and refreshed.

From I-95 in Freeport, take Exit 19, "Desert Road, Freeport." Travel
1.3 miles north on US 1 to L. L. Bean in Freeport. Here, turn right onto
Bow Street. In 2.4 miles, turn right onto Wolf Neck Road, following a
sign for Wolf Neck Woods State Park. Drive 2 miles to a driveway on the
left that leads to the parking area for Wolf Neck Woods State Park. In
season, you'll pay a day-use fee at the gate house. Off season, park off
Wolf Neck Road and walk the 0.25 mile to the trailhead.

From the southwestern side of the parking area, head into the woods
and almost immediately bear right (west) onto the Harraseeket Trail.
This level path wanders through thick woodlands and tracks across several wet areas with adequate stepping stones. Kids will have to pick up
their feet because rocks poke through the pine needle carpet and roots

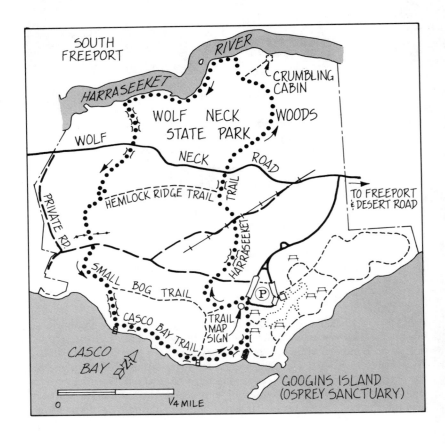

spread like a witch's fingers across the trail. At a junction with a narrow, grassy access road, continue straight (north) on the Harraseeket Trail. Children can run ahead to the lengthy, split-log bridge at 0.2 mile that spans soggy terrain. Continue straight (northwest), following arrows as a cleared swath for power lines cuts across the trail.

The trail sidesteps a tree whose roots cling desperately to a barren boulder. Who will be the first to spot a trailside spider's web? Do the kids know why spiders don't get caught in their own webs? In addition to the sticky thread it produces, a spider incorporates strands of "nonsticky" thread in its web so that it is able to walk across without getting stuck.

As the Hemlock Ridge Trail joins from the left, continue straight. After crossing another damp section on logs, walk across Wolf Neck Road and reenter the woods. Cross one more log bridge before dropping gently to the bank of the Harraseeket River, 0.7 mile from the start. As a side trail leads right to a crumbling cabin, the main trail descends to a ledge overlook of the river, 20 feet below. The trail turns left (east) to follow the riverbank, passing a chunk of ledge at 0.75 mile that broke away from the riverbank to form a steep, stark island. The trail winds above the river under a canopy of hemlocks and pines. As the slope to the water's edge lessens, indistinct side trails lead to the occasionally sandy shore while the main trail rolls in and out of wet gullies on split-log bridges. The trail angles east away from the river to wander over more streams. Kids will have fun navigating these crossings.

The trail cuts across Wolf Neck Road again, crosses another stream, switches back over a ledge outcropping on the left, and cuts back right. (This is a tricky section and the only spot on this hike where you're likely to get a little confused.) At 1.2 miles, you'll arrive at a trail junction with the Hemlock Ridge Trail, marking the end of the Harraseeket Trail. As the Hemlock Ridge Trail goes left (northeast), you bear right onto the Small Bog Trail to Casco Bay Trail, heading southeast through varied woods. The path cuts through a stone wall to cross another woods road, still meandering generally southward. At the 1.4-mile mark, continue straight on the Casco Bay Trail as the Small Bog Trail splits left (east).

As the kids run across a lengthy stretch of split logs, they'll hear the sounds of breaking waves and feel the sea breezes sweeping inland. In the daytime, the cool air over the ocean rushes inland as the sea breeze. At night, when the ocean is warmer than the mainland, the cooler air gusts out to sea. The trail reaches the edge of Casco Bay and heads left (east) to follow a manicured trail along the rocky shoreline for 0.3 mile, crossing a number of streams on sturdy footbridges. The adults can relax on the trailside benches while the kids scamper down intermittent sets of wooden steps that provide better views of the bay. The final set of stairs along this route leads to a pebbly beach. Just offshore on Googins Island the kids may spot an osprey nest in the old, broken pine. An osprey family often uses the same nest year after year for over a century, reinforcing it each fall. Look for other shorebirds here, too: sandpipers, terns, gulls, cormorants, loons.

From the pebbly beach, return to the trail and head north at a four-way intersection. Cross a substantial footbridge over a tiny gorge and shortly you'll reach the picnic area with tables and charcoal grills. One-tenth of a mile from the bay, you arrive at the parking area close to the trail map sign and the start of the Harraseeket Trail.

Note: The park is open daily from 9:00 a.m. to sunset. Fires are permitted only in grill areas. No pets are allowed.

57. Burnt Meadow Mountain

Type: Dayhike
Difficulty: Moderate for children
Distance: 2.6 miles, round trip
Hiking time: 2.5 hours
High point/elevation gain: 1575 feet, 1200 feet
Hikable: May–October
Map: USGS Brownfield

Burnt Meadow Mountain, close to the New Hampshire border, comprises three similar summits. The well-marked (though somewhat overgrown) route described here scales the eastern spur of North Peak and offers grand views beginning just 0.15 mile from the start. The broad, grassy summit gives kids room to run and adults room to spread out a feast with the White Mountains as a backdrop. The climb is somewhat steep—count on carrying preschoolers part of the way.

 From the junction of US 302, ME-113, and ME-5 in Fryeburg, take ME-5 and ME-113 heading south. In 6.9 miles, at the junction with ME-160 in East Brownfield, turn right onto ME-160 South. In exactly 3 miles, as the road bends right, park on the right-hand shoulder.

Alternatively, from the junction of ME-25 and ME-160 in Kezar Falls, travel northward on ME-160 for 8.7 miles to the parking area on the left.

The blue-blazed trail heads northwest into the woods, weaving upward on a moderate grade. At 0.15 mile, on exposed ledge, you'll enjoy your first long-range views to the southeast. Through the trees to the right (north), you'll catch a glimpse of Pleasant Mountain (Hike 58). The pitch levels through airy woodlands to an open ridge 0.35 mile from the

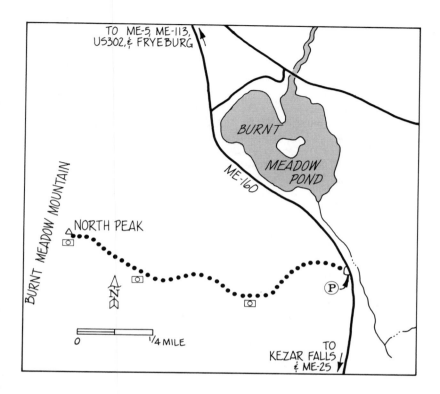

start where far-reaching panoramas persist. Fire raced across this mountain in 1947; can the kids spot any signs of the devastating blaze? (Hug a tree; do your arms reach all the way around? This is a forest of young, slender trees.)

After nearly 0.5 mile of hiking, the trail crests a shoulder and drops into a boulder-strewn sag. Assign the youngest child to find the "granddaddy" boulder off the trail to the left and assign the oldest one to point out the summit, looming ahead through the trees. After the col bottoms out in dense woods at 0.55 mile, the trail begins to wind uphill once more. Climbing westward, the path crosses more exposed granite with cairns as well as blazes marking the route. Quite a few bear dens have been found on the three mountains. Ask the children: "If you were bears, where would you sleep?"

The grade steepens at 0.7 mile and levels on a second shoulder where Burnt Meadow Pond shimmers far below. The respite is brief, however, as the trail rises moderately to curl in and out of thin woods with ever-improving views from open baldface. Can the kids see the other peaks of

Burnt Meadow Mountain to the southwest? Wildflowers fringe the trail on either side. Remember to encourage sniffing of these wildflowers, not picking.

At 1.15 miles, scramble over rock ledges and soon tackle a steep slide with precipitous cliffs approaching the trail from the left. Loose rocks make for slippery footing, so kids will need a hand. At 1.3 miles, you'll reach the broad, barren summit of North Peak. Here, grass softens the rocky terrain in contrast to the rugged trail you just climbed. The kids can run about, scouting for blueberries and mountain cranberries. Look northeast toward the Presidentials; south into a lush valley. To the northeast, Burnt Meadow Pond is a bluish puddle, reminding you of the 1200 feet you have just climbed.

After devouring a picnic lunch, head down the mountain the way you came, overlooking the two dominant shoulders you traversed on the way up.

58. Pleasant Mountain

Type: Dayhike or overnight
Difficulty: Moderate for children
Distance: 4 miles, round trip
Hiking time: 3 hours
High point/elevation gain: 2006 feet, 1500 feet
Hikable: April–October
Map: USGS Pleasant Mountain

Along the Pleasant Mountain ridge, reaching north to West Bridgton and south to Denmark, more than six summits overlook the relatively flat countryside. Most have commanding views of New Hampshire's White Mountains due to the open areas created by a forest fire some 130 years ago. Because of the not-too-tough ascent and the trailside shelters for camping, the Firewarden's Trail ranks as the most popular route to Pleasant Mountain's main summit.

From the junction of US 302 and ME-5 in Fryeburg, take US 302 East. In 6.3 miles, turn right onto Warren Road (look for the sign on a big white pine) just before Cabin-in-the-Pines Motel. In 1.1 miles, turn left onto a jeep road and park near the gate, well off the road.

Firewarden's Trail (also known as the Old Carriage Road) begins as a truck road (that may at times be open to cars). Heading east, the trail climbs gently to a fork at 0.15 mile. Bear left and soon cross a bridge over a dawdling brook where the kids can play "Pooh Sticks," so-named for one of Winnie the Pooh's favorite outdoor pastimes. Drop sticks into the water from one side of the bridge and then watch to see whose stick reappears first on the other side.

Climb easily along the brook's north bank. The pitch steepens to climb moderately through mixed woods for 0.2 mile before easing again at the 0.5-mile mark. Recross the brook shortly before you reach a clearing 1.2 miles from the start. One of our young hiking companions asked, "Does a brook have a beginning?" Yes, we told her, brooks and rivers begin as rainwater falling on the mountains and trickling downhill, seeking the easiest route for its descent. As a number of these tiny streams choose the same route, they join, forming a river.

The kids can watch for the fire warden's cabin perched on a bluff to the left; across the trail are a shelter and lean-to for overnight camping. If you're staying overnight, pause here to talk about where you'll set up camp and what you'll make for supper upon your return from the summit.

View from Pleasant summit toward the White Mountains

As the trail leaves the campsite from the right (south) side of the fire warden's cabin, it narrows to become a rugged woods road and climbs more steeply, heading southeast and then south. Keep to the left as the path splits several times (although these side roads rejoin farther uphill). Six-tenths of a mile beyond the campsite, the Bald Peak Trail intersects the Firewarden's Trail and departs left (northeast). Staying to the right, ascend gently for another 0.2 mile to arrive at the exposed main summit, referred to as House Peak in the late 1800s when a grand hotel crowned the mountaintop.

From here, the panoramic view takes in Mount Washington's southeastern face, Kearsarge North (Hike 45), Sabattus Mountain (Hike 59), and Burnt Meadow Mountain (Hike 57). The lookout tower is not open to hikers, but it would be hard to improve on the ground-level views. When you have finished admiring the truly breathtaking vistas, return to the campsite and unroll your sleeping bags or return to your car by the same route you used on the ascent.

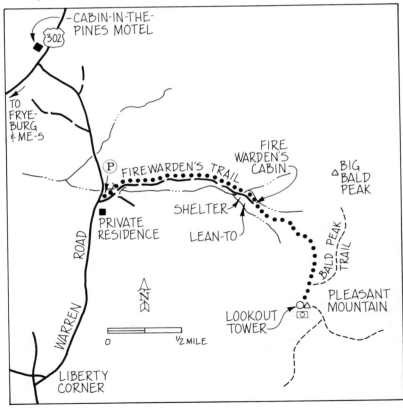

59. Sabattus Mountain

Type: Dayhike
Difficulty: Easy for children
Distance: 2 miles, loop
Hiking time: 1.5 hours
High point/elevation gain: 1253 feet, 500 feet
Hikable: May–October
Map: USGS North Waterford

Sabattus Mountain, less than a one-hour drive from the White Mountain National Forest, is the baby of the Oxford Hills family. Amazingly, this hike up a gentle slope leads to dramatic views from the vertical cliff on the mountain's southwestern face. Bring a wildflower guidebook to enhance a midday hike or a flashlight for a walk at sunset.

From the junction of ME-5 and ME-93 in Lovell, travel north on ME-5 for 4.5 miles, passing Center Lovell General Store at 3.8 miles. Turn right onto Sabattus Road (also called Sabattus Mountain Road) and drive 1.4 miles to a fork. Bear right, still on Sabattus Road (now gravel). At 1.7 miles (0.3 mile beyond the fork), park off the road near the "TRAIL" sign on the left.

Cross the road and begin an easy climb along a camouflaged stone wall through logged woods. Logging is big business in Maine: Eighty-seven percent of the state is forested. How many things can the kids name that come from trees? Follow the unblazed but well-worn trail southwest and cross a stream at 0.15 mile. Can the kids see any evidence of woodpeckers trying to root out insects living in the trunks of pine trees?

The pitch steepens after 0.25 mile of hiking, leading through a mixed hardwood forest. Three-tenths of a mile from the start, head straight across a grassy logging road. The grade gradually steepens to crest the north side of the mountain at 0.6 mile. If you are hiking in early summer, assign each child one wildflower to find along the trail: Starflower, asters, pipsissewa, wintergreen, Canada mayflower, Indian cucumber root, and trailing arbutus are all prevalent.

The trail sidesteps the remains of a fire tower on the left at 0.7 mile and quickly reaches the open summit ledges. The precipitous cliffs extend for 0.25 mile, providing tremendous views of Burnt Meadow Mountain (Hike 57) and Pleasant Mountain (Hike 58) to the south; from the ledges above the cliffs, you'll be able to see Doublehead (Hike 46), Kearsarge North (Hike 45), and the Presidential Range to the west. The shape

Hug a tree!

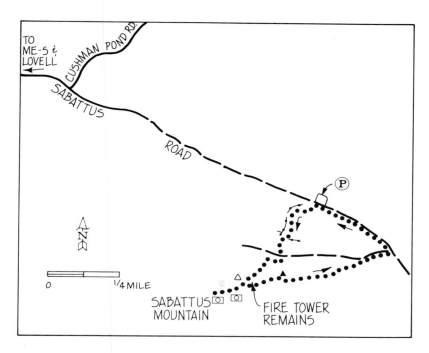

of Sabattus Mountain—mildly sloping on the northern side with a steep grade on the southern side—is called "stoss and lee," and is very common among mountains carved by continental glaciers.

After devouring a picnic lunch with this breathtaking panorama as a backdrop, follow the cliffs eastward and pick up a faint side trail. Shortly, this trail drifts northeast, away from the ridge and into the woods. The kids can watch for the peaked erratic boulder about 0.15 mile from the summit ridge. If they find egg-shaped pellets at the boulder's base or a quill or two, it probably means that a porcupine has recently called this home. The trail drops easily to cross a logging road 0.3 mile from the top; 0.1 mile later, you'll reach Sabattus Road. Turn left and in 0.5 mile you'll reach your car.

60. Bickford Brook Slides/ Blueberry Mountain

Type: Dayhike
Difficulty: Moderate for children
Distance: 4.2 miles, round trip
Hiking time: 3.5 hours
High point/elevation gain: 1781 feet, 1400 feet
Hikable: May–September
Maps: USGS Wild River (New Hampshire) and Speckled Mountain (Maine)

You'll have no trouble keeping kids motivated along this hiking route. Three major "kid" features—two water slides and a mountain summit—will keep them racing along the trail to find out what's next. At the Upper and Lower Bickford Slides, water streams down smooth rocks, collecting in pools that kids will find irresistible in warm weather. At the Blueberry Mountain summit, kids can munch on berries while the adults gaze at the view and try to name the distant peaks. A list of recommended "accessories" for the trip includes bathing suits and/or extra pairs of shoes for wading, long pants for protection through scratchy brush, containers for picking blueberries in season, bug repellant, and a camera to capture the picturesque water slides.

From the junction of US 2 and ME-113 in Gilead, head south on ME-113. In 10.1 miles, turn left into a parking area for Brickett Place (operated by the Lexington, Massachusetts, Boy Scouts), guided by a hiking trail sign.

Look for the Bickford Brook Trail sign on the eastern side of the grassy Brickett Place parking area. The trail ascends moderately through mixed woods, joining a stone wall at 0.1 mile and a White Mountain National Forest access road at 0.3 mile. Here, turn right (southeast) onto the road, climbing gently. Turn right at 0.6 mile onto the yellow-blazed Blueberry Ridge Trail as it diverges from the woods road, dropping gently southward to the bank of the cascading Bickford Brook. The kids will have fun trying to determine if a leaf boat can beat a twig boat to the next bend. Turn right and follow the unmarked (though distinct) trail for 0.1 mile into the shallow ravine carved by Bickford Brook. Drop carefully down the steep embankment for a view of the brook's sliding falls, Lower Bickford Slide. The kids may want to wade or take a quick dip in one of the icy pools.

Retrace your steps 0.1 mile to the trail junction (keep your wading shoes on for now) and cross the brook on stepping stones to begin the ascent of Blueberry Mountain on the Blueberry Ridge Trail. (Now you can put your hiking boots back on!) Climb moderately through mixed hardwoods on stone steps. Are the kids hungry enough to stop for a sandwich or a piece of fruit? Talk about what forest creatures might be snacking on right now: Gray squirrels like acorns, fungi, seeds, and berries; porcupines prefer the inner bark of trees and sweet corn; deer munch on twigs, grass, bark, apples, and acorns.

At 1.2 miles, the trail travels over sections of ledge to approach the first exposed ridge 0.2 mile later. Following cairns now, the trail weaves in and out of scrub evergreen on a moderate ascent with fine western views to the Conway region of the White Mountains. True to its name,

A young hiker leads the way across open ledges.

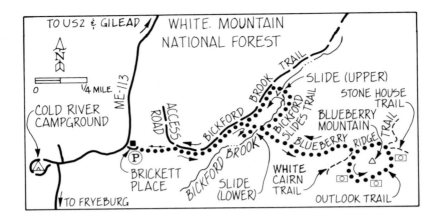

the mountain nourishes an abundance of low bush blueberries that make a perfect snack for July hikers.

As the White Cairn Trail to Shell Pond joins from the right, continue on the Blueberry Ridge Trail, following signs to Speckled Mountain. In 100 yards, at 1.6 miles, the Outlook Trail splits right. Follow this trail marked by cairns and yellow blazes to circle the broad mass of Blueberry Mountain, with frequent views in all directions. At 1.85 miles, the trail has made a U-shaped sweep to rejoin the Blueberry Ridge Trail at a junction where the Stone House Trail heads right (east). Turn left here and, 2 miles from the start, you'll reach the Outlook Trail junction to complete the loop around the summit.

Return along the Blueberry Ridge Trail to Bickford Brook. Before recrossing the brook at the 3-mile mark, turn right (east) to follow the trail to the Upper Bickford Slide. The hard-packed trail climbs easily, guided by an occasional yellow blaze. After crossing a tributary at 3.15 miles, scale a muddy embankment and recross the tributary. As soon as the slide comes into view on the left, the trail swerves left and drops down to the wide, deep pool of water at the base of the slide. On a muggy August day, you'll want to linger poolside (bug repellant is a must), although the slides are most spectacular in the springtime.

The trail crosses the base of the pool over adequate stepping stones and ascends a steep slope on the slide's left-hand (western) bank. Who will be the first to spot the cave to the left of the trail? At the top of the slide, another pool has formed that you can access by dropping steeply off the trail to the right. At 3.4 miles, the trail intersects the Bickford Brook Trail (still a woods road); turn left. The Blueberry Ridge Trail joins from the left in 0.2 mile; stay on the Bickford Brook Trail, and in 0.8 mile you'll be back at your car.

Signs point the way to North Outlook and Royce Mountain.

61. East Royce Mountain

Type:	Dayhike
Difficulty:	Challenging for children
Distance:	3.2 miles, round trip
Hiking time:	3 hours
High point/elevation gain:	3114 feet, 1750 feet
Hikable:	May–September
Maps:	Wild River (New Hampshire) and Speckled Mountain (Maine)

Even though you'll travel along the same trail both up and down this mountain, you'll be amazed at how different the route seems. On the way up, the steep grade focuses attention on your goal, the summit; on the way down, you'll be more concerned with your footing, leading to a greater awareness of your immediate surroundings. With lots of streams to cross on stepping stones and a number of challenging climbs, kids will be too busy to bicker or grumble. This is a demanding hike, best suited for older children with previous hiking experience.

From the junction of US 2 and ME-113 in Gilead, head south on ME-113. In 7.3 miles, turn right into a large parking area for East Royce Trail.

The yellow-blazed East Royce Trail leaves the western side of the parking area on a moderate, northward climb, soon curling left to head westward. In 0.15 mile, you'll cross a rock slab spanning a hurrying stream. It's always tempting for kids to conduct a few water experiments: Does a twig swim faster than a leaf? Do acorns float? How about mushrooms?

Curling westward, the trail weaves more steeply to cross another branch of the stream at 0.25 mile. Leading hikers in a northerly direction through hemlocks and birches, the trail soon swings westward on a moderate pitch. Two more stream crossings just before the 0.5-mile mark will continue to pique the kids' interest. Are any frogs poised on the bank, ready to belly-flop into the water? Ask the children if they have ever seen frogs hopping about in the wintertime. No? Actually, most frogs bury themselves in a pond's muddy bottom until spring.

As the trail continues to snake up the relatively steep slope, watch for the impressive white birches lining the trail at 0.75 mile. Here the trail becomes steeper and rockier before arching left (southwest) on a more gradual grade. Let the kids count moss-covered stones. Why does moss seem to grow so well here? Moss is one of the few plants that can survive these shady, acidic conditions. It began as a sea plant and it still requires constant moisture. In fact, it needs water to reproduce.

At 0.8 mile, the trail continues to twist and climb, briefly mounting natural stone steps before the pitch eases at 1 mile. Soon, at a junction, the Royce Connector Trail diverges left (west), leading to Royce Trail and West Royce. Remain on the East Royce Trail, heading northeast to cross another small stream trickling through a gully. The path zigzags up a moderate-to-steep slope as granite slab sweeps underfoot at 1.1 miles. A

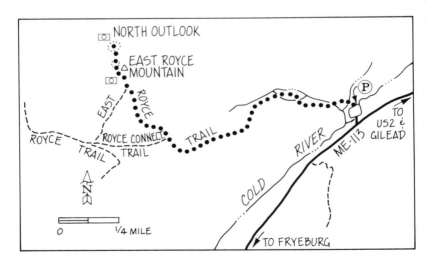

mossy ledge looms on the left. At 1.2 miles, look behind you for a fine easterly view that promises even more expansive vistas shortly.

Soon the trail opens onto exposed granite and begins bounding over steep ledge, testing the kids' agility and stamina. At 1.3 miles, the trail scales a grooved stretch of rock slab, swerving left partway up, following yellow arrows. Just under 1.5 miles from the start, a sign points to the right (north) toward the East Royce Summit (200 yards away) and toward North Outlook (400 yards away). Here, you'll have commanding views east, south, and west over the foothills of southern Maine and some substantial mountains in the Conway region of New Hampshire.

Drop briefly through a spruce forest, still guided by yellow blazes. Remind the kids that Olympian Carl Lewis can cover 200 yards in 20 seconds! Assign someone to time your group's 200-yard hike along a level ridge to the enclosed summit, marked by a rock with a yellow "X." From here, drop gently to North Outlook. You'll have one of the finest views of New Hampshire that Maine has to offer, with the Presidentials dominating the western horizon. Can the kids point to Mount Washington? (Tell them to look for its characteristic cloud halo.) The uniquely shaped Carter Dome lies to the northwest.

On the return trip, you'll be able to take in superb easterly views from the exposed ridge. Head back to your car along the familiar East Royce Trail.

62. The Roost

Type: Dayhike
Difficulty: Easy to moderate for children
Distance: 1.3 miles, round trip
Hiking time: 1 hour
High point/elevation gain: 1374 feet, 650 feet
Hikable: May–October
Map: USGS Speckled Mountain

You don't have to do a lot of advance planning to take on the Roost, a family favorite in the Evans Notch region of the White Mountain National Forest. It's a short, easy climb to the top of this hill, perfect for the little guys. Afraid the older ones will be bored? Let them race along the well-defined path to the Roost summit sign (there are no trail junctions to confuse anyone). As with so many other hikes we've included, a mini-

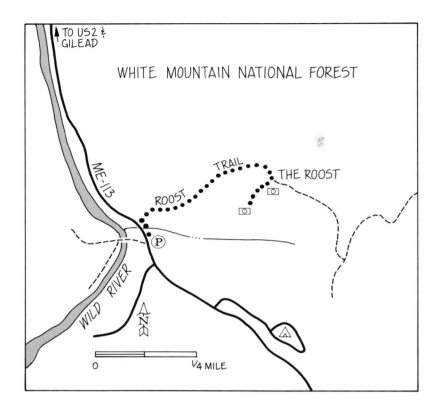

mum effort reaps maximum rewards. The views to the north, south, and west over the Wild River Valley and Evans Brook Valley are delightful.

From the junction of US 2 and ME-113 in Gilead, head south on ME-113 for 2.9 miles. The Roost Trail is on the left. Drive an additional 100 yards across a bridge and park on the widened shoulder on the left.

Walk back over Evans Brook to the Roost trailhead. The yellow-blazed trail mounts a steep flight of log stairs heading east and then settles into a moderate ascent. At 0.25 mile, the path leads through a stand of birches, then crosses a trickling stream 0.1 mile later. Do any frogs hop into the water as you pass by? Ask the kids how they distinguish frogs from toads. They probably use their sense of touch: Toads are dry and bumpy while frogs are smooth and slick. Observant little naturalists may have noticed that most frogs have teeth; most toads don't.

The trail levels at the 0.5-mile mark on exposed baldface fringed with hemlocks, spruces, and pines. A sign at the height of the land welcomes hikers to the Roost, where the grand views will delight you. Following signs to another scenic view, bear right onto a side trail as the main trail continues straight. The path then drops more gently through an evergreen forest, heading southwest. While adults anticipate the panoramas, the kids are probably more curious about the treasures closer at hand. Encourage them to locate a hole at the base of a tree. If there aren't any cobwebs covering the opening, if the leaves in front of the hole are matted down, and if there are bits of fur nearby, it is probably the home of a woodland creature.

The trail opens onto the overlook 0.65 mile from the start. Spread out your picnic lunch and take in the expansive views over the Wild River Valley, southwest to East Royce Mountain (Hike 61), and west to the more prominent peaks of the White Mountains.

Return to your car by retracing your steps.

63. Table Rock

Type: Dayhike
Difficulty: Challenging for children
Distance: 2.4 miles, loop
Hiking time: 2.5 hours
High point/elevation gain: 2405 feet, 1000 feet
Hikable: May–October
Map: USGS Old Speck Mountain

Kids are always excited about the initial leg of any hike: the challenging ascents, the anticipation of a waterfall or summit or wilderness lake up ahead, the sense of working toward a worthwhile goal. But what about the return trip, usually summed up as "retrace your steps"? Ho-hum, right? Not on this hike! The trip to Table Rock along the Appalachian and Table Rock trails is as gratifying as any ascent, but the return trip through a maze of boulders dotted with dark caves and mysterious tunnels is far from anticlimactic. In fact, it is so demanding we recommend that groups with less experienced hikers turn back after exploring the first set of caves and, yes, "retrace your steps." (Even though this increases the total hiking distance to 3.5 miles, the hike will be downgraded to a rating of "moderate.") The one guarantee we'll make to those of you who forge ahead: No one in your group will complain about the dull descent!

From the junction of US 2, ME-5, and ME-26 in Bethel, drive north on ME-26 for 12 miles to a large off-road parking area on the left (for Old Speck Mountain).

From the northern side of the parking lot, pass the wooden trail map and plunge into the woods on the white-blazed Appalachian Trail (AT). Quickly, the blazes lead across ME-26. Reenter the woods on the AT at a sign showing a hiker with a walking stick. Pass through thick woodlands and cross several halved-log bridges over wet areas and a trickling stream. In 0.15 mile, an orange-blazed trail splits right on its way to Table Rock; you follow the left-going AT. (You will be returning along the orange-blazed Table Rock Trail.) If any little hikers begin to complain, remind them that many others who have walked along this very trail did so on their way from Springer Mountain in Georgia to Katahdin

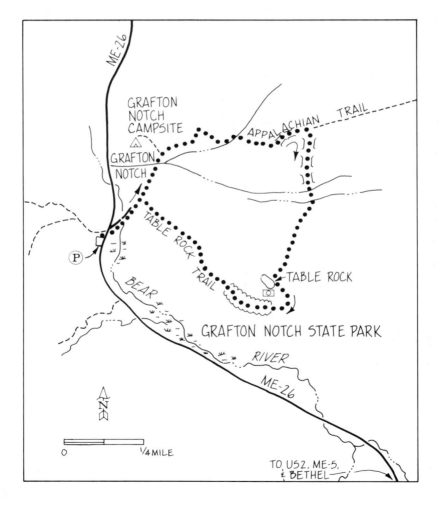

Table Rock, as seen from Route 26

in Maine, a distance of more than 2000 miles. Suddenly a 2.4-mile hike won't seem so long after all!

The trail ascends briefly but levels to cross a stream at 0.35 mile. Shortly, a blue trail parts left for the Grafton Notch campsite and lean-to. Stay right (east) on white blazes and rise on a moderate grade. A half mile from the start, the trail travels beside a stream that races raucously down the mountainside. How far will a stick tumble before a stone or fallen branch halts its reckless journey?

After the trail crosses the stream, it flattens and soon reaches a marker where it turns right (southeast) and begins climbing moderately. The wide, rugged trail narrows to cross a wet area on two split logs at 0.8 mile. Soon, the AT departs left (east) as you turn right (south) at a sign for Table Rock. Climb moderately and then more steeply for 0.5 mile to Table Rock, traversing damp sections and streams on halved logs.

You won't quibble with the name of this rock plateau, perched 1.4 miles from the start. The large, flat tabletop of rough granite 30 feet long and equally wide juts out over its supporting base. On a clear day, the **CAUTION** views of Sunday River, Old Speck, and Puzzle Mountain are delightful, although you may spend more time watching the children than the horizon (the drop-off is dangerous).

To continue along the orange trail, begin at the northeastern corner of the rock and drop into the woods. In 50 feet, turn right (southeast) into a gully. One-tenth of a mile from the rock, the path curls northeast to pass below the ledges supporting Table Rock. The trail crawls along the base of the ledges for 0.2 mile, winding through a rock labyrinth of slab caves and tunnels guaranteed to thrill every young hiker (and most old ones). This expansive rock chaos will slow you down, but the kids will enjoy every minute, although you may need to carry their packs here. The ancient Romans believed that nymphs and sibyls lived in caves like these. The kids can probably make some more accurate guesses as to what kinds of creatures call these caves home.

The trail turns left (west) away from the ledges to tumble down the rocky hillside for 0.3 mile. As the descent slackens, the path winds through a hodgepodge of rocks that makes footing difficult for another 0.2 mile. Beyond the rocky area, the path plummets for 0.1 mile before easing to drop gently toward the AT, joining it 1.3 miles from Table Rock. Turn left and retrace the initial route for 0.2 mile back to your car.

64. Step Falls

Type:	Dayhike
Difficulty:	Easy for children
Distance:	1.5 miles, round trip
Hiking time:	1.5 hours
High point/elevation gain:	1250 feet, 400 feet
Hikable:	May–October
Map:	USGS Puzzle Mountain

There's no doubt that this waterfall was created with kids in mind. Dropping 200 feet along Wight Brook in a series of cascades, Step Falls beckons little hikers to scale granite rocks alongside the tumbling water and to plunge into the deep, icy pools. (Don't forget bathing suits!) But this waterfall won't just appeal to the children—the gentle, unremitting roar will soothe and relax adults stretched out near the wading pools. If you're determined to interest the kids in family hiking, start with this one—it's a winner. And if you're a veteran hiker who enjoyed the hikes to Georgiana and Harvard Falls (Hike 37), Bickford Brook Slides (Hike 60), and Hamilton Falls (Hike 2), this, too, will make your list of favorites.

From the junction of US 2, ME-5, and ME-26 in Bethel, drive north on ME-26 for 7.7 miles. Just before metal guardrails that border each side of the road, turn right onto a gravel road and drive to a grassy parking area. (You've gone too far on ME-26 if you cross the Grafton town line, 0.45 mile north of the gravel road turnoff.)

The well-traveled trail (initially unmarked, but soon white-blazed) leaves the northern side of the parking area and ducks into the woods, passing a Nature Conservancy sign. You'll hear the whispers of Wight Brook to the left as the rocky trail leads through groves of spruce, fir, and hemlock. Can the kids tell these evergreens apart? The fir has flat needles and cones growing upright on its branches; the hemlock also has flat needles, but cones hanging from the ends of its branches; and the spruce has sharp, square needles and dangling cones.

At 0.1 mile, the sound of cascading water intensifies and a side trail branches left to approach the riverbank. Continue straight on the white-blazed trail, rising gently and avoiding the water until the 0.25-mile mark. Here, the side trail and the main trail converge along the right (northeast) bank of Wight Brook. Fifteen feet below, the water splashes and spills into a series of chilly pools. See if the kids can identify some of the trailside wildflowers and ground covers: partridgeberry, Indian cu-

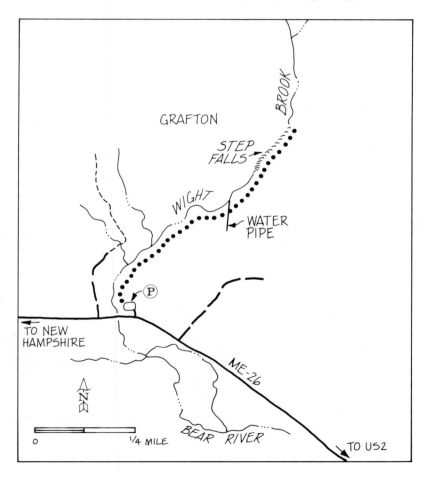

cumber, goldthread, Canada mayflower, trillium, and bunchberry.

At 0.35 mile, the trail and the river bend to the right (southeast) and again the white-blazed trail veers away from the brook to travel along an elevated ridge while an unmarked trail continues along the bank. The white trail marches through a stand of fine white birches at 0.45 mile that seems to illuminate the shaded path. Beech and sugar maple trees also dot these woods. Kids, find a maple tree to examine. Are the leaves on a given tree all the same size and shape? (No! Their size and shape vary with their age and position on the tree.) Can you guess what we make with the sap from the sugar maple tree? (Maple syrup!)

The trail begins a gradual-to-moderate ascent with the tumbling brook drowning out all other wilderness sounds. At 0.5 mile, the trail has resumed its northeasterly course. After crossing over a 10-inch water pipe, the trail emerges onto the bald rock slab that carries the dramatic falls. (Warn the kids that the wet rocks may be slippery.) Enjoy the concert of rock and water as you scale the riverside boulders or climb along the wooded trail. Near the top of the cascading falls, waterside rock slabs overlook several wide, deep pools. Stop here for a relaxing picnic lunch. The largest pool offers cautious bathers a partially submerged rock to ease themselves into the icy waters. While the "polar bears" take a dip, the others can crest the top of the falls, just 0.1 mile farther up the granite brook bed.

Return the way you came.

Note: Day use only; no fires.

Water slips down Step Falls.

65. Rumford Whitecap

Type: Dayhike
Difficulty: Moderate for children
Distance: 3.8 miles, round trip
Hiking time: 3.5 hours
High point/elevation gain: 2205 feet, 1450 feet
Hikable: May–October
Map: USGS East Andover

This trip falls into the "something for everyone" category. For anxious parents, the expansive summit and absence of precipitous cliffs make this a worry-free hike. For those who love that "top-of-the-world" feeling, the route along the lengthy exposed ridge provides postcard-perfect panoramas. For berry lovers, trailside blueberry bushes will provide a never-ending source of the tasty fruit in season. Even those spirited souls who crave adventure will be satisfied—this is a tough trail to follow due to inconsistent blazing and indistinct trail junctions. In fact, we highly recommend that you garner experience on easier trails before tackling this peak. Even veteran hikers should bring along bits of yarn and ribbon and pieces of chalk to mark the route.

From the junction of US 2 and ME-5 in Rumford Point, travel north on ME-5 for 2.9 miles. Turn right onto a paved, unmarked road and cross the Ellis River. In 0.3 mile, turn left following a sign to East Andover. In 1.5 miles, turn right onto Farmer's Hill Road. In another 0.65 mile, park on the left side of the road where there is room for two or three cars. (You've gone too far if the road turns to gravel; backtrack 0.05 mile.)

Across the road, the trail rises steeply along an old logging road heading due east through mixed woods. Coniferous trees—such as the pine, spruce, and hemlock trees you'll see—have cones; each cone is made up of scales that house seeds. If you are hiking on a sunny day, the cones will be open to allow the seeds to flutter to the ground. On wet days, the cones stay closed. (Ask the littlest hiker why conifers are sometimes referred to as evergreens.)

Climb briskly along a heavily eroded path 0.3 mile from the start; in 0.1 mile, the grade eases. The road forks at 0.5 mile: one branch continues straight (southeast), while the trail you'll take follows a severely eroded logging road that bears left (south). The path leads along the left rim of the gully until the signs of erosion fade and you travel along an old stream bed. At 0.6 mile, the trail turns left away from the dry stream bed to climb easily along an overgrown woods road. In 100 yards, head right

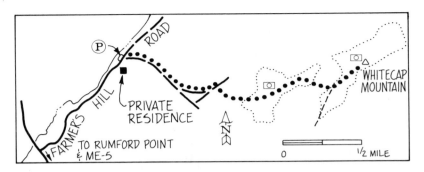

(southeast) onto a trail that leaves this waning road. Though cairns
mark this intersection, it is easy to miss.

Once you've split from the woods road, look over your shoulder for
black arrows painted on trees by the locals to guide hikers down the
mountain. Remember Hansel and Gretel? You may want to re-enact this
fairy tale, tying ribbons or pieces of bright yarn on tree branches so you,
too, will be able to find your way home.

After climbing moderately, then steeply, through mixed woods,
you'll confront a hunk of ledge at just under 1 mile. Technically, the trail
scales the ledge, but previous hikers have worn a path through the
woods, wrapping around the left-hand side to angle up the massive rock.
From the top of the rock, follow occasional black arrows, red ribbons, and
white paint blazes across exposed baldface. Here's where your chalk will
come in handy: Provide each child with a piece and let them mark the
course to avoid confusion on the return trip. (If you didn't bring chalk,
use rocks to scratch markings.)

Soon, views open to the southwest over the adjoining ridges and
Black Mountain Ski Area. Beyond Black Mountain, the White Mountains' Presidential Range dominates the horizon. The trail cuts right,
drops into a shallow ravine, and mounts another ridge to resume a moderate climb. With the summit in sight to the east/southeast, climb on this
exposed ridge guided sporadically by black arrows.

As the mountain broods over the peaceful countryside, you will crest
a stiff ascent at 1.2 miles. Here, cairns join the trail from the right. Look
over your shoulder frequently to get a sense of the return route. As
sparse cairns guide you toward the summit, the kids will scamper about
amidst the blueberry bushes. The fruit is more fun to eat than to collect
since it takes some determined picking to fill a bucket. The trail rises in
and out of woods within sight of the summit.

After emerging from a patch of thicker woods at about 1.7 miles,
dodge right, skirting another wooded section to head eastward on a moderate ascent. Large cairns point the way to the bald peak, 1.9 miles from

the start. Who can find the brass USGS survey marker at the summit? While the kids safely explore the broad mountaintop, savor the views over Baxter State Park and Mount Katahdin to the northeast, the White Mountain peaks to the southeast, and Rangeley and Flagstaff lakes due north.

After a much-needed energy break, retrace your steps to the car, paying close attention to trail markings as you descend.

66. Tumbledown Mountain

Type: Dayhike or overnight
Difficulty: Challenging for children
Distance: 6.1 miles, loop
Hiking time: 5 hours
High point/elevation gain: 2872 feet, 2000 feet
Hikable: May–October
Maps: USGS Roxbury and Jackson Mountain

When your boots are broken in and you've got some real hiking experience under your belt, spend a day exploring Tumbledown Mountain, a fascinating three-peaked mountain in the Weld region. Bring your bathing suits so you can float about in the sparkling tarn and bring sleeping bags for an overnight stay in the trailside lean-to cabin. You are not likely to run into many (or any) other hikers here, though you may witness rock climbers scaling the massive Tumbledown Cliffs.

From the junction of US 2 and ME-142 in Dixfield, head north on ME-142. In 10.6 miles, at the junction with ME-156 at Weld Four Corners, turn left, still on ME-142. In another 2.3 miles, bear left onto Byron Road following a sign to Mount Blue State Park and Webb Beach Area. In 0.5 mile, turn right, continuing on Byron Road (now gravel) as paved West Road heads straight. Two and a half miles from ME-142 (0.3 mile beyond a cemetery on the right), park on the shoulder at the base of a gravel road on the right.

Walk northwest along the gravel road. (If you have a high-clearance vehicle, you can drive this initial section and reduce the total hiking distance by 1.8 miles.) This may prove to be a tedious stretch for young hikers. Sing every song you can think of with an animal in it. Then play

A father and son approach the summit.

"Simon Says": "Simon says 'Walk like an elephant.' " "Simon says 'Flap your arms and act like a bird.' " "Now gallop like a horse! Gotcha! Simon didn't tell you!"

At 0.75 mile, side roads branch right and left. Stay on the middle road, though at 0.9 mile all roads converge at a clearing where the lean-to cabin for camping sits on a bluff to the right. The Parker Ridge Trail (the route you'll take to return from the mountain) leaves from the western side of the cabin, near an outhouse. From the cabin's northern side, find the blue-blazed Little Jackson Mountain Trail that begins as a logging road. Climb easily through a deciduous forest to a junction 0.15 mile from the cabin. Here, you stay right (following the faint blue blazes painted on stones) as a jeep road diverges left. The trail, suffering the effects of erosion, ascends moderately, heading northward. Have the kids guess why there are few large trees in this area. (Logging is big business in Maine.)

At 1.5 miles, the pitch increases. How does this typical Maine trail differ from the hiking trails that crisscross the White Mountains? In this state, you travel through wilderness along a forgotten logging road, while the Whites provide foot trails blazed especially for the hordes of hiking enthusiasts who visit each year. Nearly 2 miles into the hike, as the woods road narrows to a trail, who will be the first to notice the sounds of rushing water to the left?

The trail divides 0.2 mile later. The Pond Link Trail bears left (north) to join the Parker Ridge Trail and the Little Jackson Mountain Trail bears right (east). Head left on the blue-blazed Pond Link Trail, immediately curling left (west) toward the noisy stream. The kids will need assistance crossing the cascades on stepping stones. Do you see any raccoon tracks near the stream? Some people believe that raccoons wash their food in streams or ponds before they eat it, but this isn't quite true. They sometimes dip their food into water so that it will be softer and easier to swallow, but they aren't cleaning it. Since suburban raccoons often snack out of garbage cans, we can assume that eating dirty food doesn't bother them!

Beyond the stream, the trail climbs gently through a splendid birch forest. Look for curls of birch bark on the ground. At 2.8 miles, the trail briefly opens onto an exposed ridge with excellent southeastern views of Lake Webb. Just under 3 miles from the start, the trail finds the scrub-covered gully between the cliffs of Tumbledown Mountain and Parker Ridge and follows yellow and orange paint blazes angling left (southwest) to the top of Parker Ridge. From here, the dizzying views take in the Tumbledown Cliffs to the north and the Lake Webb area to the south. Hike along the exposed Parker Ridge to a junction at 3.1 miles where the Pond Link Trail meets the blue-blazed Parker Ridge Trail. Turn right and drop 0.1 mile to the pristine Tumbledown Pond. If you are hiking early in the morning or late in the afternoon, you may be able to spot a

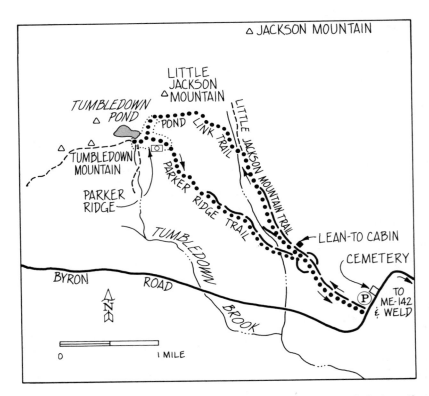

beaver—or you may hear one: Listen for the slapping of their tails against the water as they warn one another of danger. Choose a picnic spot along the rocky shore or take a refreshing dip before returning to the Parker Ridge Trail, heading eastward.

To complete the loop, follow cairns and blazes across the exposed Parker Ridge. Heading generally southward, the trail drops moderately, then inches down a rocky hillside for 0.25 mile. As it falls rapidly to the base of the mountain through a mostly hemlock forest, the trail sweeps over numerous open ledges with good views to the south over Lake Webb.

Just under 0.5 mile beyond Tumbledown Pond, the grade eases from steep to moderate. Shortly, the blazes lead across a set of dribbling streams. The trail widens into a logging road 1 mile from the pond to descend gradually for another mile. Just over 2 miles from the pond, the trail dodges left and crosses a wide, shallow brook on stones at "Sassquach Crossing." The trail climbs the riverbank and quickly arrives at the clearing and cabin, 5.2 miles from the start. Unroll your sleeping bags or march the 0.9 mile along the gravel road to your car. Whew!

67. Bald Mountain

Type: Dayhike
Difficulty: Moderate to challenging for children
Distance: 2.5 miles, round trip
Hiking time: 2.5 hours
High point/elevation gain: 2386 feet, 1400 feet
Hikable: May–October
Map: USGS Mount Blue

You wanted to take on Rumford Whitecap (Hike 65) but you decided against it, uncertain of your ability to guide the group along a confusing trail. Well, Bald Mountain in Weld is for you! It offers a similar safe, exposed summit and comparable panoramas from the lengthy, exposed ridge, but the route to the Bald summit is well marked with no trail junctions, so you're not likely to lose your way. As you hike, the kids can have their own contest to rename the mountain—there are literally dozens of peaks in Maine with the same name. (With this in mind, be sure you're headed for the right one if you're following a road map to get to the trailhead!)

From the junction of ME-142 and ME-156 in Weld, travel east on ME-156 for 5.3 miles to a small, hard-to-find shoulder parking area for two to three cars on the right. (If you miss the parking area, you'll come upon a small residential area 0.3 mile past the trailhead and the town line for Wilton in 2.3 miles.)

Alternatively, from the junction of US 2, ME-4, and ME-156 in Wilton, drive 8.9 miles west on ME-156 to the parking area.

From the parking area, the red-blazed trail heads southward and quickly crosses a stream on well-placed stones. Have the kids count how many steps it takes to get from one bank to the other. The rugged mountain trail winds on a moderate grade through stands of hemlock and birch, rising more sharply at 0.2 mile. Just over 0.5 mile from the start, the trail breaks onto exposed granite and, 0.2 mile later, scales a steep ledge where kids will scramble on all fours. You'll feel the weather here; there is no protection from sun, rain, or wind. The kids can take turns guessing what causes wind. Who guessed a change in temperature? Right! Air expands and rises as it heats up, and cooler air rushes in to take its place, causing the movement of air that we call wind.

At first, paint blazes lead along open baldface. Who will spot the first stone cairn, 0.75 mile from the start? Take turns being the leader,

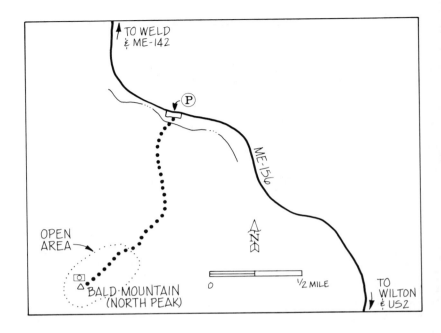

switching off each time you pass a cairn. At 0.85 mile, the trail cuts left to right across the face and quickly switches back. Look for a cairn pair (set 4 feet apart) just under 1 mile from the start. Double cairns serve the same purpose as double blazes, indicating a significant change in trail direction. Ask the oldest child to sight along the pair to establish the new direction. The trail cuts right, quickly left, to zigzag up this exposed ledge along the easiest route.

At 1.2 miles, the trail levels and dips in and out of a sag. The final ridge leads quickly to the height of the land. Here, your substantial effort is rewarded with views of Lake Webb to the northwest, Mount Blue due north over Hills Pond, Mount Katahdin to the northeast, and the Presidentials on the western horizon. Look for Tumbledown Mountain (Hike 66) to the northeast. The child who suggested the best "new" name for Bald Mountain can choose the picnic spot. On the way down, instruct the kids to watch carefully for the cairns.

68. Mount Battie

Type: Dayhike
Difficulty: Moderate for children
Distance: 1 mile, round trip
Hiking time: 1 hour
High point/elevation gain: 800 feet, 600 feet
Hikable: May–November
Map: USGS Camden

The Camden Hills, rising over Penobscot Bay's northern shore, compete with the peaks of Mount Desert Island for the title of "Finest Coastal Hiking Area in the Northeast." The summit of Mount Battie is the most popular destination for folks hiking around Camden and has long been a favorite with families. The steep climb leads in just 0.5 mile to the summit where, from ground level or atop the stone tower, kids can see boats bobbing in the bay and imagine the far-off ocean liners and battleships cutting through the open waters of the Atlantic. A map near the tower points out nearby and distant islands, peninsulas, and mountain peaks, making this a terrific first hike in the Camden area.

From the junction of US 1 and ME-52 in Camden, drive north on ME-52 for about 100 yards. Turn right onto Megunticook Street and drive 0.4 mile to the end of this residential road. Park at the gravel turnout on the left.

Locate the sign marking the Mount Battie trailhead on the northern side of the parking area. The white-blazed trail heads north over rocky, wooded terrain, then quickly swings eastward on a moderate ascent to leave behind the bustling neighborhood and the small-town traffic. In 0.1 mile, as the trail switches from right to left, heading due west, the ledge outcrops form natural steps to aid hikers on a stiff climb. Can the kids find any signs of the red squirrels so common in northern climates? Look for a "squirrel midden," a pile of scales from pine and spruce cones, near a tree stump or a log. Squirrels scrape off the scales to get at the cone's small inner seeds, a mainstay of their diet. Another sign of red squirrel activity is mushrooms drying in the crotch of a tree or spread across a tree branch.

At 0.2 mile, the trail squeezes between two outcroppings and crests a shoulder before climbing steeply once again. As the trail scales a set of 15-foot cliffs, children will have to drop to all fours to make it to the top. Here, the trail opens onto the barren ledge that it will follow for the remainder of the ascent. Look over your shoulder for expanding views of Camden and Penobscot Bay. The trail continues steeply until, at 0.35 mile, the grade eases to approach the summit on a gentle ascent. Enjoy the peaceful views from the side trails that split left and right 0.1 mile before the summit since you'll be sharing the panoramas on the mountaintop with all of those folks who drove up the auto road. Tell the kids to look for wild blueberries in season.

At the summit, kids can climb the stone tower built as a war memorial in 1921. Imagine what it must have been like to visit the hotel that sat grandly upon this spot at the turn of the century! Everyone should study the placard showing the land features of Penobscot Bay such as Owl's Head, Dead Man's Point, Curtis Island, Northeast Point, Sherman

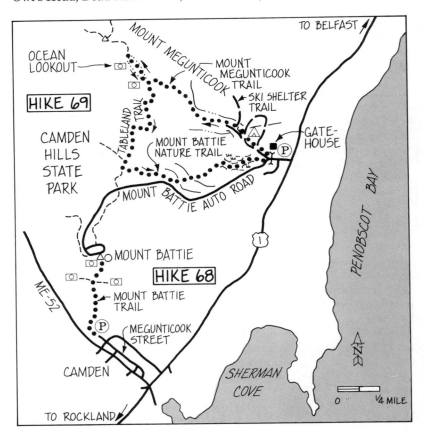

Cove, Mount Desert Island, and Seven Hundred Acre Island. You'll see many of these same places from the other Camden hikes (Hikes 69, 70, and 71).

If you are hiking in the fall, you may be fortunate enough to witness the hawk migration. Can the kids figure out how birds know when it is time to migrate? Because birds time their departures so precisely, ornithologists believe that birds use the length of the day to influence the start of their journey. As the days get shorter with the approach of winter, birds sense that it is time to begin the trip south. Many birds could withstand the frigid temperatures in the northeast; it is the lack of food during the winter that makes migration necessary.

Return to your car the way you came.

View of Camden and the harbor from the stone tower on Mount Battie

View of Penobscot Bay from Ocean Lookout

69. Ocean Lookout on Mount Megunticook

Type: Dayhike or overnight
Difficulty: Moderate for children
Distance: 3 miles, loop
Hiking time: 3 hours
High point/elevation gain: 1350 feet, 1150 feet
Hikable: May–October
Maps: USGS Camden and Lincolnville

From Ocean Lookout on a ridge of Mount Megunticook, the kids can scan Camden Harbor for windjammers and the coastal hillsides for church steeples. This hike, within the limits of most young hikers, will also challenge those with more experience since the first mile climbs the eastern side of the mountain on a steady grade with no relief. If you hike in the afternoon, you will return just in time for a picnic supper and an overnight stay at the Camden Hills State Park campground.

 From the junction of US 1 and ME-52 in Camden, drive 1.5 miles north on US 1 to signs for Camden Hills State Park and the Mount Battie auto road. Turn left here and park in the area before the gatehouse.

Head westward on the paved park road, passing the gatehouse and the Mount Battie auto road. Walk into the Camden Hills State Park campground and, 0.1 mile from your car, a sign marks the start of the Mount Megunticook Trail, initially a gravel woods road through mixed hardwoods. Do the kids hear any rustling in the forest? Have them guess what animal might be making the noises: raccoons perhaps, or a toad, or maybe a red squirrel. Red squirrels might scold you for invading their territory, but they also might climb into your pack for a closer look!

Shortly, as the pitch steepens, you'll reach a junction; stay left on the wide Mount Megunticook Trail. At another junction 0.2 mile from the start, continue straight on the Mount Megunticook Trail as the Ski Shelter Trail goes right. Immediately cross a footbridge over a brisk stream. Put the youngest hiker in charge of finding the first white blaze, indicating that this is part of the white trail system that crisscrosses the Camden Hills area.

After briefly hugging the stream bank, the trail curls westward on a moderate ascent, winding through the woods on a root-choked path. Don't be surprised if a garter, milk, or ring-necked snake (all nonpoisonous varieties) slithers across the trail. It may look to kids as if snakes have no bones at all, but in fact as many as 145 pairs of ribs are attached to a snake's sectioned backbone.

One-half mile from the start, as a brook approaches from the left, the pitch steepens and hikers climb up convenient stone steps. Shortly the brook departs and the trail levels to cut northeastward across the slope on rockier terrain. At 0.65 mile, a boulder slide tumbles toward the trail from the left. Who smells the spruce trees ahead? After the trail turns northwestward to meet a swift stream at 0.85 mile, it climbs on log steps then continues to curl west/southwest toward Ocean Lookout through more evergreens.

At a junction with the Tableland Trail 1.2 miles from the gatehouse, keep kids close as you drink in the splendid easterly views over Penobscot Bay, Maine's largest bay, dotted with dozens of islands. Can the kids see the windjammers gliding gracefully across the bay? The steeples and rooftops of charming Camden lie to the south, while to the southwest you'll see the dwarfed Mount Battie (Hike 68). Continue northwest along the Ocean Lookout ledges to explore or find an ideal picnic spot before returning to the trail junction. (The true Megunticook summit—at 1385 feet, the second highest on the northeast coast—is 0.4 mile farther to the northwest along the Ridge Trail. Its views are limited by denser woods.)

To return to your car, follow the Tableland Trail southward toward Mount Battie for a 0.3-mile moderate descent across exposed ledges and through mixed woods. Over the next 0.2 mile, the trail drops easily on rolling terrain into the saddle between Megunticook and Battie, arriving at a junction with a carriage road 0.5 mile from Ocean Lookout. Continue straight. In another 0.1 mile, after dipping through a soggy area on rock steps, turn left (east) at an intersection with the Mount Battie Nature Trail to continue the modest descent, now paralleling the auto road to Mount Battie. As the evergreen woods give way to more deciduous trees, cross two narrow streams. After hiking along the Mount Battie Nature Trail for 0.7 mile, cross a series of log bridges over trickling streams and wet areas. When you emerge onto the Mount Battie auto road, turn left and in less than 0.1 mile you will arrive at your car.

Note: The Camden Hills State Park campground (no advance reservations required) and Mount Battie auto road are open from May 15 to November 1. An entry fee is charged in season.

---

70. Maiden Cliff

Type:	Dayhike
Difficulty:	Moderate for children
Distance:	2.5 miles, round trip
Hiking time:	2 hours
High point/elevation gain:	925 feet, 750 feet
Hikable:	May–October
Maps:	USGS Camden and Lincolnville

In our high-tech world chock full of special effects, we forget that kids are still interested in simple things such as a wooden bridge over a fast-moving stream, glacial boulders perched beside the trail, a hollowed-out shell of a tree, and panoramas over a sprawling lake. The hike to Maiden Cliff offers all of these, plus the potential for a swim and picnic at Barrett Cove after the hike. Your destination is the lofty cross that perches on the edge of the cliff, erected in memory of twelve-year-old Eleanora French. On May 7, 1864, this farmer's daughter fell to her death as she chased her wind-blown hat.

 From US 1 and ME-52 in Camden, travel north on ME-52. In 2.7 miles, a driveway on the right leads uphill to a parking area.

Follow the white blazes of the Maiden Cliff Trail from the north side of the parking area up a moderate grade. The wide path continues northward, rising modestly through mostly deciduous woods. The kids can run ahead to the impressive glacial erratic, 0.1 mile from the start on the left. Who will be the first one to hear the bustling brook? At 0.2 mile, the trail approaches the narrow stream from the right. As the ribbon of water cas-

Hikers visit the cross that marks Maiden Cliff. Megunticook Lake dominates the view.

cades through a gorge, kids can toss in leaf and stick boats and witness the inevitable shipwrecks. A solid, 40-foot-long bridge spans the stream at 0.25 mile, and the trail begins a rocky, moderate ascent. Can anyone hear the rapid tapping of woodpeckers?

One-half mile from the start, the Maiden Cliff Trail meets the Ridge Trail and heads left (north). You follow the Ridge Trail right (east) on a modest ascent. After flirting briefly with the swift stream, the rocky path curls left (north) and embarks on a brisk climb. Kids will find that the ascent is easier than it looks; the rocks provide solid footing. Soon, you'll see glimpses of Megunticook Lake as the trail sweeps right (east) and snakes steeply up ledges to arrive on open baldface high over the lake and the rolling hills.

The trail intersects the Scenic Trail 0.3 mile from the Maiden Cliff Trail/Ridge Trail junction. As the Ridge Trail veers right (east), follow the Scenic Trail left (northwest) toward Maiden Cliff, 0.8 mile farther. A gradual ascent through sparse woods leads in 0.1 mile to open ledges,

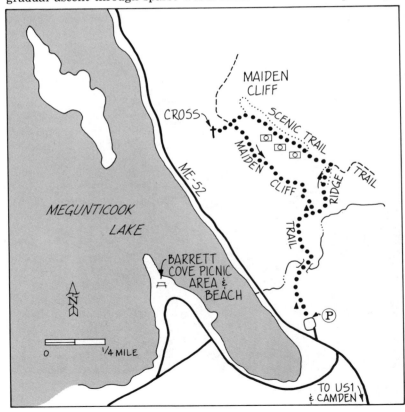

where the Scenic Trail earns its name. As you hike along this exposed area for 0.3 mile, guided by cairns and white blazes, the dizzying views to Bald and Ragged mountains, Camden Harbor, and the Atlantic are post-card-perfect. Let the kids act as photographers—you can't miss with this view. If you look left (south) to the tip of Megunticook Lake, you'll see Barrett Cove with its sandy beach and picnic area.

Along this sloping baldface the kids should be kept in sight and cautioned to step carefully. If you become confused here, remember that the trail follows the western edge of the ledges. Before the ledges end, the white blazes curl left (west) to drop off the ledges and begin a moderate-to-steep descent through the woods. The trail levels shortly before a four-way intersection with the Maiden Cliff Trail (continue straight) and then dips to the top of Maiden Cliff and the cross. Kids can safely visit the cross, but should be warned that just below the cross is an abrupt drop-off.

After admiring more spectacular views across Megunticook Lake, return to the Maiden Cliff Trail and Scenic Trail junction and turn right (southeast) on the Maiden Cliff Trail. Let the youngest member lead the group for 0.1 mile to a large tree with a hollowed trunk on the right, just the right size for a little person to step inside. Two-tenths of a mile from the cross, the trail tumbles down a pair of switchbacks. As the terrain levels, you'll see a large boulder marking the intersection with the Ridge Trail. Bear right, still on the Maiden Cliff Trail, and hike the 0.5 mile back to your car.

71. Bald Rock Mountain

Type: Dayhike or overnight
Difficulty: Easy for children
Distance: 3.4 miles, round trip
Hiking time: 2.5 hours
High point/elevation gain: 1110 feet, 700 feet
Hikable: April–October
Map: USGS Lincolnville

On the hike to Bald Rock Mountain, the end more than justifies the means. Although the initial mile or so along the gravel road may become monotonous for the little guys, the foot trail engages hikers on its final 0.5-mile climb to the summit with splendid views and—TA-DAH!—a rustic shelter for overnight camping. Because the climb to the mountaintop is not too arduous, this makes a perfect first campout for younger kids.

From the junction of ME-173 and US 1 in Lincolnville, drive north on ME-173 for 2.2 miles. Turn left at Stevens Corner onto Youngtown Road. Immediately on your left is the gravel Ski Shelter Road. Park near the beginning of the road. (A high-clearance vehicle might be able to drive the 1.2 miles on Ski Shelter Road to the Bald Rock Mountain trailhead, reducing the total hiking distance to 1 mile.)

Follow the rugged Ski Shelter Road through mixed woods. It may take some effort to maintain the kids' enthusiasm along this lengthy and rather uneventful stretch of road. They can lumber like elephants, leap like frogs, stalk like tigers, or dash like gazelles. Play "name that tune": Take turns singing the first few notes of familiar melodies while the others guess the title. For the first 0.5 mile, the road journeys south; then it gently curls westward.

At 1.2 miles, soon after the woods road crosses a stream on a camouflaged wooden bridge, the Bald Rock Trail splits left (south) over a

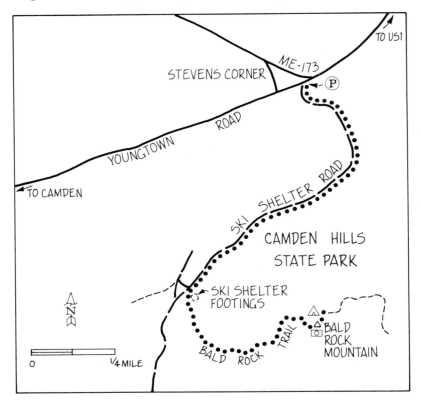

Camping shelter on Bald Rock summit

cleared knoll. At this junction you'll notice an overgrown woods road joining Ski Shelter Road from the right (north). Cut diagonally right across the knoll where you'll pass the cement footings of an old ski shelter. Shortly, a sign announces the Bald Rock Trail; from here, an old logging road will lead you to the summit in 0.5 mile.

After an initial gradual climb through an evergreen forest, rock steps facilitate the ascent up a moderate slope through mixed woods. Test the kids' abilities to identify different types of trees by feeling the bark (eyes closed, of course). At 0.35 mile from Ski Shelter Road, the trail leads over exposed granite and ledge outcrops. Look for Indian pipe, a thick, white plant with one flower that hangs from the top as if permanently wilted.

A final rise through spruce and fir trees leads to the expansive, level summit of Bald Rock Mountain. Adults admiring the commanding view across Penobscot Bay need not worry about their curious kids because the ledges drop off gradually in tiers. Looking eastward, you'll see Cadillac Mountain (Hike 75) and the other distant peaks of Mount Desert Island reaching for the ocean. To the south, over the left shoulder of Mount Megunticook, is the quaint sea village of Camden.

Heading northward from the summit through sparse woods, you'll come upon a lean-to capable of sleeping about six people, a hearth for a fire, and an outhouse. There are plenty of level spots here to pitch a tent, too. Imagine watching the evening sun illuminate Penobscot Bay before you slide into your sleeping bags! If you're not planning an overnight stay, how about building a fire and toasting some marshmallows? Afterward, retrace your steps to the car.

72. Beech Cliff and Beech Mountain

Type: Dayhike
Difficulty: Challenging for children
Distance: 3.4 miles, round trip
Hiking time: 3.5 hours
High point/elevation gain: 839 feet, 700 feet
Hikable: April–October
Map: USGS Southwest Harbor

Three million people visit Acadia National Park each year, making it one of the country's most popular national parks. Its 85,000 acres and 120 miles of trails encompass rocky peaks and shorelines, lush bogs and lakes buried within the deep valleys. The park occupies about one-half of Mount Desert Island and also includes the Schoodic Peninsula, Isle au Haut, and some small, nearby islands.

The visitor center should be your first stop. There, you can watch an introductory film, examine a large relief map of the area, and browse through maps and other publications pertaining to Acadia.

About 350 million years ago, the peaks of Mount Desert Island were as high as the Rockies. Since then, the glaciers, water, wind, and the freezing cycles have eroded thousands of feet from these rock giants. But even at their relatively minute stature, some of the island's mountains and cliffs present quite a challenge for today's adventurous families. Within the first 0.5 mile of this hike to Beech Cliff and Beech Mountain, a series of fixed iron ladders, steel cables, and handholds assists hikers in the steep climb along precipitous cliffs—too demanding for most inexperienced young hikers. In fact, we recommend that you leave a second car at the Beech Mountain parking area because it would be difficult to guide even veteran young hikers down the sheer cliffs on the return trip.

From the junction of ME-3, ME-102, and ME-198 (just beyond the causeway leading to Mount Desert Island), take ME-102 and ME-198 south toward Southwest Harbor. In 4.2 miles, as ME-198 goes left (south), continue straight on ME-102. In 8.8 miles from the causeway, turn right into the Acadia National Park Echo Lake entrance. In 0.4 mile, the road ends at a parking area.

Directions for your second car: From the Acadia National Park Echo Lake entrance, drive north on ME-102 for 2.5 miles and turn left onto Beech Hill Cross Road. In 0.9 mile, turn left onto Beech Hill Road and drive 2.2 miles to the Beech Cliff parking area.

Head down the flight of stairs at the northeastern end of the parking

Looking from Beach Cliff to Acadia Mountain

lot that leads to Echo Beach; partway down, take the Canada Cliff Trail as it splits left at a sign for Beech Cliff and Beech Mountain. The trail quickly curls around the back side of the parking area, passing a chalet-style structure and a second sign, which appropriately warns hikers that the trail is steep with exposed cliffs and fixed iron rungs to aid hikers in the climb. (Though the signs do not mention Canada Cliff, the trail scales this set of cliffs before arriving at Beech Cliff.)

Continue on a gradual ascent through the deciduous forest, dotted with birches and spruce. Do the kids know the difference between deciduous trees like oak, maple, and beech and conifers such as spruce and hemlock? (Deciduous trees lose their leaves in autumn and coniferous trees have cones and always retain some of their needles.) As Canada Cliff looms ahead on the left, who can see Echo Lake on the right?

At 0.15 mile, the trail cuts left and begins a series of switchbacks leading eventually to the top of Canada Cliff. Frequent stone steps assist in the ascent. At 0.3 mile, a side trail straight (north) leads quickly to an

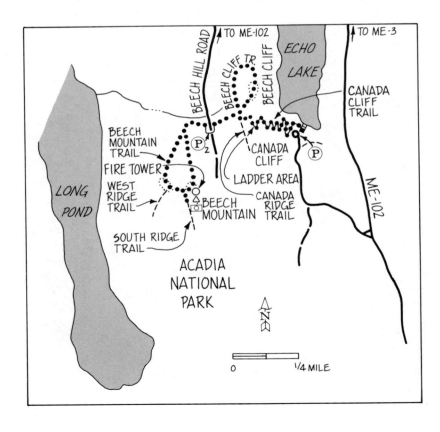

overlook of the lake. Back on the main trail, the stiff ascent continues; hikers are aided by more steps and a hand rail. Soon, overhanging ledges shelter the rugged trail. As the switchbacks tighten and the trail steepens, kids will need help and frequent words of encouragement. Handrails provide welcome assistance as the trail threads its way along the base of Canada Cliff with steep drop-offs at trail's edge.

Soon, hikers begin the assault up segments of the sheer cliffs on iron ladders imbedded in the mountainside. After climbing a ten-rung ladder, you'll follow the trail as it snakes along the base of the next section of the cliff and switches right, now traveling precariously close to the edge to eventually reach an eighteen-rung ladder. Above this ladder, a steel cable aids hikers up the continued steep ascent. Finally, fourteen- and fifteen-rung ladders bring you to a high plateau at the crest of the Canada Cliff and to a junction with the Canada Ridge Trail, 0.5 mile from the start. While the kids take a well-deserved breather, adults can enjoy the impressive view of Acadia's eastern mountains, notably Norumbega and Cadillac (Hike 75).

As the Canada Ridge Trail heads left (south), you head right (north) to the conclusion of the Canada Ridge Trail 100 yards farther along at a four-way junction. Turn right onto Beech Cliff Trail to begin the loop that circles the top of Beech Cliff. The views from the baldface over Echo Lake are among the best Acadia has to offer. As the trail winds in and out of sparse woods over the next 0.2 mile, kids can take turns listing the sounds they hear: noises from the highway, a woodpecker tapping for insects, squirrels scampering along the ground. After the trail loops back to the south, it arrives at the height of the land where far-reaching views unfold to the south over Southwest Harbor and the Atlantic Ocean. Shortly, you'll complete the loop and return to the four-way intersection.

Follow the right-hand trail for 0.6 mile to the Beech Mountain parking area; so far, you have hiked a spectacular 1.4 miles. (Even if you have opted to park a second car here, the Beech Mountain summit is just 0.6 mile from the parking area and well worth the trip.) At the northern edge of the parking lot, head back into the woods on the Beech Mountain Trail. Can the kids find any signs of the white-tailed deer that live here? In the spring, they can look for tracks in the mud; in the fall, they can try to find marks on slender trees where bucks have rubbed the protective covering off their mature antlers.

After a short descent, head left at an intersection where a stream rushes past on the right. (This section of the loop leads more quickly—and steeply—to the summit.) The familiar pattern of passing through spruce woods to arrive on exposed rock continues. As you crest the summit across a massive expanse of baldface, have the kids look for the fire tower to the south. The Beech Mountain summit is the high point on the ridge that separates Long Pond from Echo Lake on the more remote western side of Mount Desert Island, and the panoramas from the tower are every bit as splendid as you would expect. If you're hiking in the spring or early fall, have the kids watch for hawks on the hunt through their binoculars.

Locate the Beech Mountain Trail just north of the tower and follow the left-hand branch to continue the loop, guided by signs to West Ridge Trail and the Beech Mountain parking area, 0.7 mile away. Just beyond an outhouse, the trail emerges onto open ledge with delightful western views of Long Pond. Here, at a junction, the West Ridge Trail splits left. You remain on the Beech Mountain Trail, descending gradually on a wide path with frequent overlooks. Six-tenths of a mile from the summit, the two ends of the Beech Mountain Trail loop converge. Continue straight for the 0.1 mile to your second car (for a total hiking distance of 2.7 miles) or retrace your steps over Beech and Canada cliffs to enjoy freshwater swimming at Echo Lake (with lifeguard supervision) at the end of the hike.

73. Wonderland

Type: Dayhike
Difficulty: Easy for children
Distance: 1.3 miles, round trip
Hiking time: 1 hour
High point/elevation gain: 35 feet, 60 feet
Hikable: Year-round
Map: USGS Bass Harbor

Even folks confined to wheelchairs or youngsters exploring from strollers will be able to enjoy all that Wonderland has to offer because the hiking route follows an old gravel road (not open to cars). The road winds through a spruce forest punctuated with bogs to arrive at a rocky coastline. Bikinis and beach volleyball have no place here; this is a true Maine seashore. The kids will delight in scaling the massive flattened chunks of ledge that line the beach. You may decide to extend the hike to join the Ship Harbor Trail farther along the beach, or venture into the woods on the other side of ME-102A at hike's end in search of Big Heath, a quaking bog that resembles a natural trampoline.

From the junction of ME-3, ME-102, and ME-198 (just beyond the causeway leading to Mount Desert Island), head south on ME-102 and ME-198 to Southwest Harbor. In 4.2 miles, as ME-198 bears left (south),

Resting on the rocks that border the shore at Wonderland

continue straight on ME-102. In another 7.4 miles in Southwest Harbor, turn left (south) onto ME-102A. Drive 4 miles and park off the road on the left.

A footpath leads from the southeastern side of the parking area and, in 20 yards, turns right as a gravel road merges from the left. The road is dusty and dry but in the forest to each side are lush, spongy peat bogs. The trail winds easily, generally southward, through the bog areas and spruce forest. Spruce trees are common on Mount Desert Island because the meager soil adequately serves their shallow root systems. Can the kids find any spider webs hanging from the spruces' barren lower branches? Webs are especially easy to find after a rain shower or in the early morning when they are covered with dew.

Who will be the first to see the ocean? At 0.4 mile, the road splits at the bottom of its loop. You will return via the left-hand path; for now, go straight to arrive quickly at a rocky point that juts into the Atlantic Ocean, sheltering Bennet Cove to the northeast. Stop for a snack or to drink in the sights of the seashore, settling among the giant slabs of wave-worn rocks. Watch for shorebirds feeding when the tide is out and, on misty days, listen for the distant moan of foghorns.

In the tide pools—miniature oceans in a sense—kids can look for tiny fish. Hungry gulls, rainstorms that dilute the pool water's salt concentration, and the harsh sun that often overheats the shallow water combine to make life difficult for these tide-pool dwellers. Remind the kids

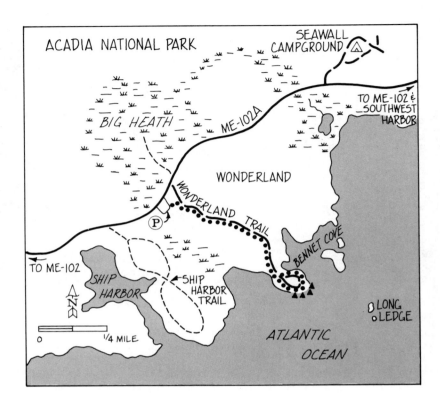

that if they pick up a sea creature to get a closer look, they should return it to the exact spot where they found it after inspection. Why isn't there a sandy beach here? For a sandy beach to occur, there must be a shoreline that does not rise too steeply, a source of sand to cover the beach, and something (like waves) to move the sand onto the shore. Wonderland's rocky shoreline obviously does not meet all of these criteria.

To complete the 1.3-mile hike, finish the loop around the peninsula, keeping Bennet Cove on your right. At the trail junction, turn right and return to your car the way you came. (To extend the hike, follow the shore in a westerly direction and in 0.6 mile you will arrive at the trail that winds along Ship Harbor and soon returns you to ME-102A. Turn right on 102A and walk 0.25 mile to your car for a 3-mile total hike. To explore Big Heath, leave the parking area and cross 102A, heading east for 50 yards. Here, an indistinct trail heads north for 0.1 mile through swamp and woods to this vast peat moss bog. Walking along the trail through the bog will remind kids of stepping on a giant trampoline. On certain sections of the bog adults can jump and create a wave under the peat. Wet feet are unavoidable. Do exercise caution here.)

74. South Bubble

Type: Dayhike
Difficulty: Easy to moderate for children
Distance: 2 miles, loop
Hiking time: 1.5 hours
High point/elevation gain: 768 feet, 700 feet
Hikable: April–October
Map: USGS Southwest Harbor

A hike to South Bubble, one of the two rounded hills of pink granite that rise over the northern end of Jordan Pond, is a relatively short, easy hike offering several points of interest for kids. They'll love circling the elephant-sized glacial boulder that rests on the eastern slope of the Bubble and they'll enjoy descending the steep rock slide to the edge of Jordan Pond. The older folks will appreciate the minimal effort required to reach this centrally located summit. Its commanding views of the surrounding peaks rival the vistas from any Acadia mountaintop.

From the Acadia National Park Visitor Center in Hulls Cove off ME-3, head south on Park Loop Road. In 3 miles, continue straight at an intersection following a sign to Cadillac Mountain. In another 3 miles, turn right into a parking area for Bubble Rock. This parking area is 2.5 miles beyond the Cadillac Mountain auto road and about 1 mile beyond the parking area for Bubble Pond.

On the western side of the parking lot, you'll find the trailhead at a sign for the paths to the North and South Bubbles, each 0.5 mile away. Head into the deciduous forest on a gradual ascent to an intersection with a wide woods road. Bear right and soon join a carriage road where a trail sign indicates that Bubble Mountain is 0.3 mile straight ahead. Go straight (northwest) on the carriage road as the woods road continues to the right. At 0.15 mile, the trail turns left (west) to climb moderately on terraced log and stone steps.

At an intersection 0.25 mile from the start, continue straight (west) on a significant grade to an intersection with North Bubble Trail, 0.1 mile later. Here, turn left (southeast) toward South Bubble, following infrequent red paint blazes. Can the kids find six erratic trailside boulders along this stretch? To the west you'll see the sheer Jordan Cliffs on Penobscot Mountain.

After sweeping over a section of baldface, the trail reaches the 768-foot summit of South Bubble, marked by a large stone cairn. From here, the kids can identify North Bubble, Eagle Lake, Jordan Pond, Penobscot and Cadillac mountains, the Cranberry Isles, and the Atlantic Ocean. They can also try to spot a bald eagle, looking for its characteristic dark body, white head and tail, and yellow beak. Early colonists named this bird the bald eagle because "bald" originally meant white, referring to the bird's white head.

Turning left at the cairn, descend eastward on a side trail to the dramatic Bubble Rock, precariously perched on the edge of the precipitous ridge. (Kids can examine the rock up close, but should exercise caution on the ledges below the rock.) A glacier deposited this erratic boulder on the South Bubble's eastern side 10,000 to 15,000 years ago. Kids, how do geologists know that this boulder was brought here by a glacier? (They

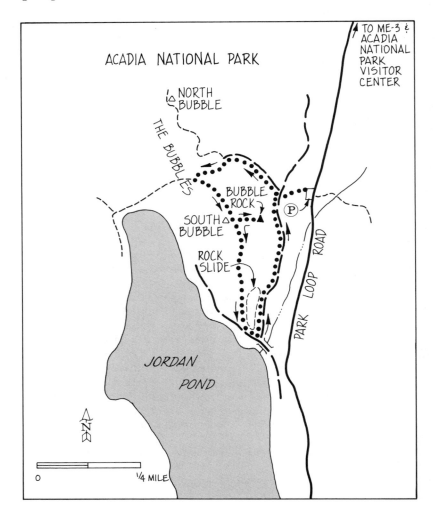

discovered that its crystals differ in size and makeup from the solid rock
underlying all of the loose soil on the island.)

Return to the cairn and follow the exposed eastern ridge of South
Bubble along red blazes, heading south on a gradual descent. As the trail
drops sharply, stay to the left (east) side to avoid straying off the route.
Magnificent panoramas of Jordan Pond, the Gulf of Maine, and the Atlantic Ocean rise to meet you. The trail winds down steeply over ledge
with several challenging spots where kids will need a hand. Now heading south toward Jordan Pond, the blazes guide hikers down a massive
(stable) rock slide into a young birch and evergreen forest to the edge of
Jordan Pond. Here, 0.4 mile from the South Bubble summit, turn left
onto a carriage road. As you follow along the water's edge, the kids may
be able to hear some of Acadia's more common frogs, which are most vo-
cal in early summer: Listen for the high-pitched whistle of the spring
peeper, the deep rumbling of the bullfrog, or the low, snoring sounds of
the pickerel frog.

Continue in an easterly direction, guided by the trail marker for the
Bubbles parking area and Eagle Lake. At the pond's northeastern corner, as a bridge stretches over a brook to the right, you turn left (north)
on an old carriage road on a gradual ascent, curling around the base of
South Bubble. Along this wide path are more large glacial erratics for
the kids to count. In 0.2 mile, ignore the right-hand side trail to the Bubbles parking lot and continue straight on the carriage road following the
sign to Eagle Lake. In another 0.2 mile, at an intersection with another
carriage road, turn right, then quickly left to arrive shortly at your car.

75. Cadillac Mountain

Type:	Dayhike
Difficulty:	Moderate for children
Distance:	4.4 miles, round trip
Hiking time:	3.5 hours
High point/elevation gain:	1530 feet, 1450 feet
Hikable:	April–November
Maps:	USGS Seal Harbor and Southwest Harbor

No monotonous woods walking for the kids on this hike! Dramatic
views over Bar Harbor will demand everyone's attention as you follow
the North Ridge Trail on its gradual climb up Cadillac's nearly barren
northern side. At the summit, the splendid 360-degree view of the island
is a real-life version of the view you had at the visitor center when you

examined the expansive relief map. Since an auto road also travels to the top, the summit is geared to tourists (in season), with a gift shop and restrooms. Take on Mount Desert's highest peak after lunch, with the sun over your shoulder, to maximize the view across Bar Harbor to the Atlantic. Or visit as the sun rises: Cadillac Mountain is said to be the first place on the eastern seaboard to greet the morning sun.

From the Acadia National Park Visitor Center in Hulls Cove off ME-3, head south on Park Loop Road. In 3 miles, turn left onto the one-way section of Park Loop Road following a sign to "Sand Beach." (Ignore the sign to "Cadillac Mountain" that points straight ahead at this intersection; this leads to the Cadillac Mountain auto road.) Drive 0.6 mile to find shoulder parking on the left. Parking is also allowed in the right-hand lane.

A log post marks the North Ridge Trailhead on the right-hand side of Park Loop Road. According to the sign, the Cadillac summit is 2.2 miles away. The trail, marked with orange blazes and cairns, reveals its true character from the start as it steadily works its way toward the mountaintop with long stretches along exposed granite baldface punctuated by short trips through pockets of birch and spruce trees. See whether the kids can tell a red spruce from a white one. The red spruce has needles that are dark green; the needles of the white spruce are light green and have a skunky smell when they are crushed.

Though the trail offers little to shelter hikers from the elements, it also offers little to block impressive panoramas toward Bar Harbor. At 0.2 mile, as the trail plateaus, look to the right (west) for a good view of Eagle Lake and straight ahead for your first view of the Cadillac Mountain summit. Two-tenths of a mile later, you will have distant views to the open Atlantic Ocean. The trail passes to the left of and below the auto road at the 0.5-mile mark and weaves through a sweet-smelling spruce forest at 0.8 mile, shortly before a sag and a small stream crossing.

At 1 mile, the trail climbs granite steps through a young birch forest toward an exposed section. Tell the kids to look back to see where the trail and roadway almost met. At the 1.3- and 1.7-mile marks, the trail again flirts with the auto road. Soon the trail sweeps across a large expanse of baldface with cairns to guide the way. Kids can plod like an elephant from the first cairn to the second, gallop like a horse from the second to the third, and so on. As the trail works it way westward, you will proceed through more frequent clusters of spruce and regain your westerly views.

The trail merges with the auto road at 2 miles, turns left, and follows this road another 0.2 mile to the summit along a stone sidewalk. It's hard to believe that the views from the peak could surpass those from the trail, but you'll have to agree they do. Glass-encased maps point to interesting landmarks and offer historical information. When you are done surveying the island, Frenchman Bay, and the Atlantic from 1530 feet, return the way you came.

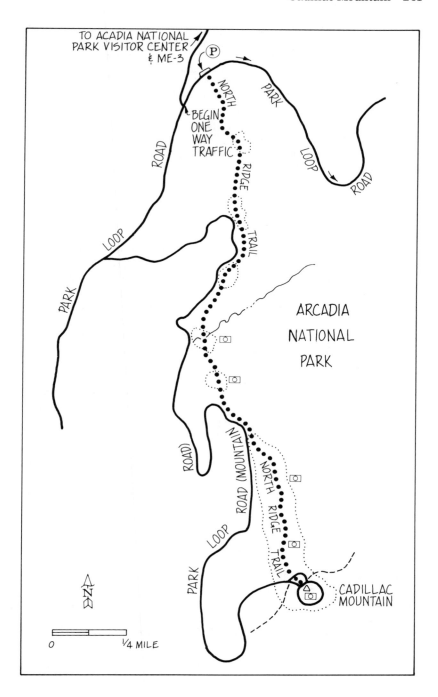

TO ACADIA NATIONAL
PARK VISITOR CENTER
& ME-3

P

BEGIN
ONE
WAY
TRAFFIC

PARK LOOP ROAD

NORTH RIDGE TRAIL

PARK LOOP ROAD

ARCADIA

NATIONAL

PARK

PARK LOOP ROAD (MOUNTAIN ROAD)

NORTH RIDGE TRAIL

CADILLAC
MOUNTAIN

N

0   ¼ MILE

76. Gorham Mountain

Type: Dayhike
Difficulty: Moderate for children
Distance: 4 miles, round trip
Hiking time: 3.5 hours
High point/elevation gain: 525 feet, 750 feet
Hikable: April–October
Map: USGS Seal Harbor

An ancient sea cave and overhanging cliffs, dramatic views, a peaceful pond . . . . This delightful hike, well marked with frequent signs, is best suited for kids with endurance and some hiking experience. Younger children can hike to the turnaround point and back, taking in the rock tunnel, cliffs, and sea cave, for a total hike of 1 mile. The bulk of Acadia's visitors converge on the island in July and August (and this hike is a popular one), so if you want to have the woods to yourself, come in early summer or fall.

Follow the directions for Ocean Trail (Hike 77). Drive another 1 mile on Park Loop Road and turn right into the parking area for Gorham Mountain Trail.

At the southern end of the parking area, look for the Gorham Mountain trailhead, announced on a log signpost. Head over exposed granite to an intersection at 0.1 mile; bear right as an unused trail continues straight. Follow the path as it curves northward through an area crowded with pitch pines. Point out to children the relatively young age of this forest. Much of the area was burned in the 1947 fire that raged for nine days on the island, destroying hundreds of palatial summer homes and the vegetation on 17,000 acres. By studying patterns of plant growth here after the fire, biologists were able to learn about the positive consequences of such a blaze. Today, carefully managed fires are used to enhance the environment by, for example, perpetuating open meadows and encouraging the propagation of species that flourish in fire-scarred soil.

As the Gorham Mountain Trail and the Cadillac Cliffs Trail intersect 0.3 mile from the start, turn right onto the Cadillac Cliffs Trail. The path, rising gradually, leads hikers through a rock "squeezer" to snake along the base of the massive, overhanging Cadillac Cliffs on the left. Soon, the kids will lead the way through a 10-foot-long tunnel created when a portion of the overhanging ledges broke off. Send the kids ahead to find the formidable cave on the left, 0.5 mile from the start. Although adults must enter and exit through the cave's large mouth, little hikers

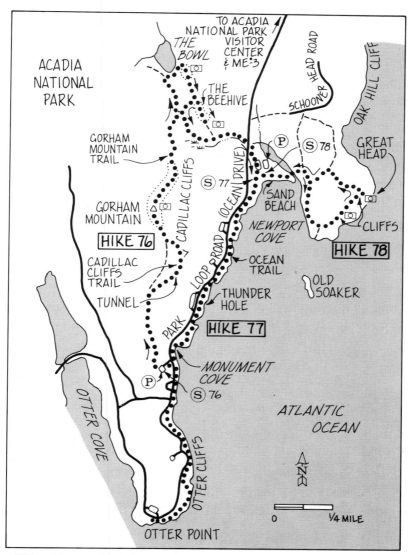

will be able to exit 15 feet up the trail (north) through a small hole. Can any of the children find the smooth boulder at the back of the cave that was worn by long-ago waves? Kids will be amazed to learn that this cave—now 200 feet above sea level, thanks to the work of the glaciers—once sat at the edge of the ocean.

The trail continues to the end of the cliffs where a steel bar handhold assists hikers on a steep ascent. At 0.7 mile, as the Cadillac Cliffs Trail rejoins the Gorham Mountain Trail, turn right. The Gorham Mountain Trail ascends moderately for another 0.1 mile to an exposed mountain ridge where the views are almost as extensive as those from the summit of Cadillac Mountain (Hike 75), the island's highest peak.

Just over 1 mile from the start, kids can look for the short, wooden cross that marks the Gorham summit at 525 feet. Continue due north over the mountain, following cairns on the generally exposed baldface. At 1.3 miles, the trail winds down off the eastern side of the baldface then dives into deciduous woods, reaching a damp sag, then tracking over rolling terrain for the next 0.25 mile. A stake marks a junction at 1.7 miles. (To the right, Park Loop Road is 0.6 mile away.) Continue straight (northwest) on a moderate ascent for another 0.2 mile to the Bowl, a pristine pond sheltered by the surrounding high hills. Turn right and follow along the southeastern bank of the Bowl, heading toward the Beehive.

Soon after the trail turns eastward over ledge on a moderate ascent, it arrives on open baldface with fine views of Champlain Mountain to the north, Gorham Mountain to the south, and the Atlantic to the southeast. At the crest, the trail turns left, dips into a sag, and meets a trail coming in from the right. Continue straight to the top of Beehive's high ledges for more dramatic island views. After the kids grab a snack to maintain their energy, return to the trail junction in the sag and turn left to begin a moderate descent. In 0.2 mile, the trail reaches another sag and trail junction. Turn left toward Park Loop Road, 0.5 mile away, on a rocky trail through a young birch forest.

Although many of Acadia's creatures are primarily nocturnal, the gray and red squirrels that are common to the area are active during the day. See if the kids can catch sight of a squirrel or a squirrel's home. These animals live in hollow trees or haphazard nests at least 30 feet above the ground. At a trail junction 2.8 miles from the start (where the Beehive Trail heads left), continue straight, crossing a boulder field, to reach Park Loop Road in 0.1 mile. Turn right and cross the road. In 100 yards, you'll arrive at the parking area for Sand Beach and Ocean Trail. Hike the final 1 mile along Ocean Trail back to your car.

If you *had* to pick an Acadia favorite, wouldn't this be it?

Bold Acadia gull

77. Ocean Trail

Type: Dayhike
Difficulty: Easy for children
Distance: 3.6 miles, round trip
Hiking time: 3 hours
High point/elevation gain: 60 feet, 100 feet
Hikable: Year-round
Map: USGS Seal Harbor

Ocean Trail, a level path that snakes along the coastline beside Park Loop Road, is Maine's version of the Newport, Rhode Island, Cliff Walk. Instead of Newport's architectural masterpieces, however, Mother Nature's handiwork is on display here. Your camera will capture the rock climbers at Otter Cliffs and the bold sea gulls that settle within arm's reach, but only a tape recorder will do at Thunder Hole, where the ferocious booms in the chasm mingle with the distant clang of bell buoys. All members of the family will enjoy this close-up look at the dramatic boundary between the ocean and the land.

From the Acadia National Park Visitor Center in Hulls Cove off ME-3, drive south on Park Loop Road. In 3 miles, turn left onto the one-way section of Park Loop Road following a sign to "Sand Beach." In another 6 miles (0.3 mile past the toll booth), turn left into the parking areas for Sand Beach and Ocean Trail. The Ocean Trail parking area is to the right and above the Sand Beach parking area.

Safe behind a sturdy fence, visitors peer into Thunder Hole.

The hike on Ocean Trail (also called Shore Trail) begins on a wide path at the southern end of the parking area where a log signpost lists the distances to points of interest: Thunder Hole, 0.6 mile; Otter Cliffs, 1.5 miles; Otter Point, 1.8 miles. With only a few diversions, the trail travels beside Park Loop Road for its entire distance, providing hikers with lovely ocean views from a considerable height. The kids can watch lobster boats chugging through the fields of brightly colored buoys. At 0.2 mile, a side trail on the left leads to an overlook of Newport Cove and Great Head (Hike 78). Walk another 0.4 mile to a flight of stairs on the left that ends abruptly at Thunder Hole, a long, deep chasm well guarded by a sturdy fence. Incoming waves crash into the back of the cavern, compressing pockets of trapped air to cause a deep boom that sounds like thunder. For the most dramatic sound effects, visit at midtide rising or midtide falling.

Beyond Thunder Hole, the trail veers left away from the road under a canopy of spruce, then quickly rejoins the auto road. Staghorn sumac borders the path; have the kids identify it by feeling its fuzzy branches. Poison ivy also grows nearby—teach the kids to identify that by sight, not touch! Ask your young companions to describe how the plant life along this trail differs from that along the inland trails. Explain that the thin soil combined with the ceaseless ocean winds and salt spray discourages the growth of all but the hardiest of plants. Those that survive hover close to the ground and have thicker, more durable surfaces and leaves.

Soon, you will catch a glimpse of Monument Cove on the left with its spectacular boulder beach. How and why does this beach differ from its neighbor, Sand Beach? As you pass through a spruce forest at 1.2 miles, point out the lichen known as "old man's beard" that hangs like Spanish moss from the branches. Numerous side trails split off to the left at the 1.5-mile mark leading to Otter Cliffs. Rock climbers often scale these sheer walls, dangling up to 50 feet above the churning ocean with belayers at the top to guide them. Can the kids see any ducks or cormorants diving into the water for small fish?

The trail continues to its conclusion at Otter Point, 0.3 mile later, where the shore is more accessible. Children can explore the shallow tide pools, examining the varieties of seaweed that cling to the rocks. Does seaweed have roots? No, it has something called a "holdfast" that helps it adhere to rocks or shells. Look for dulse, a coarse, reddish brown plant that is edible. Lay some on the rocks to dry and then take a bite! Maybe you'll find some colander, a brown, wide-bladed plant dotted with holes. (Why do you think it is called "colander"?) Kelp, another common seaweed found here, has a long, flat blade with a taillike stem that can be up to 25 feet long!

When you're ready, return along Ocean Trail the way you came.

78. Great Head

Type: Dayhike
Difficulty: Easy for children
Distance: 1.5 miles, loop
Hiking time: 1.5 hours
High point/elevation gain: 160 feet, 200 feet
Hikable: April–October
Map: USGS Seal Harbor

Great Head epitomizes what most Acadia fans love about this park; here, the mountains reach out to meet the ocean. The cliffs that rise over the rocky shoreline provide a unique look at some of the best scenery Acadia has to offer. Kids will delight in the distant rumbling of Thunder Hole and the short-range views of the nearby beach (Acadia's only sandy beach and one of the few sandy beaches on the Maine coast). This relatively easy and tremendously rewarding walk will appeal to kids of all ages and ability levels. Summer visitors can enjoy a post-hike swim with lifeguard supervision at Sand Beach.

A hiker pauses to look over Frenchman Bay from the sheer cliffs of Great Head.

Follow the directions for Ocean Trail (Hike 77). Park in the Sand Beach parking lot.

From the parking area, descend to Sand Beach by way of the stairs and cross the beach to its easternmost point with Newport Cove on your right. If the kids brought a magnifying glass, have them examine the range of colors in a handful of sand: they'll see tiny pieces of blue mussel shells, green bits of the sea urchin's shell (called a "test"), and pink potassium feldspar crystals. Cross Bear Brook and have the kids find the log post marking the Great Head trailhead. Head into a spruce forest up a flight of rocky steps. At the top of the slope, turn right onto a grassy trail following red blazing. Soon, the trail becomes hard-packed, and then rocky as it sweeps along the top of the ridge through a deciduous forest. Who can imitate the sound of the waves exploding on the rocks below? The trail switches back left over rock ledge to arrive at the height of the land and then marches southward.

Shortly, at a junction 0.3 mile from the start, a trail splits to the left (east) as you continue straight. You will complete a loop and rejoin the trail here. Look west to see beyond Newport Cove and Sand Beach to the Beehive and Champlain Mountain. The path continues on a gradual descent along the ridge rising 100 feet above Frenchman Bay. From the southern tip of the Great Head peninsula, look for the Old Soaker, a rocky island (or shatter zone), where the schooner *Tay* was destroyed in 1911. Today, the wind and waves sometimes expose pieces of the wrecked ship on Sand Beach. As the trail swings along Great Head's southern point, brave and surefooted children can carefully scramble closer to the water's edge.

The path curls north and sweeps across exposed rock guided by cairns with precipitous cliffs on the right. After descending into a wet sag, it arrives on another section of open baldface—the summit of Great Head—with splendid views. Here, at 0.7 mile, the cliffs plummet 100 feet to the choppy surf below. To the north, you can see the former John D. Rockefeller house and Champlain Mountain. Look to the northwest for the Beehive, east across Frenchman Bay to the Schoodic Peninsula (can you see Egg Rock Lighthouse?), southwest for Otter Cliffs. Point out to the kids that the pine trees are "wind-flagged," that is, the branches appear to grow on just one side of the trunk because of the action of the wind. Watch carefully for the cairns and paint blazes that will guide you left (northwest) back into the woods. At 1 mile, turn left (west) at a trail junction, following the sign to Sand Beach as the right-hand (northern) trail heads for Schooner Head Road.

The return trip begins on a rocky, gradual ascent where the trail quickly curls south on orange blazes, reaching a crest on exposed baldface with more dramatic ocean views. After following the level ridge top for 0.1 mile, the trail turns right (west) and shortly intersects with the section of trail traveled earlier, just above the switchbacks. Turn right and return to your car.

79. Bar Island

Type: Dayhike
Difficulty: Easy for children
Distance: 2 miles, round trip
Hiking time: 1.5 hours
High point/elevation gain: 100 feet, 150 feet
Hikable: Year-round
Map: USGS Bar Harbor

The hike to Bar Island, a satisfying short hike in a less crowded area of Acadia, will bring out the adventurous spirit in every member of the family. Hikers cross over to the island along a sandbar at low tide, head to the eastern tip of the island for an oceanside picnic and return before the rising water has covered the sandbar (at high tide, to a depth of 6 to 8 feet!). Put an older child (with adult supervision) in charge of keeping track of the time and tide schedule. If you would like more time to explore, plan a private, extended stay on Bar Island between twice-daily low tides!

From the junction of ME-233 and ME-3 in Bar Harbor, drive 0.1 mile on ME-3 West and turn right onto Cottage Street following signs to the waterfront. In 0.3 mile, turn left onto Bridge Street. Travel another 0.1 mile to the intersection with West Street and park along West Street (near Bridge Street).

Check the tide schedule (at the Acadia National Park Visitor Center or the Bar Harbor Chamber of Commerce information station) to confirm that the sandbar is exposed and the tide is receding. Walk down Bridge Street to the tidal bar and head across toward the island. Distances are often deceiving: Can the kids guess the distance from the mainland to the island? (Four-tenths of a mile.) Though the sandbar (more accurately, a tombolo) may be spongy in places, it won't be hard for the kids to avoid wet feet. Bare feet won't do since in places the sandbar is coated with sharp pieces of shells, due in large part to the gulls. Watch as they fly up and drop mussels or other creatures onto the hard surface below in an attempt to shatter their shells. The kids will be tempted to comb the sand for beach treasures now, but urge them to wait until the return trip when parents will feel less anxious about the impending high tide. Kids may want to poke a stick into the ground at water's edge to see how high the tide will rise while they are hiking.

Once you have reached the island, head through a gate and into the

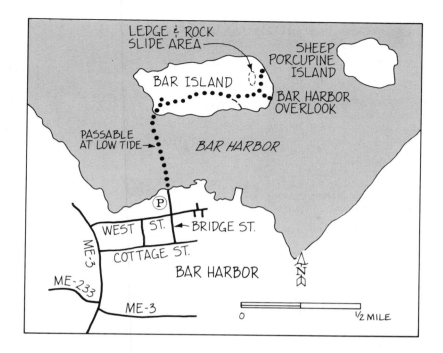

woods, where you'll begin a gradual climb on a wide gravel road. In 0.15 mile (all mileages are from the start of the island walk), the road passes along the right side of a meadow fringed by deciduous, pine and spruce trees. Here, point out to the kids the cropped view of Mount Desert Island's higher peaks. In 0.25 mile, the gravel road continues straight at a sign indicating a private residence. You turn left onto a grassy foot trail to Bar Harbor Overlook. Watch for an old foundation off the trail to the right. Remind the kids that where there is a cellar hole, there is often an old well nearby that may no longer be covered.

At 0.4 mile, a side trail swings right to an overlook where hikers can survey tranquil Bar Harbor. Back on the main trail, the path curls left, sidestepping a high ledge and a rock slide on the left. As you approach the island's eastern shore, the path ends in disarray at the rocky beach bordered by a thin ribbon of evergreens. Pick a resting spot from among the large flat boulders rimming the shore. Enjoy a snack or picnic lunch. With one eye on your watch, reverse direction and hike back to your car. (As you cross the tombolo, look for driftwood, gull feathers, and varieties of common shells such as periwinkle, whelk, clam, and mussel.)

Note: No camping or fires allowed on Bar Island.

Important Addresses and Phone Numbers

General

Appalachian Mountain Club
5 Joy Street
Boston, MA 02108
(617) 523-0636
  Publishes *AMC White Mountain Guide, AMC Guide to Mount Desert Island and Acadia National Park, AMC Guide to Mount Washington and the Presidential Range,* and *AMC Maine Mountain Guide.* Develops and maintains trails and facilities; sponsors outings.

Appalachian Trail Conference
P.O. Box 807
Harpers Ferry, WV 25425
(304) 535-6331
  Publishes *Guide to the Appalachian Trail in New Hampshire and Vermont.* Coordinates those who maintain the Appalachian Trail.

Branch of Distribution
U.S. Geological Survey
1200 South Eads Street
Arlington, VA 22202
  Publishes free pamphlet and an index to topographical maps.

DeLorme Publishing Company
Main Street
Box 298
Freeport, ME 04032
  Publishes an *Atlas and Gazetteer* for Vermont, New Hampshire, and Maine with state information and detailed local maps.

New England Trail Conference
33 Knollwood Drive
East Longmeadow, MA 01028
  Publishes *Hiking Trails of New England.* Provides information about trail and shelter conditions throughout New England.

State Police (Vermont, New Hampshire, Maine)
1-800-525-5555
  Calling this number from any of the three states will connect you to the appropriate police department.

Vermont

Ascutney Trails Association
32 Elm Street
Windsor, VT 05089
  Publishes *Guide to the Trails of Ascutney Mountain.* Maintains the mountain's trails and shelters.

Green Mountain Club, Inc.
P.O. Box 889
Montpelier, VT 05602
(802) 223-3463
  Publishes *Day Hiker's Guide to Vermont* and *Guide Book of the Long Trail.*

Green Mountain National Forest
Forest Supervisor
P.O. Box 519
Rutland, VT 05701
  Publishes maps and guides of the national forest. Maintains trails, recreational areas, and campgrounds.

Vermont Department of Forests, Parks, and Recreation
103 South Main Street
Waterbury, VT 05676
(802) 244-8711
  Publishes free trail maps, *Vermont State Parks and Forest Recreation Areas,* and *Vermont Guide to Primitive Camping on State Lands.* Maintains trails, campgrounds, and recreational areas in state parks and forests.

Vermont Travel Division
134 State Street
Montpelier, VT 05602
  Will send a copy of the *Vermont
  Official State Map and Touring
  Guide* upon request. This lists most
  of the state's public and private
  campgrounds.

Westmore Association Trail
  Committee
c/o Mrs. Arthur Poisson
RFD 2
Barton, VT 05822
  Publishes free maps and guides of
  Lake Willoughby region trails.
  Maintains area trails.

Williams Outing Club
Williams College
Williamstown, MA 01267
  Publishes trail guide and map of
  area trails. Maintains trails in
  northwestern Massachusetts and
  southwestern Vermont.

Woodstock Park Commission
Woodstock, VT 05091
  Publishes free map of local trails.
  Maintains trails in Faulkner and
  Billings parks.

New Hampshire

Appalachian Mountain Club
Pinkham Notch Camp
Box 298
Gorham, NH 03582
(603) 466-2727
  Provides general hiking information
  for the White Mountains region.

National Weather Service
Concord, NH
(603) 225-5191
  Broadcasts forecast for White
  Mountain region each morning.

Office of Vacation Travel
Box 856
Concord, NH 03301
(603) 271-2665
  Provides information on state parks
  and park campgrounds.

Society for the Protection of New
  Hampshire Forests
54 Portsmouth Street
Concord, NH 03301
(603) 224-9945

  Publishes *Trees and Shrubs of
  Northern New England*. Protects
  mountains, forests, and wetlands of
  the state and promotes conservation
  and wise forestry practices. Manages
  a number of properties, including
  land on Monadnock and in Kinsman
  Notch.

White Mountain National Forest
United States Forest Service
P.O. Box 638
Laconia, NH 03247
(603) 528-8721

Maine

Department of Conservation
State House Station 22
Augusta, ME 04333
(207) 289-2791
  Publishes booklets: *Public and
  Reserved Lands* and *Outdoors in
  Maine.*

Department of Conservation
Bureau of Public Lands
(see above address)
(207) 289-3061
  Provides free publications regarding
  recreational opportunities on
  Maine's public reserved lands.

Maine Appalachian Trail Club
P.O. Box 283
Augusta, ME 04330
  Publishes the *Guide to the
  Appalachian Trail in Maine.*

Maine Audubon Society
188 US Route 2
Falmouth, ME 04105
(207) 781-2330

Maine Coast Heritage Trust
167 Park Row
Brunswick ME 04022
(207) 729-7366
  Private, nonprofit land conservation
  organization.

Natural Resources Council of Maine
271 State Street
Augusta, ME 04330
(207) 622-3101
  Private, nonprofit environmental
  group.

The Nature Conservancy
P.O. Box 338
122 Main Street
Topsham, ME 04086
(207) 729-5181
  Sells guide to Maine chapter
  preserves.

Index

CYNTHIA and THOMAS LEWIS are residents of East Sullivan, New Hampshire. Cynthia ia a full-time mother and author of several books, including *Mother's First Year*. Tom is an environmental chemist. Avid outdoorspeople, they have explored every corner of New England together on a tandem bicycle and on foot, and are the authors of *Best Hikes with Children in Connecticut, Massachusetts, and Rhode Island* (The Mountaineers). They now share their outdoor adventures with their two children, ages five and three.